Flashpoint: World War III

Flashpoint: World War III

Andrew Murray

Pluto Press

LONDON • CHICAGO, IL.

First published 1997 by Pluto Press
345 Archway Road, London N6 5AA
and 1436 West Randolph,
Chicago, Illinois 60607, USA

British Library Cataloguing in Publication Data

ISBN 0 7453 1073 7   hbk

Library of Congress Cataloging in Publication Data available

Murray, Andrew.
  Flashpoint: World War Three / Andrew Murray.
    p. cm.
  ISBN 0–7453–1073–7 (hbk.)
  1. World politics – 1989–   2. World War III.   3. International
relations.   I. Title.
D860.M88   1997
909.82´0 – dc21
                                                              96–47672
                                                                   CIP

Printing history   99   98   97   5   4   3   2   1

Designed and produced for Pluto Press by
Chase Production Services, Chadlington, OX7 3LN
Typeset from disk by Vera A. Keep, Cheltenham
Printed in the EC by J. W. Arrowsmith Ltd, Bristol, England

For

Jack Murray

Contents

Preface   ix

   Introduction   1

1 A History of Wars   9

2 The World Economy and the Nation-State   18

3 The End of the USSR   38

4 The Great Powers – the United States   51

5 The Great Powers – Europe   59

6 The Great Powers – the Far East   89

7 The New World Order   104

8 Currency Conflict   119

9 The Division of the World   127

10 The Technology of War   150

11 Flashpoints   156

12 The Third World War   165

Notes   176

Index   188

Preface

Kohl, Mitterrand, Yeltsin and Thatcher have all warned of it since mid-1994. On the other side of the world, China and Taiwan have gone to the brink of doing it.

War is once again on the international political agenda. The fall of the Soviet Union was meant to mark a new era of peace. Instead, it has raised the spectre of war once more. The world needs to know why.

This book intends to outline the forces pushing the world towards a third world war in the next century. It starts with a bit of speculation to dramatise the general point, but thereafter I seek to rest the case on evidence already to hand in the development of the world economy and in the words and deeds of the major powers themselves.

The Introduction, besides including the fantasy scenario of the start of a third world war, outlines the general argument of the book. Chapter 1 is a survey of world war and its causes in recent world history. Chapter 2 considers the 'globalisation' and 'end of the nation-state' arguments now fashionable, and looks at the actual development of the world economy. Chapter 3 looks at the consequences for world peace and great-power relations of the collapse of the socialist Soviet Union, the most important single change in international politics since the end of World War II. Taken together, these four chapters define the background to contemporary world politics.

The next three chapters examine the current position of the great powers – their economic situation and their new policies. Chapter 4 deals with the United States, Chapter 5 with the European powers – Germany, France, Britain and Russia – and Chapter 6 with Japan and China.

I then look at the main symptoms of great power rivalry in the world today. Chapter 7 considers the most important of the actual wars which have followed from the declaration of 'a new world order' – in the Gulf, Yugoslavia, Rwanda and Somalia. It deals with these wars from the perspective of how each reveals conflicts between the great powers, rather than from the general (and well-known) perspective of who did what to whom. Chapter 8 looks at the role of currency and 'currency crises' in expressing the contradictions in the world system today. Chapter 9 views the emergence of power 'blocs' in Europe, Asia and the Western hemisphere as being the start of a new division of the world between competing national capitalisms.

The last section of the book deals directly with how the world could move from here to war. Chapter 10 concerns developments in military technology, while Chapter 11 identifies the specific 'flashpoints' around the world which could trigger a war. Chapter 12 examines the politics of war, both from the point of view of the ruling classes which would start it, and of the popular politics which must oppose it.

By and large, this book draws on sources in the establishment press. If there is a new trend towards conflict between great powers, that trend must be reflected in the *Wall Street Journal*, the *Financial Times*, *Business Week* and contemporary literature – and it is.

Finally, this is a book with a purpose. By raising awareness of the new great power rivalry, it hopes to focus the attention of the Left and of peace movements on the new political tasks which this situation calls for.

I would like to thank all the staff at Pluto Press for their assistance – Roger von Zwanenberg and Robert Webb most notably – and three other people whose support helped make this book a reality: Seumas Milne, who gave considerable encouragement from the beginning and offered many useful comments on and corrections to the text; Frances O'Grady, an inexhaustible source of warmth, friendship and intelligent observation; and, particularly, Jennie Walsh, whose personal and practical contribution, ranging from keeping the author on course to preparing the index to the book, was essential and is warmly appreciated.

Finally, special thanks to Jessica, Jack and Laura Murray. Their optimism, sense of justice and energy in good causes – shared with children throughout the world – buoyed me up throughout the writing of *Flashpoint* and is a daily reminder that the logic of war is not the only, or even the most powerful, force which shapes our future.

Andrew Murray
London, November 1996

INTRODUCTION

The 'Lvov Incident'

Once despised as a pointless talking shop, the eyes of the world were fixed on the European Assembly, meeting in Strasbourg on 26 April 2010. Cable News Network cameras relayed the image of the German Foreign Minister, representing the European Union Council of Ministers, mounting the rostrum to address the deputies.

> As a result of the continued incursion of Russian troops into Ukrainian territory, and in response to requests for assistance from the Lvov government, the Council of Ministers has today authorised the Bundeswehr, together with the joint Franco-German Corps and other combat units of the West European Union, to take such measures as may be necessary to repulse the aggressor and ensure the integrity and independence of the sovereign Ukrainian state. The Polish Republic and the Czech government have agreed to open their territories to expedite the necessary military operations.

His words were greeted with cheers from German and Austrian MEPs above all – but a walk-out from British Euro-parliamentarians, both Labour and Conservative. The House of Commons approved a government declaration calling for an immediate halt to 'rash military actions which are fraught with the most dangerous consequences for world peace'. Privately, the government approved the dispatch of an urgent mission to Moscow to discuss what assistance, if any, it could offer Russian President Alexander Lebed in resisting the German move east. Publicly, the chief of the French General Staff resigned in protest at his government's participation 'in an action inimical to the national interests of France'. Anti-war demonstrations swept Paris and other French cities.

Turning from his TV set in the Oval Office, President Quayle ordered his staff to prepare an address to Congress declaring US support for the 'strong German lead in seeking to stabilise the European situation' and pledging that, in view of the 'special relationship between the US and Germany', US forces in Europe would be ready to act in 'defence of Europe' against any Russian military operations against the Baltic republics or beyond the old

1

Soviet state border elsewhere. He then called the Pentagon, ordering US forces around the globe into the highest state of
combat readiness. Forces based in Kuwait moved pre-emptively
into southern Iraq, citing the provisions of the treaty imposed on
the post-Saddam Hussein puppet regime in Baghdad by the US.

Within 48 hours, war had broken out along a frontier stretching
across Europe from north to south. Declaring 'general solidarity
with the European Union decision', the Fini government in
Rome ordered an Italian march into Slovenia 'to safeguard against
Russian-supported Serb aggression'. With German and US logis-
tical support, the Turkish army began its long-prepared invasion
of Armenia, coordinated with an Azerbaijani offensive from the
east. Russian troops moving south to assist the Armenians faced
organised disruption of their supply lines by guerilla forces from
Chechnya, Ingushetia and Georgia. The Greek military began to
mobilise, and sought urgent word from London as to whether the
privately promised military assistance from bases in Cyprus for
such an eventuality would indeed be forthcoming.

The Serb government immediately declared war on Germany
and 'any other state which takes up arms against the great Slavonic
peoples', a category which almost immediately came to include the
Croat nationalist dictatorship. As the Serb army began to burst out
of the Slavonian enclave, rumours swept Zagreb that the Croat
government had already fled to Berlin. The Albanian and Mace-
donian governments both issued declarations of neutrality, more
in hope than expectation; their pacific stance being in any case
undermined by the eruption of clashes between the forces of the
two countries.

In Ukraine itself, forces loyal to the nationalist Lvov government were in full retreat from the combined forces of the Russian
Army's 1st Ukrainian Front and the army of the pro-Russian Kiev
government. The Russian Army's 2nd Ukrainian Front meanwhile headed south-west to link-up with the Transdenestr Army
in Moldva, already locked in combat with the joint Romanian-
Moldvan armed forces.

In the north, the vast Russian army garrisoned in the Kaliningrad region moved south into Poland to obstruct German military
operations and the Russian Baltic Fleet put to sea from its Kron-
stadt base. The Baltic republics were warned that failure to break
relations with Berlin immediately would be regarded as an 'un-
friendly act' by Moscow.

All but one of the 14 nuclear powers issued statements in the
first 72 hours pledging not to 'go nuclear', although each entered
important caveats along the lines of 'unless national survival ren-
ders the consideration of all measures imperative', in the words of
the Russian statement (which also indicated that the five missile

sites which had been under the control of the Lvov government had been secured by Russian commandos). There was silence from Israel.

The so-called 'smart weapons' deployed by the leaner, meaner NATO forces were doing enough damage in any case. CNN broadcast the first pictures of a Belorussian village destroyed by cruise missiles after being mistaken for a missile site within four days of hostilities starting. It was only the first such catastrophe, but it was the last such broadcast. Time Warner boss Ted Turner was told by the Secretary of State himself that pictures undermining the morale of Washington's German ally could not be tolerated.

With all the mayhem in Europe, it was scarcely surprising that President Quayle, who had in any case a sub-Reaganesque attention span, did not bother to study a top secret CIA report drawing attention to the eight incursions into Philippine territorial waters by the Chinese navy over the last week; nor had he yet read the National Security Council analysis – Military-Strategic Implications of the Japanese Lead in Semiconductor Technology Application – which had been on his desk for the previous month.

He had, however, read a sheet of paper from his staff advising that in order to secure the support of critical Republican senators for his re-election, he should deliver on his promise to support the long-anticipated declaration of independence by Taiwan. He was sure that the Chinese threat to invade in the event of such an act was all bluff . . .

Mitterand's Warning

. . . Meanwhile, back in the real world, 1995: 'Nationalism is War. War is our past. It can also be our future' (François Mitterrand, speech to the European Assembly).[1]

Just two months after his valedictory address to the European Assembly, the French President's government expelled five agents of the US Central Intelligence Agency from France in the first diplomatic incident between two 'free world allies' caused by economic espionage.

On the other side of the world, a few months earlier, the US had come off worst in a military conflict with China – although this was only a secret Pentagon 'war game' looking at possibilities for the next conflict Washington would have to fight.[2]

The US and Russian foreign ministers met to agree that their post-communist 'honeymoon' was over,[3] in part due to the bloody war in Chechnya; whilst in Somalia, US and Italian interests were fighting – literally – for control of the country's banana trade as the Marines pulled out, their 'humanitarian' mission apparently complete.[4]

And within twelve months, Mitterrand's warning of war had been explicitly echoed by two other powerful European leaders – German Chancellor Helmut Kohl and Russian President Boris Yeltsin. When such figures as these speak, it is as well for us to listen.

After the proclamation of a 'new world order' over the ruins of the Berlin Wall, international politics are taking a 'familiar shape, one that would be recognisable to Lord Palmerston. We are watching the rebirth not of empires, but of quasi-imperial spheres of influence',[5] according to a *Guardian* writer, recalling the nineteenth-century British statesman whose single-minded pursuit of national interest disguised as diplomacy played a signal part in the rise and consolidation of the British Empire.

He might have added that the history of the twentieth century displays all too vividly where these politics lead. When the *Financial Times* bemoans the 'recurrence of these ancient faultlines – reminiscent of European politics before 1914',[6] it leaves unspoken the implications of the parallel.

Former British premier Margaret Thatcher differed from Kohl and Mitterrand only in seeing the crisis in international relations as developing over a longer time-scale. She told an audience in the symbolic setting of Fulton, Missouri, where Churchill had delivered his 'iron curtain' speech 50 years earlier, that

> what we see here in 2096 is an unstable world in which there are more than half a dozen great powers, all with their own clients, all vulnerable if they stand alone, all capable of increasing their power and influence if they form the right kind of alliance, and all engaged willy-nilly in perpetual diplomatic manoeuvres to ensure that their relative positions improve rather than deteriorate. In other words, 2096 might look like 1914 played on a somewhat larger stage.[7]

But Thatcher does not need to speculate about 2096. Her words define 1996 precisely.

Certainly, François Mitterrand, who shared with Deng Xiaoping the distinction of being the last world leader who was politically shaped before World War II, would have needed no reminding of the parallels between the beginning and the end of the twentieth century. His spectacular flight into besieged Sarajevo, focus of Europe's first post-Cold War 'hot war', in 1992 took place on the anniversary of the assassination in that very city of Archduke Franz Ferdinand of Austria-Hungary, the event which provided the immediate *causus belli* of the first great world conflict.[8]

This acute sense of historical aptness makes it all the more likely that Mitterrand was aware of the implications both of his words to the parliamentarians of the EU and of the actions his government took against the CIA Paris station a few weeks later.

However, even if all the parallels are drawn, and all the storm signals explicit, the political imagination still recoils from the logic of the development of events – that the main emerging trend in world politics is towards a third world war arising out of conflict between the great powers.

Haven't nuclear weapons made that unthinkable? Doesn't global economic integration make conflict unnecessary? Wouldn't the United Nations step in? Isn't the nation-state becoming a thing of the past?

The answer to these questions, as this book will set out to prove, is no. They are, in fact, the bromides behind which the unthinkable is actually being thought; contemporary equivalents of the view that no nation would dare challenge the might of the British Navy before 1914, that no politician would lead a nation to war after the experience of 1914–18 and so on.

Undoubtedly, the new situation demands more than just a political re-evaluation: it calls for a reversal of assumptions that have been deeply rooted for 50 years. Ever since 1945, we all *knew* where and how the next war would start. Airport fiction and the training manuals of General Staff academies all sang from the same sheet: the red menace would roll in from the east, perhaps through Germany's Fulda Gap, perhaps into Yugoslavia. Communism was the aggressive enemy, and the 'free world' stood united against it, preserving the peace through its nuclear deterrent above all. The next war, if it happened, would be between capitalism and socialism. [9]

That war, of course, never happened. Indeed, the flood of revelations which have emerged from the Moscow archives since the demise of the Soviet Union indicate that it was never going to happen. (The nature of Soviet policy is examined in greater detail in Chapter 3.) Despite supposedly combining overbearing military might and unabated aggressive designs on the world, the Soviet government never showed the slightest intention of launching the third world war. Indeed, the actual history of the Soviet Union is of two great defensive wars for survival (1918–21 and 1941–5) against invasion by capitalist powers.

So, although the 'war of Soviet aggression' is one of the great non-barking dogs in the night of world political history, all the rhetoric and propaganda of anti-communism concealed one of the most compelling and critical political facts of the twentieth century – capitalism causes wars. More specifically, world wars have only ever grown out of rivalries and antagonisms between the great powers which stand at the apex of the global economy.

In that sense, not the smallest of the achievements of the Soviet

Union is that by its existence and, since 1945, its strength, it curtailed the most disastrous of capitalism's tendencies – the tendency to launch wars of ever greater intensity and destructive horror. The Cold War was, in Europe at any rate, a longer period of peace than any in its history since the industrial revolution.[10]

If political leaders and hordes of editorial writers are again speculating on the possibility of war, it is not because of the Soviet Union, but because of its absence. As anti-imperialist scholar Frank Füredi has noted: 'With the disintegration of the Soviet Union, the cement of anti-communism could no longer bind together the western powers.'[11] The 'cement' was the fear of social revolution which the Soviet Union embodied, with its 70-year history of getting along without capitalists and its diplomatic, economic and sometimes military support for peoples in various parts of the world fighting for social change and national liberation.

The smashing up of the Soviet Union has released the demons of inter-capitalist rivalry in two distinct ways. First, it has rendered obsolete many of the forms and structures of great power co-operation which have developed since 1945. NATO has been left floundering around for a new role. Questions have been raised about the composition of the United Nations Security Council. 'Special relationships' have been shown to be only skin deep, and based mainly on fear of communism.

Second, the restoration of the capitalist system – in the most primitive and barbarous form – in the former USSR and the countries of eastern and central Europe has opened up new areas for capital investment and new markets for profitable exploitation by big business. Inevitably, different interests collide in the scramble for influence in these virgin territories – witness, for example, the spread of the Deutschmark zone into eastern Europe, the complications this is causing for France, the threats emanating from Russia.[12]

However, the overthrow of socialism is only one of the factors that have made for the return of the spectres of 1914. This would not on its own destabilise the relations between the Western powers were the conditions for such a destabilisation not already present. The most important such condition is the decline of the post-war US economic and industrial hegemony, which the requirement of the Cold War for continued US military leadership had masked (and also exacerbated through the financial demands it made on Washington).

In 1945, the United States, flushed with the boost given to its manufacturing industries by World War II, accounted for over half of worldwide industrial production. The British Empire ranked second in the capitalist world, massively indebted but still on its feet. France was striving to recover its world economic position lost as a result of military defeat in 1940 and subsequent German occupation. Germany was in ruins, while Japanese business was striving anxiously to reorganise under US occupation.

Fifty years later, the United States does not produce more than 20 per cent of the world's industrial output, the dollar is fast losing its pre-eminent position amongst the world's currencies, and US industry has found itself losing one market after another. Japan's economy, on the other hand, looks set to overhaul the US fairly soon, perhaps by the turn of the century. Germany has become the mightiest economy in Europe, and is in the leadership of an emerging European bloc (substantially overlapping with but not confined to the member states of the EU) which could be economically more powerful than either the US or Japan. Within this bloc and beyond it, Britain and France both struggle for their special interests, although as relatively weakened powers. And, to the east, a new, embryonic, Russian imperialism could emerge, with its own developing sphere of influence – mainly among former Soviet republics, but also beyond. On the other hand, Germany, the US and (in Central Asia) Turkey are competing with Russia for influence in parts of this territory.

Under this new situation, it is clear that the political structures of the world since 1945 – the alliances, special relationships, spheres of influence – are increasingly at odds with the actual strengths and possibilities of the powers. Hence the insistent impetus towards a new redistribution of world political power, the disintegration of a global (i.e. US-dominated) capitalist bloc and its replacement by competing regional groupings, and rivalry for control of new markets for investment.

Currency crises, the expansion of NATO, the attitudes towards the wars in the former Yugoslavia, the rifts in the British Conservative party over European policy, the argument over the composition of the UN Security Council, the virtual economic annexation of Mexico by the US, are all part of a single connecting thread – all expressions of these rising contradictions in the 'new world order'.

The institutions of the international order appear all but impotent before these contradictions. The most venerable – the United Nations – has suffered a complete fiasco in Bosnia as a result of its failure to operate a policy around which all the great powers can agree. A wistful New York firefighter, seconded to Bosnia under the UN's auspices only to learn that his own government would no longer allow him to serve, told the BBC that if the US government continued like this 'the UN will go the way of the League of Nations, and that led straight to world war two'. Every word from the right-wingers increasingly ascendant in

Washington indicates that the US government is dead set on this course – pursuing US interests without regard to whatever restraints may be imposed by multilateral forums. Proposals to expand the membership of the United Nations' decisive Security Council to Japan and Germany will, if accepted, most likely extend this paralysis rather than end it.

The newest international institution – the World Trade Organisation, designed to enforce free trade policies around the globe – is doing no better. No sooner had it opened for business in 1995 with an agreed set of rules and procedures than the world's largest trading nation, the United States, unilaterally disregarded it by slapping tariffs on Japanese luxury cars as part of its intensifying trade dispute with Tokyo.

The conflicts, negating the hopes of a 'new world order' and the bodies designed to promote it, do not themselves appear out of nowhere. They are, as we shall try to elaborate, inherent in the present phase of world capitalism, a period of increasing chaos and disorder, symptomatic of the clash between the vast development of the productive forces worldwide and the incapacity of the economic system to harness those forces for the general good.

On the one hand, new technology has multiplied the productive potential of the world economy; on the other, living standards have regressed throughout much of the world over the last ten to fifteen years, and stagnated in much of the remainder. In 1995, people in Latin America, Africa, most of the Middle East, eastern Europe and the former Soviet Union live worse than they did in the mid-1970s. Over the same period, real wages for workers have stagnated in the United States. Wealth has been redistributed in favour of the already wealthy. Unemployment has risen throughout the developed countries and has remained at mass levels. The post-war welfare systems have come under attack throughout western Europe, under conservative or social-democratic governments alike. Yet this has coexisted with a general rise in production, despite two major slumps, a range of new technical developments from the Internet to robots and CDs, and a consistent rise in corporate profits.

The central argument is that these facts are connected to the speculative scenario outlined at the start of this Introduction. A connection, but not an inevitable one, or one the world must inexorably travel through. The main purpose here is to help inspire the action which can ensure that the last world war remains just that – the last one. To uproot the causes of war means to struggle against the prevailing world economic and political system, a prospect which seems particularly difficult and sometimes fruitless at present. But the consequences of passivity will be worse.

CHAPTER 1

A History of Wars

In order to understand great-power rivalry today, it is worth taking a brief look at the issue over the last hundred years or so in order to establish where such rivalry springs from.

As capitalism has given us a 'world economy', it has also given us 'world war', a uniquely twentieth-century creation. The emergence of world wars as the decisive events in the development of human society on the planet is not due to technology, transport or communications (although it would be impossible without them). It arises out of the logic of the development of capitalism as a world system. War extends the competition inherent in capitalism – the struggle of companies for markets and profits – to the level of conflict between nation-states which are themselves the expression of capitalist interests.

The existence of a number of states dominated by capitalist interests does not in itself mean that conflict automatically follows. If one country is at a higher level of development, with vastly superior technology, productivity and industrial capacity, its capitalists could expand peacefully into the markets of other states. Likewise, even a group of powerful nation-states at the same level of economic development need not clash if there are still unexploited markets and territory in the world – zones into which each can expand, negotiating to avoid conflict.

History gives examples of both situations, sometimes pertaining for a considerable period of time. But it gives still more dramatic examples of the opposite – periods when there have been a number of leading capitalist states at approximately the same level of development at a time when there has been no 'virgin territory' in terms of unexploited or uncontrolled markets to commercially conquer. The powers controlling particular markets, by and large in the interests of their own national capitalist groups, may not necessarily be the most dynamic or productive. The rising economic powers find themselves beating against the existing world power relationships, with no new areas to expand into, hemmed in by the vested interests of the established powers. Conflict follows.

This has proved to be the main common thread in the history of the relations between the major capitalist powers over the last 125 years. Britain, being the first country to integrate the advances in

industrial technology of the late eighteenth century with an established system of commercial capitalism, built a worldwide hegemony based on its economic might, disposing of its French and
Dutch commercial rivals from the recent past as challengers for
future world leadership en route.

A virtual industrial monopoly led, when combined with vast
naval resources and accumulated mercantile capital, to a virtual
trading monopoly and then an expansive colonial empire and a
still wider zone of financial and trading control. At its peak this
included most of Latin America, Turkey and much of Asia as well
as the formal British Empire.

Yet other nations – Germany, the United States, France and
Japan above all – developed industrially, eroding Britain's unique
advantages. Starting after Britain, they often built higher levels of
technology into their industries from the start. Britain, meanwhile, did not renew its industrial capacity and infrastructure on
the basis of competitive technology, preferring to invest ever-
larger sums in protected colonial markets which could not be
penetrated by a competitor, however superior its industrial effi-
ciency. Under these circumstances British leaders retreated somewhat from their earlier state religion of 'free trade' to doctrines of
'imperial preference' and what today might be called 'managed
trade'.

The business interests of the United States were still, at the turn
of the century, mainly concerned with their rapidly growing
domestic market, and were disinclined to get involved in a war to
redivide the world. But while Britain retained its colonial and
financial hegemony intact, there was no easy way for the rising
business leaders of the German Empire to expand into the new
markets to the extent which they felt their powerful industries
merited.

German companies enjoyed a particular lead over the British in
productivity in the leading edge industries at the turn of the
century. If Britain still led in coal and textiles, it was German
companies which were most adept at applying new technologies in
industries like machine-building and chemicals, sometimes establishing a near-monopoly position in strategic products. British
interests often retained, through colonial and trade privileges,
markets they would have lost to German concerns had the previous doctrine of 'free trade' been impartially applied. It was only
in 1914 that Britain's rulers noticed their complete dependence
on imports from Germany of such vital items as ball-bearings
and advanced electric generators, and the great relative under-
development of their light engineering and steel industries.[1]

The years before 1914 were years of various 'war scares' in North
Africa, of intense Anglo-German naval rivalry and of developing

chauvinist politics in both countries, including the demonisation in each of the other. But the fundamental rivalry which impelled the world towards war in 1914 was the commercial rivalry of the British Empire, determined to preserve its position, and Germany, determined to undermine it. Given the growing inter-connections in the world economy, the fact that other powers also had an interest in preserving or acquiring colonial possessions, and that any rearrangement of the geopolitical map of the world could either profit or disadvantage them and their banks and big companies, it was never likely that any conflict could be confined to Britain and Germany alone. And, of course, World War I began as a war pitting the enfeebled Austro-Hungarian Empire against Serbia and its imperial Russian ally, immediately over the balance of power in the Balkans.

France and Britain fought alongside each other, a fact that would have astonished the military leaders of both countries a century earlier. However, the Battle of Waterloo in 1815 had marked the definitive defeat of France in its struggle for European supremacy with Britain, and its defeat by Prussian armies in 1871 had made abundantly clear its weak position relative to Germany; furthermore its inferior industrial base made playing a powerful independent role almost impossible by 1914. The united Germany which had been forged by Bismarck in the wake of the 1871 victory changed the balance of power in Europe for good, giving Germany both the capacity as well as the desire to challenge the status quo in international politics.

For example, in 1870, Britain mined 112 million tons of coal against 35 million in Germany, while in 1913 the relative figures were 292 million to 277 million. Still more striking, pig iron production in the two countries was 6,055,000 tons to 1,262,000 in Britain's favour in 1870. In 1913 the relative figures were 10,425,000 for Britain and 16,632,000 in Germany. However, Britain had, in 1904, 50 colonial banks with 2,279 branches while Germany had only 13 such banks with just 70 branches in the colonies.[2]

So the nature of what generations called the Great War was not primarily rooted in geography, diplomacy, the personality of the Kaiser or the Tsar, but in the logic of international competition between capitalist nation-states. The former factors did, of course, play a role in the course of the conflict and in its exact configurations. But it was the clash of economic interests that played the main part in unleashing the war. The 1914–18 war broadly pitted those great powers satisfied with the status quo or, like Tsarist Russia, anxious about any consequences of an attempted disturbance of it, against the power which needed a reordering of the world to allow its monopolies their place in the sun.

Russia's place in the anti-German coalition was enough to dispel any notion that the war was being fought for a particular set of values or freedoms. Britain's strategic interests led it to overlook the differences between its political system and that of the Russian Empire. However, it is important to understand that, while the tendency towards war was inherent in the world situation before 1914, the particular shape of that war was not inevitable or god-given. Britain could easily have clashed with Russia over its expansion southwards towards India, or with France over Middle Eastern and North African policy.

Equally importantly, war was preceded by numerous efforts to reach a mutually acceptable accommodation between the interests of the powers. Africa was divided, naval treaties were signed, trade agreements made and unmade in an endeavour to achieve peacefully the division and redivision of spheres of economic influence which the rise of new powers like Germany so obviously demanded. What made this impossible in the end was the limited room for manoeuvre in a world economy already complete and carved up – finally, something given to one power and its business interests had to be taken from another.

Once embarked upon, World War I proved impossible to stop, contrary to most expectations at its outset. Each power declared that it was a war for 'national survival' in which the alternative to victory was to be crushed and to lose its place in the world order completely. In this, the conflict exactly reproduced the nature of monopoly competition, in which the stronger company ultimately puts the weaker out of business, swallowing up its assets and taking over its markets. And that, indeed, was the peace which the victors imposed on the vanquished. Germany was deprived of all its colonies, had its border territories detached and was subjected to a crushing reparations regime, all designed to ensure that it could not rise again as a major imperialist competitor. The Austro-Hungarian Empire was completely broken up, its territory being fragmented into several wholly or partially new states.

Before arriving at that point, however, humanity's first exercise in world war had already produced two contradictory results. It had drawn the world still closer together, by involving both Japan and, more significantly, the United States in what 50 years earlier would have been a purely European war. No great power anywhere could afford to be a mere spectator in a major redivision of the world. Yet on the other hand, the war had set in motion an unprecedented process of fragmentation, with the departure of the now Soviet Russia from the system as a whole

This contradiction of integration and disintegration defined the agenda of world politics for the 30 years after 1917. The existence of an increasingly powerful socialist state changed every calculation. It did not remove or displace rivalry between the capitalist powers, but it embodied a serious new complication – the prospect of revolution. In their hearts, even if they seldom announced it as public policy, many politicians from the ruling classes resolved that they would rather suffer any humiliation at the hands of another state that at least accepted the values of western imperialist 'civilisation', than they would run the risk of a revolution in the name of another civilisation entirely.

This determined, in turn, the development of events towards World War II. In 1919 and for some time thereafter France wished to see Germany kept down, the better to secure its own hegemony in continental Europe. However, when it became obvious in 1940 that Germany was crushing France rather than the other way round, most of the French ruling class collapsed gratefully into Hitler's arms the better to forestall a recurrence of the 1871 Paris Commune on a grander scale. Given a choice of occupation or revolution, most of the French establishment chose occupation.

Britain, however, gave priority from the start to rebuilding its former enemy as a barrier against Bolshevism while the British Empire was inflated to its greatest ever extent, in part thanks to the addition of several former German colonies. So the basic causes of World War I were reproduced and intensified by the peace settlement at its conclusion.

These problems were exacerbated by the global slump which followed the stock market crash of 1929. This stimulated the rise of the 'war party' to the leadership of Germany, above all, and more broadly led to the formation of trade blocs and cartel arrangements by powers still concerned with forestalling socialism at any price. As contemporary writer R. Palme Dutt put it: 'Tariffs are a weapon of conflict of modern monopolist capitalism. Their aim is, by securing unlimited exploitation of the home market, to use this as a base for conquering foreign markets and for conducting warfare against foreign rivals.'[3]

The rise of Hitler, the most lurid political consequence of the world slump, was a product of the tendency towards war inherent in the situation, rather than a cause of it. The roots of Germany's pre-1914 dissatisfaction with the world order (a powerful domestic industry with limited access to foreign markets, above all) had been made still greater by the punitive Versailles peace. Its industries, speedily rebuilt in spite of the reparations, still sought new outlets and markets. The lands to the east of Germany, in particular the vast territories and natural resources of the USSR, beckoned – with the new advantage that such an enterprise could be presented as not just mere German acquisitiveness but as a signal contribution to saving capitalist civilisation from the Bolshevik menace. This central thrust of German policy pre-dated the advent of Hitler to office. The head of the great chemicals monopoly IG Farben wrote in 1931, two years before the Nazi take-over: 'The narrowness of the national economic territory must be overcome by transnational economic territories . . . For a final settlement of the problem of Europe . . . a close economic combine must be formed from Bordeaux to Odessa as the back-bone of Europe.'[4] It was in order to form such a 'close economic combine', which bears more than a passing resemblance to the present-day EU, under the direction of Farben and the like, that Hitler was entrusted with power by the German establishment of 1933.

Britain, more than ever a satisfied power despite its continuing economic underperformance relative to its rivals, based its policy on the assumption – mistaken, as it turned out – that Germany too could achieve satisfaction without striking at the vital interests of the British Empire. This line persisted even after the declaration of war in September 1939 – indeed, the French and British general staffs showed considerably more vigour in planning anti-Soviet military action as a result of the Finnish war that winter than they did in preparing any moves against Germany. Collaboration by the capitalist powers against communism remained a serious policy option even after the European powers were formally at war with each other. Had the Nazi–Soviet non-aggression pact not been in place, such co-operation could well have become a reality, however much the pact was a shock to the anti-fascists of 1939.

However, the war of London's dreams – pitting Germany against the USSR – never began until well after it was clear that only the former's defeat could give Britain a hope of preserving its place in the world. World War II was the product of deeply conflicting interests and goals on the part of the different powers (and some-times within them). Its anti-fascist content is indisputable, but the war was not the product of fascism in particular, but of the capital-ist system in general.

This was much clearer in relation to the conflict in Asia, which saw Britain fighting to preserve its imperial possessions, the US seeking to expand as the hegemonic power in the Pacific and Japan determined to expel both in order to establish its own unchal-lenged 'Greater East Asia Co-Prosperity sphere'. As with the 'close economic combine' in Europe urged by the boss of IG Farben, this has proved to be an enduring aspiration, outlasting several changes in political system. This character of the Far Eastern conflict explains the widespread view in India, Burma and Indo-China that there was little to choose between the warring parties, an attitude that sometimes extended to support for Japan's war propa-ganda about the desirability of expelling the decadent Western colonialists from Britain and France. 'Nirad C. Chaudhuri, an

ardent admirer of the British Empire in India, has written about
the whole-hearted partisanship felt towards the Germans and
Japanese by the Indian people, and the eager expectation of a
British collapse ... Scholars of Vietnam, Cambodia, Burma, Malaysia, Singapore and the Philippines have found a positive impact in
the Japanese invasion', according to an Indian writing in a British
conservative journal.[5]

Asian anti-colonialists had, surprisingly, an ally in Washington.
While the US directed its military activities in the Pacific exclusively against the Japanese, its diplomatic struggle was as much
directed against the British Empire, and at replacing British influence everywhere from Australia to the smallest protectorate with
the domination of the dollar. It used the slogan of 'decolonisation'
and the rights of all people to independence – an idea which
Churchill, the arch-opponent of any such right, had been forced to
sign up to in the Atlantic Charter. 'The wartime archives amply
reveal that the sense of historic antagonism between Britain and
the United States continued to exist along with the spirit of co-
operation generated by the war', according to one historian, who
adds that Roosevelt 'made it no secret that he deplored British
imperialism in India and in all other parts of the world. He found
it easier to talk to Stalin and Chiang Kai-shek than Churchill
about the future of the British Empire.'[6] But behind Washington's
idealistic anti-colonial rhetoric was a desire to extend its own
sphere of influence.

The conclusion of this hybrid conflict was pretty much in line
with 'worst case scenarios' for all of the powers which had started
it. Only the world's two leading economic powers, the US and
the USSR, which had been neutral at the start of the war, came
out of it ahead. Socialism emerged greatly strengthened, despite
the devastation wrought by the Nazis on the USSR, expanding
throughout eastern Europe and, shortly thereafter, to China as
well. The US, in 1950 home to 50 per cent of world industrial
production, emerged as the only real winner among the capitalist
states. Germany and Japan were knocked out and under military
occupation, while Britain and, still more, France, were seriously
weakened and under a degree of economic occupation. The skids
were clearly under the established empires, leaving the US to fill
the vacuum in every sense except that of formal and direct political
sovereignty.

These two consequences of the war marked the last great shift in
world politics before 1991. A united world capitalist bloc was
rebuilt under the hegemony of a single power, the US, which had
such a commanding economic position as to be able to impose its
will, with the minimum of negotiation, on all other capitalist
powers. The latter were, moreover, in mortal fear of the Soviet

Union and the newly strengthened socialist bloc and world communist movement. After two wars which were the culmination of rivalry between the great powers, these powers were at last able to form a common front on the basis of anti-Sovietism.

One by one, the pillars of this new system of collaboration were put into place: NATO (the first-ever all-embracing military organisation of the great powers), Bretton Woods, the World Bank and the IMF. The aim was three-fold – encircling and menacing the USSR and its allies, keeping the Third World tied closely to the interests of the great powers despite decolonisation in the 1950s and 1960s, and integrating as much of the world as possible under US leadership. As part of this strategy, the pre-war ruling classes were firmly re-established in West Germany and Japan as strongholds against communism by a US government which could not conceive of them ever becoming serious economic rivals to the vastly-powerful US corporations. Stalin, however, writing in 1952, did predict the course of events.

> Let us pass to the major vanquished countries, Germany and Japan. These countries are now languishing in misery under the jackboot of American imperialism. Their industry and agriculture, their trade, their foreign and home policies and their whole life are fettered by the American occupation 'regime'. Yet only yesterday these countries were great imperialist powers and were shaking the foundations of the domination of Britain, the US and France in Europe and Asia. To think that these countries will not try to get on their feet again, will not try to smash the American 'regime' and force their way to independent development, is to believe in miracles.[7]

Big-power jockeying for position never entirely abated, of course. The Suez crisis of 1956, with Washington refusing to back the Anglo-French attack on Egypt, was the most obvious example. Nevertheless, for the first time the conflict between capitalist nation-states over markets and spheres of influence did not dominate world politics. Only gradually did classic inter-imperialist rivalry begin to reassert itself, as the conditions which gave rise to the 'united front' of the post-war years began to dissolve.

The US started to go into relative economic decline. Japan and the Federal Republic of Germany began to develop their economic power once more, even while the US started to lose its competitive edge. This movement of history was exacerbated by costs of the Vietnam War, which forced the US to end the convertibility of the dollar into gold, and thereby destroyed the main pillar of the post-war economic order.

This slow decline fell a long way short of eliminating the United

States' enormous strategic superiority in the world at large. Her military might remained dominant, but Washington was no longer the sole economic great power. Having welcomed the evolution of the Common Market as cementing western Europe together against the threat from the east, it now found the European allies sometimes following their own policy *vis-à-vis* the Soviet Union. Trade frictions with Japan also began to multiply. These growing problems between the great powers, and between all of them and the weaker third world, did not, however, pull apart the anti-Soviet alliance. It was only with the end of the USSR after 1989 and the end of the Cold War which demanded US military leadership that the latent problems of great power rivalry began to reassert themselves – leaving the twentieth century in much the same position as they found it, with rival powers manoeuvring for advantage, forming blocs and shaping new, independent, military and geopolitical strategies.

CHAPTER 2

The World Economy and the Nation-State

The arguments about the world economy today often echo those of the period before 1914. The following exposition on the peaceful effects of global economic competition was made by a leading socialist, the German Eduard Bernstein, shortly before World War I, an event that dramatically refuted almost everything he said:

> The economic development of nations will intensify their enmity: what nonsense! As if nations were petty shop-keepers competing for a limited clientele such that a gain for one necessarily represented a loss for the others. A mere glance at the development of the commercial relations among the advanced countries demonstrates the fallacious character of these ideas. The most industrially developed countries are simultaneously competitors and customers of one another; likewise their trade relations expand simultaneously with their mutual competition . . . the era in which peoples attempted to subjugate one another is finished in Europe and the same will more and more tend to be true in Asia. We have entered a new epoch, an epoch in which international law will prevail.[1]

Bernstein was not alone. Two months before the start of the 1914 war, the Socialist International praised big business for its promotion of international co-operation.[2] If social democrats seem stuck for new policies today, they are also stuck for new illusions.

The view that we are seeing the dawning of an era of world peace because of the global expansion of capitalism is being propounded with renewed vigour today. The key buzz-word is 'globalisation', denoting the increased integration of the world capitalist economy. This globalisation is supposed to eliminate many of the functions and rivalries of the nation-state and, with them, the prospect of a repetition of the two world wars of the twentieth century.

We shall argue here that, beneath the surface movement of things, the actual direction of development is *away* from 'globalisation', if that term has any meaning, towards a *dis*integration of the world economy and towards new clashes between various capitals organised in the form of nation-states.

Some of the consequences of this 'globalisation' were suggested in an article on the significance of the new developments in the *Financial Times*:

> Globalisation has been one of the more significant developments in the industrialised world over the past 15 years. Driven by the desire to produce and sell goods in more than one market, it has led to the spread of corporate operations across borders through international investment, trade and collaboration for purposes such as product development, sourcing and marketing ... As many as one in 10 jobs a year have been destroyed by this process. But it has also created jobs on a similar scale. It is because globalisation has so far taken place mainly within the group of industrialised countries that the destruction and creation of jobs on this scale has been politically and socially acceptable.[3]

Another, more severe, view of the actual state of the world economy was given by David Henderson, a former head of economic research for the Organisation of Economic Cooperation and Development (OECD), at a conference hosted by British Prime Minister John Major in 1992. He said that in many areas the policy of OECD member-states 'continue to have significant disintegrating effects within the world economy ... the tendency over the past decade or more has been to maintain and even reinforce such policies'. Henderson instanced the drift towards 'managed trade' (the ante-room to protectionism) as the prime example of this, adding that 'the world economy in October 1992 is further away from full integration than it was in June 1914'.[4]

So what is new and what has changed? There has, of course, been much that is new in the last 20 years which has led to the talk of a fresh phase in capitalism's development. First, it has become once more the almost universal economic system across the planet. It has been at least provisionally restored in the USSR and eastern Europe, and, in the wake of that development, has drawn back into its orbit nearly all those countries which had previously existed to some extent or other outside the capitalist system under the economic and strategic umbrella of the Soviet Union. Even China and Vietnam, which remain formally attached to a socialist system, are increasingly integrated into a world economy that is unarguably capitalist.

This geographical extension of the scope of capitalism has been matched by an intensification of almost every *international* aspect of the system – trade, capital flows, currency movements, globally organised production – relative to most of the post-1945 period.

For the largest corporations and for the great financial institutions the process of turning a profit may combine financing, production, distribution and marketing operations from several countries under closely integrated central control. However, this process is far from representing a 'globalisation' in the sense of blurring the divisions between the major nation-states.

'Globalisation' is an extension of the already existing power relationships in the world economy, in which the controllers of capital in the great powers seek to reinforce and intensify their exploitation of the rest of the world. It is the carrying forward of the process of competition to a new level – not one in which the world economy functions as an integrated whole without divisions or rivalries, but one in which the whole world becomes the arena of struggle for supremacy between the various capitalist groups, organised through trans-national corporations, banks and global financial institutions, cartels and alliances, trading blocs and, ultimately, the power of nation-states.

Role of the Nation-state

Much mystery surrounds the nation-state. For some, it is an eternal element of the human condition, something which has always been and will always be, passing more or less unscathed through epochs, social systems and economic transformations. For others, it is already as good as dead, reduced to a mere husk by the globalisation of economic power, retaining merely the shadow of its pomp while the substance has removed elsewhere.

Unlike nations or states, both of which have a fairly long historical lineage, the nation-state is, by and large, a creation of the last two hundred years or so – broadly, the era of capitalism. European history is full of states (like the Holy Roman Empire or the Empire of the Russian Tsar) which exercised authority over diverse collections of peoples, some of which considered themselves as nations and some of which had a more limited sense of identity. More recently, there have been multi-national socialist states, based in principle on the equality of different nations, like the USSR, Yugoslavia or Czechoslovakia. There were also peoples who came to see themselves as 'nations', like the Germans or Italians before the mid-nineteenth century, divided between any number of states of their own; and nations like the Poles or the Irish, long prevented from creating any state whatsoever by oppressing powers, but retaining a strong national identity nevertheless.[5]

The nation-state owes its rise to eminence, at least in most parts of the world, to the need for ruling classes to secure a stable, extended basis for the accumulation of capital, with an integrated market, common laws, language, currency and customs. In some cases, where the nation was already fairly well developed, like England, the transformation of the feudal state into the modern nation-state included a measure of continuity; although even here the nation-state's territory was extended by the annexation of Scotland. These, however, tend to be the historical exceptions, numbering only half a dozen or so and confined to parts of western Europe and Japan alone. Few 'nation-states' can plausibly trace a lineage back before the emergence of the world capitalist system. The nation-state, according to *The Economist*, is 'a pretty recent arrival on the political scene and has the resilience of youth'.[6] It is a political structure which still provides the most favourable conditions for the accumulation of capital.

British writer Anthony Brewer accurately summed up the symbiosis of the nation and the state under capitalism:

> Capital and the nation-state have grown up together . . . the existence of a state (and the extension of its boundaries to the point where the resistance of other nation-states limited further expansion) created and delimited national interests, national markets and so on. Each capital looked to its 'own' state for support against other capitals forming in other nation-states and, through the common need for state support, formed an alliance with other regional capitals within the same nation.[7]

Of course, it is also obvious that the capitals operating through the nation-state do not call a halt to their expansion at the point where they meet the boundaries of other nation-states. Whether or not they proceed to an attempt at formal annexation and extension of their 'own' state authority (and this has happened repeatedly), each national capital cannot but seek to expand at the expense of the subordination of the capitals of other lands.

This does not mean that the functions of the nation-state may not be changed or constricted by economic developments, or even that some particular nation-states may disappear, merge or change shape. Some states in Europe, for example, have lost much of the capacity to carry out autonomously some of the range of functions which used to characterise all nation-states. This is rather similar to the way in which the concentration of capital through agreements, mergers, take-overs and so on reduces and finally eliminates the independent operation of separately organised capitals in a particular branch of industry. In the case of nation-states, their abolition has almost always been the consequence of war, in which a temporarily victorious state might subordinate other nations to its authority. And, of course, in the 'third world', many states have never been permitted significant capacity for independent action in the first place, despite possessing all the formal attributes of sovereignty.

But none of this abolishes the nation-state as such. It merely defines the differences in power between them. To see the abolition of the nation-state as a whole, we would first have to see the emergence of international corporations based on the merger of different national capitals in a particular branch of industry, the organised division of the world between such monopolies, operating on the basis of a single monetary system and a unified trading system, and the creation of international bodies of authority (a global state) to regulate their competition and impose their will on the peoples of the world.

In principle, that would be the final destination of the present economic development. It would not be a world of peace, since there would still be innumerable social conflicts, but it would be a world in which war between nation-states would no longer occur, because nation-states themselves would have been superseded by the development of a fully integrated international economic system and would remain in form only, if at all.

However, such a perspective exists in principle alone – if economic development could be reduced to the unimpeded progress of a sort of mathematical model, that is where the world would end up. There is, first of all, no sign of the international fusion of capitals becoming a serious tendency within the world system. Many observers mistake the global extension of the operations of US or Japanese or French companies (sometimes by buying up a foreign rival) as being equivalent to their merger into a non-national whole, a point examined in more detail later. Secondly, the world currency and trading systems are in important respects operating to a common standard less than before. This is because the overwhelming predominance of one capitalist power willing and able to enforce uniform rules, which has been the prerequisite for such a world order hitherto, is absent and not in sight of return – unless one of the existing powers is able to effectively 'knock out' one or more of its rivals. There is no currency on a 'gold standard', for example, and no power imposing uniform trading rules.

More serious, however, is the fact that if the progress towards monopoly in an industry proceeds through tariff barriers, cartels, price-fixing, hostile takeovers, etc., behind a veneer, at best, of 'gentlemen's agreements', the elimination of nation-states could only be completely accomplished (under capitalism) through force. The first steps may be peaceful – one can envisage a hypothetical Franco-German 'cartel' gently laying Belgium to rest, or even Germany swallowing up Austria which in turn might absorb Slovenia without shots being fired. But even within the EU the possibilities of the peaceful absorption of the British state by the German state are non-existent, to say nothing of the ending of the Russian, Japanese, US or Chinese nation-states.

So the tendency towards creating a single global economy, which is certainly inherent in capitalism, can really only proceed through the further strengthening of the already strong nation-states, the subordination of the weaker ones, and the intensification of competition between the survivors.

The point has been well made by leading African scholar Samir Amin:

> The United States and Japan are not merely geographical areas of a world economy under construction. They are and will remain national economies, with a state that ensures the continuance of national structures while grabbing the lion's share of world trade. Fanatics of liberalism will tell us that this is a rearguard action. It may come down to this over the next couple of centuries, but it is a vanguard action from the perspective of the next couple of decades.

According to Amin 'no supranational state is visible on the horizon. This is the first major source of the chaos that the new globalization will bring in its train.' Elsewhere, he writes that while we may witness the emergence of a global capitalism which negates the previous relationship between capital and the state 'the construction of a unified American-European-Japanese state is not likely in the foreseeable future. The contradiction will therefore remain and necessarily generate a new source of global disorder.'[8]

As Amin indicates, such steps as have been taken in the direction of forming a 'global state' highlight the impossibility of such a project at present, rather than its feasibility. The United Nations is the only global body with the potential to dispatch armed forces. Yet those forces are sub-contracted to the UN by nation-states, and are incapable of embarking on any major operation without the support of the US – support which is never forthcoming unless the US government also controls the operation, in essence making the UN another arm of US policy. Despite peace-keeping operations of limited utility by any standards, there is no sign of any of the powers agreeing to cede any real military authority whatsoever to the UN.

On the economic front, the long-established IMF and World Bank are both broadly under US control. Both play a role in enforcing the great powers' control over the 'third world' – imposing austerity, demanding privatisations, etc. – but neither are generally a force in the development of the major economies themselves, or in the relationships between them. The newly formed World Trade Organisation has not got off to a propitious start, since the leading traders apparently continue to prefer to resolve their differences (or descend into protectionism) bilaterally.

The 'G7' – the cartel of rich nations – has been the most significant force in attempting to forge a common economic policy among the big powers. The regular meetings of the leaders of the seven biggest capitalist powers began in the 1970s, essentially as a result of the decline in the capacity of the US to direct international economic affairs on its own any longer. The regulation of currency exchange rates, attempts to co-ordinate growth and to deal with crises like the prospect of mass debt defaults by Third-World states in the early 1980s have been the basic stuff of its agendas.

Nevertheless, it is hard to say what exactly has changed as a result of its endeavours, or what would now be different had the G7 never summitted together. None of its agreements have stuck for long, as currency values and economic policies have gone their own, diverging, ways. The G7 has neither been able to develop a long-term, effective plan for the integration of the major economic blocs, nor to work out a way to manage their divergences.

Since the G7 started meeting, the world has gone through two wrenching recessions, the number of unemployed has soared almost everywhere, currency values have fluctuated wildly, there have been perennial trade rows and the stability of the world financial system has regularly been called into question. If the G7 was born out of the end of the era of US leadership, it has neither been able to provide a collective substitute nor produce one of its own to take over the baton. Indeed, right under the G7's noses the most likely contender, Japan, has entered its worst economic downturn for 60 years. Broadly, the G7 has turned out to be less than the sum of its parts, its failures vividly illustrating the limits of economic co-operation between nation-states.

This failure is not irrational, nor the result of misjudgments which could be set to rights under more enlightened leadership. Much as capital increasingly tends to disregard the significance of national boundaries, the main corporations remain firmly attached to their home base. It remains far easier to achieve a commanding position in a national market, with the profits which would follow, and then look for that market to organically expand into contiguous territories (which is broadly the strategy being pursued by Japan and Germany at present), than it is to pursue global hegemony in a particular industry – although Japanese domination of certain electronics and computer-related industries provide a particular, and contentious, exception. And the attachment to the state is no less than a necessity for realising a profit both at home and abroad – without the functions discharged by the state the great arms monopolies, oil companies, banks and so on would often be floundering. For all the talk of 'free competition', 'open markets', 'free trade' and so on, each state shores up its own companies with a variety of financial, diplomatic and political supports, as we shall see.

Some of the fashionable arguments for the end of the nation-state are intellectually threadbare. For example, Kenichi Ohmae, the top Japanese management consultant guru, takes as exhibit A for his case the demise of the Soviet Union.[9] Now the Soviet Union was about as far from being a classic nation-state as possible – it was a multinational federation. Indeed, its multi-national character, like that of Yugoslavia, was a factor exploited in promoting its collapse. One of the US Marines' top planners, Colonel Thomas Linn, likewise cites developments in the Soviet Union and Yugoslavia as part of a trend of 'disintegrating nation-states'.[10] In fact, the end of the USSR and Yugoslavia has given rise to more than a dozen *new* (or re-created) nation-states, each with their own currencies, customs barriers, etc., a circumstance which has in practice facilitated the restoration of capitalism in many of the new countries.

Ohmae also argues that nation-states are being replaced by what he calls 'region states' like Silicon Valley in California. Only two of his tenuous examples actually cross a national frontier, however. One of those, the San Diego/Tijuana zone across the US–Mexican border, illustrates the real point more precisely. No-one crossing that border could miss the fact that one had passed from one state to another. Besides the strict immigration controls for those heading north (but not south), average income levels are about 10 per cent in the poverty-wracked Tijuana end of the 'zone' of what they are in southern California. The contrast better illustrates the core-periphery nature of the emerging economic blocs rather than the disappearance of the nation-state as a distinct economic entity.

Other arguments are, however, more deeply rooted in the actual developments of the late twentieth century. When seeking to establish the historical redundancy of the nation-state, pundits usually point to the growth in foreign investment (that is, investment by a capitalist concern based in one country in another country), the growth in trade (the movement of goods and services between countries) and the enhanced role of trans-national corporations (companies conducting business operations in more than one country) as the main causes. These are buttressed by forms of communication which can link investors and permit the transfer of funds around the world in next to no time, and which are furthermore not easily amenable to control by national governments.

To take foreign investment first. The figures are certainly

impressive. In 1993 big businesses in the US invested $69 billion abroad, those in the UK 25 billion, France 22 billion, Germany 20 billion and Japan 18 billion. Figures like this prompted the chief economist for the giant Royal Dutch/Shell oil monopoly to enthuse that 'increases in FDI flows have reached the threshold where they create a qualitatively different set of linkages between advanced economies'[11] comparable to the role played by trade in the 1940s. Certainly, they are testimony to the growing internationalisation of economic life, but not to a 'globalisation' in which there is no conflict between the capital flowing out of the different nation-states.

Overall, the role of such capital flows is not as great as this sort of analysis assumes. Foreign direct investment (FDI) accounted, in 1991, for 7.2 per cent of world output, sharply up from 4.4 per cent in 1960, but less than the 9 per cent it represented in 1913. World FDI inflows account for 2.9 per cent of world gross fixed capital formation. Only in Britain do FDI flows exceed 10 per cent of domestic fixed capital formation.[12]

Of course, other forms of foreign investment must also be considered – portfolio holdings of foreign stocks and shares, bank loans, etc. However, the largest capitalist nation-state, with by far the largest number of investors, is rather home-loving here as well: 94 per cent of the stocks owned by Americans are US issued, a sign of what the then vice-chairman of the Federal Reserve, Alan Blinder, called an economy more closed than is generally perceived, one which left Americans 'more able to control our own destiny'.[13] In Japan and Germany, the banks are notoriously fixed on investments in their domestic industrial giants. So while the big corporations and banks clearly seek profit-making opportunities around the world, the inter-penetration of the different national economies is not nearly great enough to justify talk of an integrated world economy. In the words of the chief commentator of the *Financial Times*, 'globalisation is, if not a myth, a huge exaggeration'.[14]

Such capital flows do indeed undermine the sovereignty of third world nations, which find themselves forced to adapt to the rigors of 'globalisation' as they were forced to submit to colonialism and neo-colonialism in past generations. With limited internal resources of capital, and dependent on technology transfers from the big powers for the development of industries which can compete on the world market (using cheap labour as their sole 'asset'), the globalisation imposed by New York, London, Frankfurt, Paris and Tokyo and policed by the IMF and the World Bank does indeed devalue their hard-won sovereignty and tend towards the reduction of 'self-determination' to a purely formal and legalistic assertion.

This was even conceded by the editor of the *Wall Street Journal*. Robert Bartley observed that 'China is much less vulnerable than Mexico' to economic collapse 'because it is much less integrated into the world economy'[15] – that is, subordinate to Wall Street and the City of London.

The real nature of foreign investment was declared in the OECD's proposal to draft an international agreement on the protection of foreign investment, equivalent to worldwide trade agreements like GATT. The *Wall Street Journal* reported: 'There won't be a long-dragging debate in Geneva between GATT's haves and have-nots if the OECD can help it. In order to set the highest possible standards for the [Multilateral Agreement in Investment] the drafting will be exclusively in the hands of the OECD's 25 industrialised democracies.'[16] It is clear whose interests the rules on foreign investment are going to protect and promote.

The vast figures for international capital flows do not signal an integration of the financial interests of the main powers. Capital does indeed tour the globe, with over one trillion dollars (one thousand billion) being transferred on foreign exchanges daily, mainly through London. However, the capital utilised in this and other forms of speculation is not rootless – it is controlled by a definite (and, through merger, diminishing) number of financial institutions, often American. The *Wall Street Journal* commented: 'Heard all about the globalization of finance? Forget it. What's really happening is the Americanisation of finance ... seven of the top ten merger advisers are American, the top four global underwriters of stock offerings in the past three years have been American firms.'[17] And, indeed, Wall Street firms have been swallowing up their London-based rivals to strengthen their own competitive position.

Regulation of the giant financial enterprises is likewise nationally based in the main, even if it performs an international function in limiting the dangers of a bank failure or collapse in one country (like Barings in Britain or Daiwa in Japan) from spreading to the worldwide system. The regulatory system established over the last 20 years has worked to eliminate smaller banks and helped concentrate power in a fewer, bigger, institutions mostly based in New York, London, Frankfurt and Tokyo which are now competing all the more ferociously with each other.

The whole process illustrates the conclusion drawn by one of Bernstein's opponents, the Bolshevik Nikolai Bukharin, who wrote in his work *Imperialism and World Economy*, published in 1916: 'the process of the internationalisation of economic life is by no means identical with the internationalisation of economic interests'.[18]

The growth of the international aspects of 'economic life' is, overall, at least as great today as it was before 1914. But, equally, this has not given rise to one common worldwide 'economic interest'. Instead nation-states, prematurely declared dead and buried, continue to be the vehicle for the expression of differing interests, even if they all compete with one another on a global plane.

Trade

This point is still more apparent when world trade is considered. On the one hand, not only has world trade expanded as a proportion of global economic activity, but also a new policing body – the World Trade Organisation – has been established, ostensibly to enforce the principles of free trade. Yet on the other hand, the actual movement of policy in the major states is away from free trade and towards various forms of protectionism, alongside the division of the world economy into a collection of trade blocs. The development of these blocs is examined later, in considering the unfolding redivision of the world by the leading powers. Here it is necessary to note that, far from representing a 'globalising' trend in economic affairs, one smoothing out contradictions between nation-states, developments in trade are actually signalling a fiercer struggle between them.

That world trade policy is at a turning point is beyond doubt. Both the last head of the General Agreement on Tariffs and Trade organisation and the first leader of its successor body, the WTO, have issued dire warnings. The former, Peter Sutherland, left office warning of a reversion 'to the laws of the jungle. That leads to tension which ultimately leads not only to economic conflict but political conflict';[19] while the latter, Renato Ruggiero, came into office declaiming against a protectionism which 'will destroy resources and encourage nationalism and violence'. He reminded a London audience of the old aphorism: 'If goods cannot cross frontiers, soldiers will.'[20]

Despite such imposing speculation, there are still plenty of frontiers closed to plenty of goods. As with foreign investment, the figures for foreign trade paint a different picture to the one imagined by the partisans of the globalisation thesis. Take the ratio of merchandise trade (imports and exports combined) to GDP for the big powers over this century and you get the results as shown in Table 2.1.

As Table 2.1 reveals, trade is not, overall, a bigger factor in international economic life than it was before World War I, although it is now bigger than in the years since World War II.

The first problem with securing free trade is that there is no power strong enough to impose it. The same factor which undermines currency stability, the absence of any state able to plausibly

Table 2.1: Ratio of merchandise trade to GDP[21]

	1913	1950	1994
Britain	45%	37%	44%
Germany	36%	21%	40%
France	36%	22%	35%
Japan	31%	18%	15%
United States	11%	9%	18%

guarantee the value of its currency in gold, undermines free trade, which has only prevailed as the general norm in the nineteenth century, under British domination, and after World War II, under that of the US. British and US interests were served at these points in history by as many open markets for them to penetrate as possible, since their advanced industrial capacity would, under those circumstances, be at an advantage. Now, qualified free trade – for free trade in some goods or services but not others, against protectionism in some parts of the world but not others – are the best any world leader can manage, however much homage they still pay to Adam Smith.

The new attitude to trade was exemplified in 1995 by the bizarre spectacle of the chief of French car giant Peugeot urging China to maintain its trade barriers, which the Beijing government was considering reducing, in order to keep imports out and thus the profits of his company's two new factories in China up. Monopolies promote competition in one part of the world, where it may suit them, while seeking to restrict it where they need to in order to secure continued profits. The big trans-nationals seek to combine a dominant position within their own 'bloc', buttressed by barriers of one sort of another where necessary, alongside privileged access in as many external markets as possible. Few, if any, genuinely look for a worldwide 'level playing field' in their own industry, while each runs for the assistance of 'their' nation-state in securing the right 'tilt' in the right place – the US for its car industry and defence contractors, Japan for its rice farmers and construction firms, France for its film-makers and agricultural sector, and so on. For such groups, protectionism offers the guarantee of a higher rate of profit than could be secured in 'free competition' on a global basis.

Despite all the free-trade fanfare which accompanied the conclusion of the GATT Uruguay round, the pundits are pessimistic. The *Wall Street Journal*, for example, commented:

> Today's blocs constantly seem to be oozing into each other . . .
> The bloc's benign character could change, however . . . even

now, the blocs are infected with protectionist policies. The EC heavily subsidises its farmers and curbs outsiders' access to European markets; the US extends similar protection to its textile and sugar industries. Japan's structural restrictions make it more difficult for European or US firms to reach Japanese consumers than for Japanese firms to sell to European or US consumers.[22]

Or, as *The Economist* editorialised: 'The barriers politicians have lowered can be raised again . . . Protectionists such as Ross Perot and Sir James Goldsmith, who demand that the trends of global integration be halted and reversed, are frightening precisely because, given the will, governments could do it.'[23]

These fears appear to be well founded. Let us examine the record of the US alone. The consistent pattern has been to try to push down barriers against US-made goods in other countries, while maintaining identical restrictions in their own country. This practice has led to disputes with Canada over beer (1994), Japan over cellular telephones (1989), Japan and Brazil over orange juice (1988), South Korea over beef (1988), Canada over timber (1986), Japan over semiconductors (1985), Japan over leather (1985), Brazil, South Korea and Taiwan over shoes (1982), Taiwan over refrigerators and watches, the EU over a range of agricultural products and so on.[24]

This conflicting pattern, whereby the major trading nations attempt to protect their own industries from imports while removing barriers to those same industries' exports, is likely to get worse. Political support for open markets is slipping fast in the US, particularly in the wake of the free-trade agreement with Mexico, which has cost US jobs while making the economy to the south dependent on US taxpayer guarantees. NAFTA, 'the engine of hemispheric growth', *Business Week* reported, 'has produced a dangerously weak partner for the US. The implication is that, far from triumphing around the world, the free-market model has hit a wall.'[25]

The shape of things to come was signalled when the Clinton administration tore up the rules of the new World Trade Organisation within weeks of its inception by threatening unilateral sanctions against Japan over motor car components, rather than waiting for the WTO to examine the controversy. Far from promoting the ideals of an integrated 'global' economy in which all play by the same rules and the ownership of a company is immaterial, the US speaks exclusively for the interests of General Motors and Ford in the car trade dispute with Japan, for General Electric when trying to open up the German power-generation market, for Archer Daniel Midland on agricultural commodity trade, for Lockheed, Boeing and Martin Marietta in arms sales. And what holds true for the US government holds true for other states as well.

Even the bloc supposedly most advanced on free trade matters, the EU, is riven by disputes between its component nation-states. One day's headlines on a single page of the *Financial Times* tells the story: 'EU energy liberalisation put in doubt' (because of French objections to competition in the sector); 'Dublin tries to avert big EU farm fine' (because of irregularities in its meat market); and 'Denmark seeks curb on state aid to Germany's shipyards'.[26]

Indeed, the great economic powers unite in the trade field only when it comes to devising new forms of protectionism against the third world. For example, the United States government has recently raised the question of 'intellectual property' to a matter of high principle in trade agreements. This is another form of disguised protectionism by the economically powerful, designed to perpetuate the control over technology of US, Japanese and western European big businesses, while locking the industries of poorer countries into a dependence on them. As Noam Chomsky has pointed out,[27] these are demands for the international control of processes which the US and other big powers never recognised when they were developing. They are another clear sign that the supposed restructuring of the world economy around 'globalist' principles masks the continuation and intensification of the domination of the giant trans-national corporations.

We are not yet in a worldwide trade war, although the big powers have been to the brink several times. Certainly, the actual position in relation to world trade lends no comfort at all to the 'end of the nation-state' thesis. The growth of protectionist sentiment, interacting with aggressive competition for markets, has in the past been the scene-setter for conflict on an altogether different plane. Bukharin wrote in 1916 that 'tariff wars . . . are only partial sorties, they are only a sort of testing the ground. In the long run, the conflict is solved by the interrelation of "real forces" i.e. by the force of arms.'[28] Or, as anti-imperialist scholar A. Sivanandan has put it more recently: 'Trade no longer follows the flag, the flag follows trade . . . governments must follow in capital's wake to set up the political and social orders within which it can safely and profitably operate – if needs be with force.'[29]

Trans-national Companies

The final foundation of the case for the globalisation of capitalism has been the emergence of trans-national corporations (TNCs) over the last 30 years or so. Their size and scope has been well documented. The biggest – the great industrial monopolies –

generate annual revenue larger than the gross national product of all but the biggest states. Their operations normally cover every continent. Not only are their products sold ubiquitously, but they are often produced in dozens of different countries. In a further stage of integration, the final commodity in industries like motors and electronics is often itself the product of parts made in a variety of different countries, as the controlling company seeks to ensure that every element and process in the finished goods is made as cheaply as possible.

There are various ways to rank these super-giant companies. The most comprehensive listing is the Global 1000 published annually by the US magazine *Business Week*, which ranks all monopolies (industrial, services and banking) from all countries by market value, that is the worth of the company based on the price of its shares on the stock exchange. The 1995 list is full of familiar names – Shell (no. 2), Coca-Cola (no. 6), Toyota (no. 7), Microsoft (no. 20) – as well as those perhaps only recognised in big business circles themselves – Sanwa Bank (no. 12), Allianz Holding (no. 31).[30]

Taken together, the list is revealing about the distribution of power within world capital today. Of the 1,000, the G7 powers – the US, Japan, Germany, Britain, France, Italy and Canada – together provide the 'home base' for no less than 862, with the US alone accounting for 396 of the monopolies on the list. Japan ranks second, with Britain in third place, testimony to the high degree of monopolisation in the British economy, the highest anywhere in the world. By sector, banks are in the lead, with twice the aggregate market capitalisation of second-placed telecommunications, though overall it is industrial corporations which are predominant.

The outstanding question, however, is to what extent are these giants of the world economy detached from the nation-states which gave birth to them? Are they not so much trans-national (operating across borders) as 'multinational' (not having a single country as a home base)? A very few companies on the list might qualify for that description: Royal Dutch/Shell, Unilever and Reed Elsevier are all Anglo-Dutch in their capital structure and could therefore be considered at least 'binational', as could the Swedish-Swiss giant ABB. More arguably, other Swiss-based companies like Nestlé and Roche, whose value and operation are so out of proportion to the economy of Switzerland, are, in fact, capitals which have had to detach themselves from the nation-state to some extent in order to prosper in the world economy and could be dubbed 'denational'. But the vast bulk of the 1,000 big monopolies all have a national identity, however far-flung their operations, and a close relationship with their own nation-state; its officials, regulators, bankers, diplomats, generals, and so on. Indeed, around three-quarters of wealth produced under the aegis of TNCs is still produced in their home countries, according to a detailed demolition of the globalisation thesis by British academics Paul Hirst and Grahame Thompson, tying the corporations still more closely to the governments of their own nation-state.[31]

There are of course, a host of cross-border relationships between companies of different lands – cartels, 'strategic alliance', joint ventures, and so on. Relatively few of these prove durable, however, either running their course after a particular project, or breaking up under the pressure of the divergent strengths of their different parts after a time. The 'alliance' between German aerospace giant Daimler Benz and Dutch airplane maker Fokker is one recent example. An exception is the European aerospace cartel Airbus Industrie which has survived to date, largely because it is operating in worldwide competition with one other major monopoly – Boeing – and the European companies forming the cartel could not challenge the US company in most markets except in collaboration. Such arrangements may become a larger factor in Europe, although generally under the direction of German interests. Cartels between the blocs, however, are few and far between and have not proved very durable.

If the TNCs have no doubt as to which nation-state to turn to in order to advance their interests in competition with rivals, neither does the nation-state itself lack clarity as to which big businesses are 'ours' and which 'the enemy'. Senior US trade official Jeffrey Garten debunked the globalist myth when he pointed out that 'the most ubiquitous multinational companies are American'. Unconsciously echoing British imperialist Cecil Rhodes, who described the acquisition of empire at the turn of the century as a 'bread-and-butter issue' to prevent Britain's poor from starving and rising up against the system, Garten explained that US trade hegemony was needed because 'millions more high-wage jobs must be generated, not just in the interests of a vibrant economy but also for social cohesion'.[32] The former head of French Intelligence Pierre Marion said of the US that 'in economics, we are competitors not allies'.[33] Clearly 'we' refers to the fusion of the French nation-state, one of the most venerable, with French big business. Other countries have drawn the same conclusion, since government support for the international activity of its own monopolies is growing almost everywhere. Japan spent $146 billion on export support for its monopoly corporations in 1993, France 35 billion, Germany 23 billion, the US 19 billion and the UK 9 billion.[34]

Trans-national corporations retain their strong identity as partners in the 'enterprise' of their home nation-state. Even those analysts seeking to bury the nation-state find themselves drawn back to it when considering the real dynamics of TNC behaviour. For example, British journalists Mathew Horsman and Andrew Marshall portray TNCs as being above and beyond governments, but then admit: 'The TNC also demands a constant, secure environment and local politics may not provide this. In the extreme if they are not getting the environment they require they may import, to put it euphemistically, security: through requesting military intervention from their home country.'[35] We have already seen a number of 'extremes' in which such an importation of security has, appropriately presented, been exactly what happened. United Fruit, at any rate, have yet to invade anywhere, but they have not had any trouble getting invading done when necessary. Britain's giant arms companies – Vickers, British Aerospace and others – looked to their nation-state to protect their interests by trying to expel an embarrassing critic of the Saudi Arabian government from London.

This all reinforces the central point about the contemporary nation-state – that it is an organised expression of monopoly capitalist interests, with different roots and shaped by different forces to be sure, but as unvarying in its aims as a cartel, a trade association or a trans-national corporation in advancing the strategic interests of its 'shareholders', the big business interests.

We are seeing the development of capitalist competition with renewed intensity – fewer and fewer larger and larger companies fighting for market share and profit in a world already carved up between them. Protectionism and currency manipulation are the first signs of the extension of this competition to the level of monopoly capital organised through the nation-state, but clearly not the last.

World Economy

Naturally, one cannot treat the world economy as if it were exclusively concerned with the inter-relationships of the big powers and the leading monopoly groups. That is one side of the picture alone. The world economy embraces the activities of over five billion people, most of them not resident in the G7 powers or in their immediate circle of satellites, which are taken together as the 'developed world'.

For all the turmoil of the twentieth century, it is a fact that the powers around which the world economy was based in 1900 are the same powers as exercise a hegemonic role today, at the end of the century. Of course, their ranking has changed and been reshuffled – Britain has slipped, the US and Japan have risen. However, the 'core' and the 'periphery' of the world economy remain basically as they were. Where at the start of the century one might speak of a handful of industrial powers controlling a large agrarian or semi-agrarian hinterland, today the same powers control the capital and technology of the system, exporting lower-technology and lower-value (having set the terms of trade which assign different values to identical quantities of labour) work throughout the same hinterland.

While some Third World countries live better than 20 years ago and many live worse, rarely has any of them looked like breaking into the ranks of the world's economic elite. Mexico's illusions have been cruelly dashed. South Korea, perhaps, displays the greatest potential for storming the club of the super-rich – however, it is still hemmed in by Japanese economic power, as discussed in Chapter 9. Other Asian countries, or city-states, have grown very fast in recent years, but none are remotely near playing a controlling part in the world economy equivalent to that of the G7 powers.

Historian Paul Kennedy, looking into the next century, sees only a continuation of this situation:

> As we move into the next century the developed economies appear to have all the trump cards in their hands – capital, technology, control of communications, surplus foodstuffs, powerful multinational companies – and, if anything, their advantages are growing because technology is eroding the value of labour and materials, the chief assets of developing countries. Although nominally independent since decolonisation, these countries are probably more dependent upon Europe and the United States than a century ago.[36]

In fact, as Kenichi Ohmae noted, 'the absolute gap in GNP per capita between developed and developing economies has substantially widened. In other words, the road has gotten tougher at the same time as the hurdle has gotten higher.'[37]

Recent developments in the world economy have reinforced this relationship at every point, most notoriously through the 'debt crisis', which saw the historic flow of capital from the developed to the under-developed world reversed, and the states of the Third World pressed into IMF-directed debt bondage for the further enrichment of the big powers. Between 1983 and 1987 alone, $100 billion was transferred from the poorest countries to the richest through the mechanisms of the debt 'crisis'. Foreign aid did not increase at all in the same period.[38] Recent UN figures highlighted the growing gulf: the wealth of the 358 billionaires in the world was greater than that of countries home to around half the world's population added together. In 70 countries, average incomes in

1995 were less than they were in 1980, and in 43 less than they were in 1970.

The consequences of all this have been vividly impressed on the world in the endless pictures of poverty, starvation, disease, social breakdown and local wars in Africa, Latin America, the Middle East and many parts of Asia. The world economic order treats billions of people as objects of exploitation, whose interests need to be taken into account even less now that the ideological alternative embodied in the Soviet Union is considered to be no more.

In view of this situation, which all the great powers together seek to perpetuate, it is scarcely surprising that some see the contradiction between 'North' and 'South' as being the main, or only significant one, left in the world. Indeed, the opposition of the great powers to the peoples of the world is one of the critical factors which will shape the politics of the next century. It is embodied in the resistance of the people of Somalia to the 'human-itarianism' of the US marines, in the determination of Cuba to maintain its independence and its socialism, in the uprisings in the Mexican state of Chiapas and in the continuing struggle of the mass of the Arab people for unity and emancipation, and many other places as well.

However, if it seems bad enough to see humanity divided be-tween a handful of rich powers living at the expense of the rest of the world, the full picture is worse when one understands that those same powers see the world as a battleground to be fought over as well as a site for endless exploitation.

The system of exploitation is, of its nature, also a system of war. The vast profits accruing to the TNCs and banks of the Global 1000 and beyond represent a pool of surplus capital seeking the highest possible rate of return around the globe. Over the last ten years or so, some of this capital has been absorbed in the 'privat-isations' of industries which have become a feature of national economic policy almost everywhere – each privatisation is, of course, a 'once-only', and there is not an infinite number of them. Some capital has moved into the 'emerging markets' of Latin America and Asia, which have a limited capacity to absorb the sums concerned, and involve a high element of risk, as the Mex-ican crisis illustrated – again, much of this money (which may be as much as $50 billion in 1996) is oriented towards once-only privatisations. Some money (mainly German) has started heading into the former socialist countries of Europe. All of these oppor-tunities offer outlets for surplus capital, and prevent the competi-tive struggle reaching fever pitch at present.[39]

In the end, however, there are likely to be great sums of money in the hands of big business with no high-profit home to go to. It is then that the choice will arise most starkly: either a sharper, nationally based struggle for markets which could guarantee a continuance of these profits, or an international change in the prevailing economic system.

Not all socialists had it wrong before 1914. Bernstein's fellow German Rudolf Hilferding concluded his great work *Finance Capital* with words of obvious relevance to today:

> The opening up of the Far East, and the rapid development of Canada, South Africa and South America, have made a major contribution to the dizzy pace of capitalist development, interrupted by only brief depressions, since 1895. Once this development begins to slow down, however, the domestic market is bound to feel the pressure of the cartels all the more acutely, for it is during periods of depression that concentration proceeds most rapidly. At the same time, as the expansion of the world market slows down, the conflict between capitalist nations over their share in it will become more acute, and all the more so when large markets which were previously open to competition ... are closed to other countries by the spread of protective tariffs.[40]

Hilferding's book was published in 1910. But his description of the situation provides a general principle which holds true of the world in 1997, the world of falling real wages, growing poverty, mega-mergers and trade skirmishes.

CHAPTER 3

The End of the USSR

When historian Eric Hobsbawm sought to frame his 'short twentieth century', he chose 1991 as the year to mark the end of the epoch which began with the start of World War I in 1914. For it was in 1991 that the most enduring and significant legacy of the events set in motion in 1914 finally came to an end with the dissolution of the Union of Soviet Socialist Republics. More than the fall of the Berlin Wall and the restoration of capitalism in eastern Europe, the overthrow of the socialist system in its heartland, and the consequent disintegration of the first multinational socialist state, marked a signal transformation in world politics and society scarcely less significant than the October Revolution of 1917 itself.

It is not necessary here to examine all the reasons for the triumph of capitalist counter-revolution in a country of which Fidel Castro said in 1992 'its existence was as sure as the sun appearing in the morning, for it was such a solid, powerful, strong, country that had survived extremely difficult tests'.[1] However, some understanding of the unravelling of Soviet power is essential for grasping the main features of the 'post-Soviet' world situation.

The matter was put fairly simply by Lenin after the Revolution:

> We are living not merely in a state, but in a system of states, and the existence of the Soviet Republic side-by-side with imperialist states for a long time is unthinkable. One or the other must triumph in the end. And before that end comes, a series of frightful collisions between the Soviet Republic and the bourgeois states will be inevitable.[2]

Perhaps Lenin would have been less surprised by the demise of the Soviet Union after over 70 years in a hostile world environment than by its survival for so long, the more so since there was no shortage of 'frightful collisions' throughout those years. These included the wars of intervention by 14 different capitalist powers between 1918 and 1921, the Nazi invasion of 1941, the provocations of the Truman doctrine of 'rolling back communism', the wars in Korea and Vietnam, the restrictions on trade and economic relations, the blockade of Cuba, a variety of political and propaganda campaigns and, finally, an endless arms race pumped up to breaking point by the Reagan administration.

Nevertheless, this litany represents only one side of the factors which drove the Soviet Union into decline, stagnation and eventual collapse. V. M. Molotov, for many years Soviet Premier and Foreign Minister, speaking near the end of a life which paralleled closely that of the state he served, offered this assessment:

> Our country moved to the front line, so to speak, and has lived with two fundamental problems since the onset of the Revolution, which it could not surmount in a brief period and which are not yet fully surmounted. The first is our internal backwardness. To move to the most advanced positions for the destruction of capitalism and the building of Socialism in a backward country – that, after all, is a Herculean task ... The second problem is that the developed capitalist countries have remained capitalist. That is the external factor ... These are the two problems, not to mention others, with which we must cope. They present colossal difficulties which might be overcome only under special conditions.[3]

In this sense, the defeat of the Soviet Union was a victory for imperialism contingent upon its earlier success in preventing the spread of Socialism into the major developed countries. That latter victory having been achieved, the demise of the Soviet Union became all the easier to bring about and, in the end, was almost inevitable. When the most advanced sectors of the global economy remained under the control of capitalism, and while the whole system of international exploitation which made the masters of New York, London, Tokyo, Bonn and Paris masters of most of the rest of the world as well stayed intact, the pressures on the Soviet Union were never going to be less than formidable.

From 1917 on, the Soviet Union was the central question in world politics. The policies of all the major powers from then until 1991 turned largely on how to deal with the Soviet state and the threat to the capitalist system which it could not help but represent. The common thread uniting all the big powers in the 1930s, for example, was 'fear of Bolshevism'. This nightmare lay behind both the support given by German big business to Hitler in his rise to power, and the subsequent 'appeasement' of him by the British ruling class. The Chamberlains and company did not wish to avoid war with the Nazis because of a misplaced pacifism or humanitarianism but because they wished to use Hitler to destroy the Soviet Union for them and because in the event of war with Germany 'whether we win or lose, it will be the end of everything we stand for', as one British minister remarked in 1938.[4]

After 1945, anti-Sovietism became the entire content of the

foreign policy of the world's predominant power, the US. Alliances, bases and treaties had one purpose only: containing the spread of socialism and undermining its main support, the Soviet Union. World politics as seen from Washington, London, Bonn and Paris was viewed almost exclusively through an anticommunist prism.

The reasons for this were relatively straightforward. For all its deficiencies, the USSR represented the 'spectre' of the *Communist Manifesto* made real. It embodied the possibility of a society without capitalists, and constituted a real base of support for those opposing the big powers around the world. It was, moreover, an extremely powerful state with every possibility to give effect to its political intentions.

The changes in world politics since the collapse of the USSR show just what a difference its existence made. Not only has capitalism – often in its most primitive forms – been reasserted across half of Europe, but those states throughout Africa and Latin America seeking an independent path of development have been forced back into the arms of the big powers (with the exception of Cuba) and liberation movements struggling for independence or social justice have been put in vastly more unfavourable positions. Moves towards a new international economic order have stalled, and the remaining socialist states have seen little alternative to their incremental adaptation to the prevailing market economy. And, far from enjoying a peace dividend, working people in the more developed capitalist nations have faced ceaseless pressure against the 'welfare state' and wage levels from newly emboldened ruling classes no longer having to look over their shoulders at a rival system run without them, however tarnished it may have become.

Already the world is clearly missing the presence of the USSR in terms of the maintenance of peace. For 70 years it was drilled into all of us that the Soviet Union was the main source of international instability and the principal source of the war danger. In reality, as noted earlier, the stronger the Soviet Union was, the more stable Europe was and the more remote the prospect of a general war. No one in successive Soviet leaderships seemed in the least bit interested in starting a war, despite continued helpful advice from Western media to the effect that Moscow enjoyed a massive military superiority. The socialist societies nurtured no interest groups which could hope to profit from war.

Of course, this situation was less than ideal. Vast sums of money were squandered on armaments, and a variety of conflicts broke out in Asia, Africa, the Middle East and Latin America. The tensions generated by the Cold War hindered progressive and democratic developments in many countries. There is no sense in which the Cold War was a golden age of world peace. Nevertheless, it unarguably provided a brake on the 'hot war' tendencies inherent in an unchecked great power rivalry.

This could not have been made clearer than in a 1988 article by leading US foreign policy expert Dimitri Simes, who explained in the *New York Times* exactly what the decline of the USSR (then obviously under way) would mean for US foreign policy: 'The apparent decline in the Soviet threat . . . makes military power more useful as a United States foreign policy instrument . . . against those who contemplate challenging important American interests.' If concerns over Soviet counter-action declined, he wrote, this could give the US greater opportunities to use military force in a crisis. He gave as examples the Middle East, Cuba and Nicaragua and, given subsequent history, who can dismiss this as the meanderings of one scholar?[5]

The whole movement for the independence of Third-World countries from domination by the big powers has been weakened by the absence of the 'Soviet threat' to this state of affairs. Nations and movements challenging the US and its allies have lost the diplomatic, political, economic and military support which they derived from the Soviet Union. With the absence of such backing, some movements and governments have collapsed, while others have had to settle for compromise and half-way positions. Cuba is economically besieged, Afghanistan is in chaos and turmoil, reforms have been rolled back in Nicaragua, the Palestine Liberation Organisation has had to settle for much less than 'half a loaf' and every government must accommodate the IMF – yet the Emir of Kuwait and the scions of the House of Saud remain on their thrones (if a trifle precariously). The movement for national independence in the Third World, such a major element of world politics for four decades after World War II, has suffered the most serious reverse.

So the capitalist world's antipathy to the Soviet Union was not misplaced. It grew out of a clear sense of its class interest. Only the tactics with which it pursued the undermining of the Soviet system changed over time. After World War II, direct military confrontation gradually receded as an option, largely on account of the increased strength of the USSR. Even when the US had a monopoly on atomic weapons, Washington could not be certain that a sufficiently strong nuclear blow could be struck before the Red Army had time to overrun all of western Europe.

The foundations for 'peaceful coexistence' were laid by the failure of the campaign to 'roll back communism', culminating in the defeat of the Hungarian insurrection of 1956 and the failure of a number of efforts to overthrow Fidel Castro's government in Cuba in the early 1960s. Coupled with the growth of 'strategic parity' between the armed forces of the USSR and the US through the 1960s, including the development of the Soviet nuclear deterrent, the capitalist world was more or less forced to come to terms with its adversary.

This coincided with a weakening of the role of the US following its defeat in Vietnam and the gradual shift in relative economic power between the big powers, giving rise to a period when those powers suffered what seemed to be an almost uninterrupted series of defeats. Angola, Mozambique, Ethiopia, Nicaragua, Afghanistan, south Yemen, Laos and (after the fall of Pol Pot) Kampuchea gained revolutionary governments to some degree or other aligned with the world bloc headed by the USSR, while other strategic allies of Washington either fell to radical forces (Iran) or seemed in imminent danger of doing so (El Salvador). Left-wing parties also gained ground in a number of western European countries.

In reality, this picture overstated the real weakness of the big powers and the Soviet Union's actual strength. 'Strategic parity' was a considerable burden on a Soviet economy which increasingly came to lack the means to effectively modernise its industrial infrastructure, while the failure to heal the rift with China multiplied the USSR's military problems at the same time as diminishing its global political resources. The new spread of impoverished allies in need of assistance further complicated the global balance.

Nevertheless, the 1970s saw a weakening in the drive to destroy 'communism', largely because there seemed to be no obvious or remotely safe way to do so. The advent of Reagan and Thatcher at the turn of the decade reversed this policy. The US-led arms race unleashed (at enduring cost to the health of the US economy) by Ronald Reagan had as its aim not the launching of a world war, which remained far too risky an enterprise to be easily countenanced, but the bankrupting of the Soviet Union – by leading it into trying to maintain a military parity it could no longer afford and thereby forcing it into a strategic submission.

A great volume of literature has now documented the extent to which this process of pressure and internal decay found an expression within the leadership of the Soviet Communist Party.[6] A significant element led by Gorbachev and including Politburo members Yeltsin, Shevardnadze and Yakovlev came to see the only solution for the Soviet Union as lying in adaptation to the capitalist world. The shift in world politics towards a new hegemony for the great powers therefore pre-dated the actual demise of the Soviet Union by a few years. From 1986 onwards, Soviet diplomacy was increasingly oriented towards concessions to the US and other big powers (notably Germany) – long-held Soviet positions in arms control negotiations were unilaterally surrendered and support for left-wing governments in many parts of the world was bit-by-bit abandoned. This new policy, elaborately disguised by an appeal to 'universal human values', culminated in acquiescence in the extension of NATO eastward through the annexation of the German Democratic Republic by the Federal Republic, the collapse of the Warsaw Pact and support for the US-led war against Iraq.

Gorbachev read the formal obituary for revolutionary policy in the Soviet Union when he told a special meeting to celebrate the 70th anniversary of the October Revolution that 'a safe world will have to be built jointly with capitalist countries', amidst speculations as to how capitalism would develop better if it forsook militarism and neo-colonialism and gave 'universal human values . . . top priority'.[7] Gorbachev's hopes regarding improved behaviour from the US and its allies were dashed with the invasion of Panama and the Gulf War of 1990–1, as fine expressions of militarism and neo-colonialism as one could wish to see, but the Soviet leader supported the latter anyway.

However, this disintegration of the ideological and political 'threat' from the USSR served to stimulate disagreements between the big powers as to how to proceed, much as they all welcomed the demise of the socialist system. The crumbling of the USSR created a whole new area for competition rather than co-operation.

The US administration, which had played the largest part in the whole anti-Soviet offensive, initially favoured an orderly Gorbachev-led capitalist restoration throughout the Soviet Union, believing that Washington could thereby play a hegemonic role in the process through its influence over (control of?) the government in Moscow. Thus George Bush told a Ukrainian audience in July 1991: 'God bless the Soviet Union.' The US President was subsequently rather unfairly criticised for what was seen as a faux pas – in fact he had merely been endorsing the result of the referendum on the USSR's future earlier in the year which had, in the Ukraine as elsewhere, produced a huge majority for maintaining the union. This was a democratic inconvenience which Washington, Yeltsin and the Ukrainian President Kravchuk were to overlook before too long.

France, too, showed no great enthusiasm for a splintered Soviet Union, correctly fearing that only the newly reunited Germany would benefit from such an implosion. Nevertheless, the tide turned against those banking on Gorbachev delivering Soviet socialism bound hand and foot to the table of the G7. By mid-1991 he was so obviously losing his grip on the situation, having reduced to a shambles the Communist Party which had brought him to power, that he was sent packing from the economic summit to which he had gone begging for funds. By the end of the year, Gorbachev was gone, the USSR was gone and the big powers found themselves in a new world order, each with their own priorities and prospects.

The end of the Cold War and the 'communist threat' mythology which had sustained it has had a contradictory effect on the relations between the big powers. On the one hand, the absence of the USSR not only removed one of the major restraints upon the reassertion of rivalry, which the changed economic positions of the US, Japan and the western European powers were otherwise impelling, but also gave that rivalry a new field of expression across the territory of the dismembered socialist community. On the other hand, and in the short term only, it gave those rivalries a new possibility of temporary abatement in so far as fresh markets were opened up for the export of surplus capital, easing one of the principal symptoms of crisis in the world economy.

One of the main trends in world politics over the next several years will be the transition from the first phase, of the peaceful expansion of capitalism into the new territories in eastern Europe and the former USSR, to the second phase, in which conflicts and clashes amongst the competing powers and also between those powers and the peoples and states of the region will emerge. The passage from the one phase to the next looks likely to be rapid.

The initial phase – the establishment of a capitalist system in Russia with the full involvement of the great powers – is in full swing, 'dripping from head to toe, from every pore, with blood and dirt', in a way not seen in Europe since Karl Marx's original description of the genesis of capital. Rudi Dornbusch, professor of economics at the Massachusetts Institute of Technology and no critic of capitalism, was as blunt as Marx could possibly have been: 'Yes, there are opportunities in Russia – enough to get many thousands of criminals instant wealth. But that wealth is created by corruption, theft and violence on a scale probably unprecedented in history. The other side of this coin is mass poverty . . .'[8]

Indeed, the whole experience of Russia since 1991 (and much of eastern Europe from 1989) is a salutary lesson to anyone who might believe that capitalism is a superior system of society. Its advent over the sixth of the earth represented by the territory of the erstwhile USSR has been marked by leaps backwards by almost every measurable indicator of social progress. The scale of the regression has no peacetime parallel and finds a precedent only in the aftermath of defeat in war. However, even Germany and Japan recovered from the devastation of World War II a great deal faster than Russia will recover from the comeback of capitalism.

According to the International Labour Organisation (ILO),[9] the GDP in Russia has fallen as follows:

1991	−12.5%
1992	−19.2%
1993	−17.0%
1994	−16.0% (estimate)

The figures for other ex-Soviet republics are still more dramatic, particularly in the Caucusus region. These figures have stark implications for the ordinary people of the former USSR. The same ILO document reports estimates that as many as 100 million people are now living below the official poverty line, with average real family incomes falling by up to 26 per cent. In a separate study, the ILO estimates that unemployment in Russia is five times the official total of around 2 per cent and that life expectancy is dropping sharply – from 65 years to 58 for men and from 74 years to 72.5 for women – a phenomenon it attributes to 'the stress and insecurity triggered by economic change'.[10] The capitalist returns with the grim reaper a pace behind.

But he does not come for all alike. The social stratification associated with capitalism is also back with a vengeance. The *Financial Times* reported that 'heads of Russian private and state enterprises are raking in huge salaries even where factories are technically bankrupt and workers are not being paid'. One example cited told of workers in an engineering factory being left unpaid for two months in the summer, while the plant director got through 4.7 million roubles in the same period.[11] One can fairly assume that the only threat to his enhanced life expectancy will come from the gangland killings which appear to have replaced five-year plans as Russia's main regulator of economic activity.

The emerging capitalist class is moving whatever money it can get its hands on out of the country as fast as possible. Possibly as much as 15 per cent of Russia's shrinking gross domestic product was spirited out of the country in 1992 alone, the first year after the end of Soviet power, according to a World Bank official.[12] Small surprise that capitalism and criminality are regarded as more or less the same thing. The Russian State Duma (parliament) has estimated that 80 per cent of all enterprises are engaged in corruption, and 50 per cent run by organised criminal gangs.[13] The new ruling class 'trembles on the surface of society rather than being accepted by it', in the words of one experienced observer.[14]

Nevertheless, the more cultured and civilised business leaders of the West have found themselves well able to operate in this market. US businesses have led the way, investing over $4,000 million in Russia in 1991–3. In the same period, French concerns invested $1,536 million and German 1,482 million. These amounts are relatively small in proportion to the size of the Russian economy, however. Clearly Russia and the other ex-Soviet republics are not yet a major destination for surplus capital.

That has not stopped the great powers staking out positions for the future, nevertheless. Germany has extended its growing sphere of influence in eastern Europe into the ex-Soviet republics as well. The Estonian currency, for example, pegged itself to the deutschmark immediately it separated from the rouble. As a consequence, the German currency is now parked where the German army was in 1941, at the gates of Leningrad (St Petersburg). The Baltic republics would almost certainly be incorporated in any 'deutschmark zone' which might emerge from the wreckage of the EU's schemes, and possibly in an expanded NATO as well.

In the southern parts of the ex-USSR great power rivalry is also finding sharp expression. Turkey is promoting its influence in the Moslem republics of Central Asia and Azerbaijan, pursuing a 'tempting vision . . . of exercising a network of political and economic influence over the 60 million Moslems of Azerbaijan, Turkmenistan, Kazakhstan, Uzbekistan and Kyrgyzstan'.[15] It is pursuing this through bank loans, food exports and involvement in the exploitation of the great natural resources of the region. The Turks are not alone. 'Israel's march into Central Asia has been led by hard-headed businessmen able to see great potential in a seeming economic and political minefield', a *Jerusalem Post* journalist reported.[16]

And, still more crucially, US business is moving into the Central Asian region in a big way, looking in particular to lay its hands on the huge oil and gas resources there. The US deputy energy secretary, Bill White, toured the republics, accompanied by officials of the National Security Council and the State Department 'to galvanise the southern republics of the former Soviet Union into standing up for themselves' and to 'face down what they see as Russia's attempt to impose a stranglehold on the development of the region's resources'.[17] Mr White's motives were not, needless to say, altruistic. US companies have made multi-billion dollar investments in oil in Azerbaijan, and in gas in Kazakhstan and elsewhere. As a result, Washington has adopted a new policy 'designed to break Russia's grip on Central Asia's oil exports . . . both to help ensure the survival of independent states in the region and to protect US corporate interests'.[18]

The stage is therefore set for a renewal of the nineteenth-century 'great game', in which the imperial powers – mainly British and Russian – manoeuvred to control the same region. The prizes are enormous, and the risk of conflict is therefore correspondingly high. The Russian foreign ministry recently warned against 'regional powers' attempting to 'create wider communities under a national or religious banner' or establish a military presence in the region.[19] Russia's new rulers are as good as their word. Certainly, the whole direction of Russian policy has been towards the re-creation of a strong 'imperial presence' in the territories of the old Soviet Union wherever possible, and in the republics to the south of Russia in the first instance.

The pro-Turkish President of Azerbaijan was overthrown and replaced by a more amenable leader, an ex-member of the Communist Party Politburo. The Kazakh military has been largely reintegrated into the Russian, and its president has called for a single parliament and currency as well.[20] Georgia has moved back into the 'rouble zone' and accepted a Russian military presence, as has Armenia. The Tajik government is wholly dependent on Russian military support in the face of an insurgency directed from over its border with Afghanistan. It is not simply pressure which is bringing about this alignment. The integrated nature of the old Soviet economy makes building links with Russia easier, and a counter-weight against China's growing power may be seen as desirable by the new post-Soviet rulers of the Central Asian republics, in every case identical to the Soviet rulers, having shed communism in favour of a motley mix of Islam, nationalism and exotic personality cults.

Where this logic is insufficient, violence is deployed by the Russians in pursuit of a re-created empire, as the case of the brutal crushing of Chechnya showed. This war, with the aim of subordinating the small nation of Chechnya to the Russian Federation, was, in fact, a microcosm of the new politics of the region. At heart, the issue was about oil, gas and pipelines, and the great power jostling for control over these resources and their delivery.

The oil of Azerbaijan, the oil and gas of Kazakhstan and the other riches which have lured billions of dollars eastward can only be converted into profits once they are shipped out of their countries of origin and into the world market. The importance of this cannot be overstated. Kazakhstan has been referred to as 'the next Kuwait', and recent history has made it all too apparent what lengths the US and its allies were prepared to go to in order to secure the old Kuwait. Russia, under its present rulers, is not likely to be any more generous, as the people of Chechnya have now discovered.

For it is the Chechens' misfortune to sit bang on top of the pipeline route preferred by the Russians to transport both oil from Baku in Azerbaijan and from the huge Tengiz field in Kazakhstan, to the exploitation of which the US oil giant Chevron has committed $20 billion. And these are only the tips of the iceberg, perhaps. Reserves below the Caspian Sea could be larger than those in Kuwait and Iraq, and would certainly dwarf those in Alaska.

'The Caspian and Kazakh basins are going to be the major source of world energy in the twenty-first century. The reserves are up there with the Persian Gulf', a US National Security Council official, playing the now mandatory 'security' role of speaking up for US big business, commented.[21] For this reason, the US has been pushing for the pipeline to go south, through its NATO ally Turkey, rather than through the Russian-controlled route through Chechnya to the port of Novorossisk. The head of Turkey's pipeline-building firm says bluntly 'the pipeline is a strategic issue. The country controlling the pipeline will have a lot of influence over the oil-exporting countries.'[22] Without the pipeline, Turkey's hopes of a new empire in the lands of Tamberlaine the Great will be set back, along with the US enterprise of prising the southern republics away from Russia and into the arms of the oil monopolies. For Russia, vast revenues for transporting the oil across its territories and effective means of subordinating the governments of the republics beckon.

The Russian moves to re-establish hegemony over Georgia are also connected to the pipeline issue, since they place a possible alternative route from Azerbaijan to the Georgian port of Poti under effective control from Moscow as well, probably ensuring that such a route will not be built, costing Georgia up to $250 million a year in lost revenues.[23] So too is Russian support for Armenia in its war with Azerbaijan over the disputed region of Nagorno-Karabakh. 'There is no way we will allow a resolution of the conflict that benefits Turkey', a Russian diplomat is quoted as saying,[24] referring to Turkey's strong pro-Azeri position. This has led Russia to appear once again as the protector of beleaguered Armenians against the Turks and given it a lever of its own to influence the now somewhat more tractable government in Baku.

Indeed, Russia is taking pipeline politics still further west. Another pipeline deal, to transport oil and gas from Bulgaria through Greece, has been signed as part of an emerging anti-Turkish alliance between Russia and Greece, also reflected in the two countries' support for Serbia in the Yugoslav crisis and Greek reservations about the eastward expansion of NATO. The pipeline deal diminishes Turkey's importance while promoting that of Greece.[25]

Britain is the final major player in the 'great game' being contested over pipeline routes – British Petroleum has joined the US companies Amoco and Pennzoil in investing in Azerbaijan. Britain's position is nothing if not clear: 'Whatever is good for BP is fine by us', says Her Majesty's man in Baku, Thomas Young.[26] British Gas is also involved in the exploitation of Kazakhstan's resources, and no doubt the British ambassador to the Kazakh capital of Almaty is equally sure where he is taking his orders from.

The situation along Russia's southern flank is only the clearest expression of the competition which will emerge in the wake of the collapse of the USSR. New states have emerged, sometimes for the first time in the relevant nations' history, each with their own agenda but with very limited means of advancing it, each unstable and looking for protectors among the big powers, who scramble for the right to take resource-rich pseudo-states under their wing. Often these new states are themselves home to national minorities with their own demands and movements – like the Russians in Moldva, separated from Russia by the Ukraine and fearing the designs Rumania may have on reincorporating the regions it lost in 1940 to the USSR.

The Ukraine itself is clearly pregnant with the possibility of conflict, divided between a Russian-oriented and heavily industrial east, and a nationalistic west, located in the parts of the republic annexed from Poland in 1939. According to the *Financial Times*, xenophobia and neo-fascism prevail in the politics of the latter, while nostalgia for Soviet days is strong in the former. 'Ukraine for the Ukrainians' shout the western Ukrainians; 'union with Russia' and 'life was better under the Communists' say the eastern.[27] Russia's conflict with the Ukraine over control of the Crimea, most of whose people wish to be reattached to the Russian Federation, is a further source of friction. The US and Germany have clearly declared for an independent Ukraine, primarily as a means of weakening their Russian rival. Germany is in the lead, here, too. It has established a council for the deepening of economic relations with the Ukraine, and the burgeoning Ukrainian fascist movement is closely aligned with German sympathisers.[28]

The ex-Soviet republics have embarked on a sort of national nightmare since the destruction of the USSR. They pull away from Russia and are pulled back by economic interest and Moscow's own *force majeure*. US interests advance in one direction, German in another, all over the bodies of the slain of Chechnya, Nagorno-Karabakh, South Ossetia, Tajikistan and elsewhere. The voice of reason was surely that of the justice minister of the doomed Chechen Republic who said that while Chechen citizens could recognise the legitimacy of the USSR, having taken part in the referendum to endorse its continued existence, they could never accept the imposition of the Russian Federation by Boris Yeltsin, who had unconstitutionally destroyed the USSR.[29]

He was unconsciously echoing the Albanians from Kosova who declared that they could be Yugoslavs but never Serbs. The destruction of the multinational socialist states of Europe is not the least of the disasters visited by imperialism on the twentieth century, and like other such catastrophes visited on the peoples by the great powers, the danger is that it merely previsions still greater misfortunes.

CHAPTER 4

The Great Powers – the United States

The vast changes in the development of the international economy and the end of the capitalist–socialist confrontation (for the time being at least) have inevitably changed the circumstances and strategies of all the major powers. The old alliances are fading away, or are at least under strain, new blocs are emerging and solidifying, and new points of conflict are starting to aggravate international relations.

Henry Kissinger, a sophisticated servant of US diplomacy for the last quarter of a century, defined the new world politics thus: 'The absence of both an overriding ideological or strategic threat frees nations to pursue foreign policies based increasingly on their immediate national interest. In an international system characterized by perhaps five or six major powers and a multiplicity of smaller states, order will have to emerge much as it did in past centuries from a reconciliation and balancing of competing national interests.'[1] Curiously, given his expansive erudition, Dr Kissinger did not note that such reconciliation and balancing has, in the end, been the product of victory and defeat in war for the major powers and their satellites.

It is therefore all the more necessary to examine the economic and diplomatic position of each of the 'five or six major powers'. No longer are they bound into a more or less monolithic bloc. Each now has its own specific interests, based on its economic prospect and carried through into its strategic choices.

Conventionally, the great powers are held to be the overlapping members of the G7 group of the leading capitalist countries and the five permanent members of the United Nations Security Council. The first group comprises the US, Japan, Germany, France, Britain, Italy and Canada; the second, the US, Russia, China, Britain and France. Italy and Canada are not studied in detail here, although the impact their position has on the whole picture will be touched on at points later on. While economically significant, neither power has the capacity for independent political action which the others possess; their history, economic weight relative to their neighbours, more limited military means and internal problems make them followers rather than leaders in the new dance of the great powers. This chapter looks at the position of the US. The following two will examine the European powers and the Asian giants.

At the top of the heap remains the United States of America, endlessly described as the 'sole remaining superpower'. The US economy is, as it has been for all of this century, the world's most productive. Its armed forces are, by most measures, the world's mightiest. It is the only power with truly global interests – investments everywhere, bases everywhere, alliances everywhere – and is therefore the power with the most interest in a new *world* order which it can control. As a consequence, the voice of Washington and Wall Street is still heard the loudest in the counsels of nations.

Yet if one is to look at what is changing, it is the facts, and the consequences, of relative US decline which are the most compelling. In 1950, the gross national product of the US was greater than that of the USSR, the UK, Japan, Germany, France and Italy *combined*. By 1980, the latter six powers produced half as much again as the US.[2] From 1950 to today, the US share of world production has declined from about one-half to about one-fifth.[3] In 1970, the US was home to 64 of the 100 largest industrial corporations in the world and 19 of the 50 biggest banks. By 1993, only 30 of the top 100 monopolies and 5 of the top 50 banks were American.[4]

These figures do not, in themselves, constitute a sign of sickness in the US economy. It could be argued that they merely reflect the inevitable recovery of other powers from their prostrate economic position immediately after World War II. More alarming for Washington is the relentless rise in the nation's indebtedness. In 1916, this amounted to 2 per cent of national income. It rose to just over 100 per cent at the end of World War II, before declining to 26 per cent by 1980. Ronald Reagan's voodoo economics had pushed the figure back up to 46 per cent by the time he left office. Subsequent attempts to reduce the vast trade and budget deficits which are Reagan's legacy have made little dent in that figure.[5] Still more critical in its long-term implications is the decline in investment in the US economy, which is in itself sufficient indication that there is little prospect of the problems going away. In 1979, investment per capita was $2,352 in the US, as against $2,257 in Japan and $1,918 in Germany. By 1993 the respective figures were $3,927, $6,914 and $4,112.[6] While the US matches Japan and Germany in defence-related research spending, non-defence research and development is only 1.8 per cent of gross national product, as against 2.6 per cent for Germany and 2.8 per cent for Japan.[7] These figures are at the root of the diminishing position of US corporations in many major industries, including such strategically vital ones as machine tools.

As discussed in detail in Chapter 8, the dollar has also declined sharply over the years against the deutschmark and the yen. On the basis of all of this, it cannot be the case that the US will remain the world's most productive economy indefinitely.

These general indicators of a declining economy have been met by the US ruling class in the same fashion as the masters of the British Empire met the reality of their decline after World War I – a retreat from free trade towards a measure of protectionism and a sweeping attack on the living standards of workers. The change in US global economic policy is seen in the creation of a hemispheric trade bloc, as a US-dominated sphere of influence, to mask the loss of its position as the leading power in the world economy as a whole, in much the same way as British industry looked to 'empire preference' when it lost the capacity to dominate world markets. This policy has been complemented by a drift towards managing trade with nations and blocs outside the NAFTA area.

US capital has been exceptionally adept at boosting the production of surplus value and profit levels within a context of diminishing market share. Probably the most impressive symptom of this is the situation with regard to real wage levels for American working people, those who have actually built the most productive economy on earth. The stark fact is that average weekly earnings are now lower in real terms than they were in 1959.[8] Given that the US capitalist class and sections of the working population have certainly seen their income rise over this period, it is obvious that millions of working-class Americans now live worse than in the 1950s. During the Reagan years, it is estimated that real income for working-class families fell by 20 per cent, far more than it had risen in the 1970s.[9] For the workforce as a whole, real wages fell by 13 per cent in the 20 years to 1992.[10] Over 35 million Americans are officially classed as poor, more than 14 per cent of the population – and this in the richest country on earth.[11] The rudiments of welfare in the US are now under sustained attack from the reactionary Congress elected in 1994, with even Democrat leaders joining in the assault.

This is only one side of the picture, of course. Social inequality has grown exponentially. Today, the top 20 per cent of the population control 45 per cent of the nation's wealth, and the bottom 20 per cent just 4 per cent, the greatest gap since records began.[12] The remuneration of the chief executives of big corporations, which in 1974 was already a generous 35 times greater than the average wage paid in their companies, had by 1995 reached a staggering 150 times greater.[13]

These are not the reversible results of recession, they represent deep-seated features of the development of the US economy in its present stage, where the ruling class is struggling against fiercer competition than ever and is battling to reverse its relative decline at the expense of ordinary Americans as well as at the expense of the rest of the world. Recent booms have made hardly a dent in the downward pressure on real wages – they have been booms for profit only.

This is the domestic background against which the rulers of the US have to reorient themselves in the new world situation – define their strategic choices, maintain their existing positions of economic influence and extend them where possible. Within this framework, US foreign policy is taking a different shape, with the single-minded hostility once directed towards the USSR now finding new enemies in the commercial rivals of US business. In essence it is grappling with how to maintain US world hegemony from a position of relative economic weakness and without the strategic glue of anti-communism.

The new thinking which increasingly informs, in different ways, the mainstreams of both the Republican and Democratic parties, was spelt out dramatically in a Pentagon defence planning document drawn up in 1992. This official report, which was leaked to the *New York Times*, indicated the priorities for the US in the post-Soviet world which was then just emerging amidst extravagant propaganda of a new dawn for humanity.

The aim outlined in the document was to ensure that no rival for world leadership should emerge to challenge the US in western Europe, Asia or the former USSR. This meant that the US must retain sufficient military might to deter any nation or group of nations from challenging American primacy and that the US itself 'must account for the interests of advanced industrial nations to discourage them from challenging our leadership or seeking to overturn the established political and economic order'.

The Pentagon called this 'benevolent domination by one power', which sought to achieve the goal of preventing Japan or Germany from pursuing a course of arms build-up, including acquiring nuclear weapons (which is well within their technical means), by integrating them into a US-dominated system of security which would take account of their interests as well. 'Nuclear proliferation . . . could lead Germany and Japan and other industrial powers to acquire nuclear weapons to deter attack from regional foes. This could start them down the road to global competition with the US and, in a crisis over national interests, military rivalry.' Such thinking goes a long way to explain the Clinton administration's zeal in using the nuclear weapons issue to provoke North Korea – the need to deprive Japan of a pretext for acquiring such armaments for itself.

The Pentagon also urged that Washington should 'seek to prevent the emergence of European-only security arrangements which would undermine NATO' and that the US should explicitly guarantee eastern Europe against Russia, with the extension of the EU into the region as fast as possible being the first step towards putting this security 'guarantee' in place. Here again we see the overlap between the strategic objectives of the US and resurgent and reunited Germany.[14]

In Asia, the Pentagon looked to maintaining a number of states in a military balance, while preventing either a dominant regional power or a power vacuum emerging. The seven hypothetical wars the document envisaged for purposes of illustration covered every part of the world – the Middle East, the Baltic ex-Soviet republics, Panama and Korea among them. Little wonder that the document gave rise to 'fretting', in the words of one reporter, amongst Washington's allies.[15]

That this report constitutes a basic strategic document for the maintenance of US hegemony in the world can be seen from the fact that its precepts have so obviously guided much of Washington's international behaviour ever since – its alliance with Germany over Yugoslavia, the attempts to contain China and Russia, its harassment of North Korea, intervention in Somalia and Haiti, and so on.

The Pentagon merely articulated more bluntly what has since become the common currency of American politics. Both parties have moved towards an aggressive 'America First' rhetoric, whether it is the Japan-bashing of the trade warriors in the Clinton administration or the virulent anti-United Nations isolationism of many elements among Newt Gingrich's Republicans. Alliances and multilateral institutions which were tolerated for the sake of the united anti-communist front are now scorned and down graded, to be replaced by an exclusive emphasis on the economic and strategic needs of US corporations.

This is in turn reflected in the new role of the CIA in spying on the commercial secrets of countries still nominally Washington's allies – witness recent complaints from Japan and the actual expulsion of US 'diplomats' from France. Even during the Bush presidency, the CIA was moving in this direction. Its then director William Webster said: 'Our political and military allies are also our economic competitors. The national security implications of a competitor's ability to create, capture or control markets of the future are very significant.'[16] President Clinton was reported to have 'ordered the CIA to make economic espionage with America's trade rivals a top priority', and was apparently delighted with the spies' role in recent car trade negotiations with Tokyo.[17] Such activity has nothing to do with the struggle against communism, or the 'strategic interests' of the United States as they would normally be understood.

The blending of economic and security concerns was further

underlined by President Clinton's creation of a National Economic Council in the White House, with the same status as the
National Security Council, the home of Ronald Reagan's network
of drug-smugglers, gun-runners and money-launderers in the anti-
communist cause. 'We're now going to develop an economic strategy much in the way we developed a national security strategy to
fight the cold war', one Clinton official explained, while another
added: 'I'm tired of a level playing field, we should tilt the playing
field for US business. We should have done it 20 years ago.'[18] US
ambassadors are now being turned into super-salesmen – 'the main
brief of a US ambassador in Clinton's new world order is to *get* the
order for whichever US company happens to be in town that week',
according to *Newsweek*.[19] Just as the CIA now spies for General
Motors and IBM, ambassadors are there to represent Microsoft or
Exxon. US big business is delighted, since it used to have to pay
people to do this kind of work for it. The burden is now borne by
the American taxpayer.

The 'America First' approach, straightforward as it may sound,
does raise a complication for the Pentagon planners, however. Not
only are the interests of US business far too extensive, as British
historian Professor Kennedy has pointed out, for the US state to
be able to defend them all by force; even the thought of doing so
contradicts the stated aim of ensuring that Washington heads off
the military ambitions of Japan and Germany by speaking up for
their interests as well. One cannot stand for 'America First' and
then expect the protagonists of 'Deutschland uber alles' and 'the
Japan that can say no' to happily shelter under your strategic
umbrella.

The truth is that the US has no intention of giving more than
a moment's thought to the interests of Japan and Germany, or
Britain and France for that matter. The aim is rather to disguise, as
in the Gulf War, the interests of US monopoly capitalism as being
the interests of the 'international community', in much the same
way as every ruling class over the last 150 years has presented its
interests as being those of 'the nation' (and before that those of
God).

What is harder to disguise is the growing weakness of the US,
despite its continued military and political pre-eminence. This is
the problem which afflicts those calling for a return to a 'big stick'
foreign policy, defined by one expert as 'a foreign policy that first
and foremost protects its interests with power'.[20] The heyday of
the 'big stick' was the presidency of Theodore Roosevelt, who led
the US on its upswing to becoming the world's dominant power, at
a time when the US economy was outstripping all rivals and the
country was on its way to becoming the world's creditor. No such
easy option presents itself to today's senators and congressmen,

grappling with a national debt in trillions of dollars and a budget deficit in hundreds of billions. Who will pay for the big stick? Bonn and Tokyo may have been begrudgingly prepared to write the cheque for it in the Gulf War . . . but if the stick is to be wielded against them?

And, indeed, the stick is shrinking. US troop levels in Europe have been reduced by two-thirds. The Pentagon has been forced out of the Philippines already, and there is pressure to reduce its presence in Japan. To be sure, this is a relative decline, which still leaves the US stronger than any one single potential adversary. But the new limitations have been recognised in the shift in Pentagon war-planning from 'win-win' to 'win-hold-win'. The former indicated the US capacity to fight and win two major conflicts in different parts of the world simultaneously. The latter calls on the military to do no more than hold on in one of the two conflicts until the first has been victoriously concluded, releasing resources for the second. It no longer sounds like the strategy of a superpower. Hence the congruence between Clinton's position, that the US will not act alone as a 'world policeman', and that of the neo-isolationists in Congress unwilling to sanction any overseas entanglement.

Nevertheless, the US alone of all the powers is at least able to contemplate engagement with each of the power blocs emerging in the world today – Europe (with the leading US role in brokering a Bosnian peace settlement) and the Far East (where the administration has played a big part in the launch of the Asia-Pacific Economic Conference), as well as 'its own' bloc in North America. Clinton's policy does indeed seem aimed at keeping a US foot in every door through aggressive economic diplomacy and preventing rival blocs solidifying against US interests. It must be doubted, however, that the US can bring sufficient weight to bear in all economic theatres to stop other monopoly interests prevailing and itself being forced back on the exclusive leadership of its own backyard bloc in the North American Free Trade Area (NAFTA).

The new US policy has emerged against this broad picture. Rather than world leadership backed up by overwhelming force, it consists of the following principal features:

- The construction of a hemispheric trade bloc under US control, with the NAFTA as the first major step.
- Alliance with Germany as far as European affairs go, supporting the creation of a German-dominated zone in eastern and central Europe directed against Russia above all. This amounts to a new special relationship, at the expense of Britain.
- An aggressive struggle for markets in the Third World

backed up by a willingness to take the lead in great power action against troublesome independent-minded nations like Iraq, Libya, North Korea, etc. where a consensus of common interest can be created, and a willingness to advance exclusively US interests where possible.

• Prevention of either China or Japan attaining hegemony in the Asia-Pacific region, through continued US involvement.

These points define the areas where the US may be willing to risk conflict in the future, conflicts which it will face as a declining power, strong enough to fight for its interests, but too weak to any longer simply impose them. Much as it may not like it, Washington now has to negotiate with other powers, build precarious alliances, bluff and counter-bluff, in order to get its own way. The most powerful, but no longer omnipotent, stronger than all, but relatively declining, US power is bound to become a more volatile element in international affairs.

CHAPTER 5

The Great Powers – Europe

Germany

No country has seen its position in the world alter as a result of the end of the socialist–capitalist confrontation more than Germany. Firstly, the rapid annexation of the territory of the former German Democratic Republic by the Federal Republic swelled Germany back to its rank as easily the most populous state in Europe west of Russia. Secondly, its already emerging role as Europe's leading economic power was reinforced. Thirdly, its diplomacy was removed from the constraints placed upon it by the Cold War, and by the division of its own territory in particular. The 'economic giant' neither could, nor wished to, be a 'political pygmy' any longer.

And as Germany has changed because of changes in the world, so the world around Germany has had to adapt to the new position. From being (arguably) first among equals in a European Community headed towards some form of federation in which leadership would have to be shared with France at least, Germany now has a whole new range of strategic options. The most historically evocative option is a resumption of its 'eastward orientation' in the new form of the creation of a Deutschmark bloc which will include Poland, the Czech Republic, Hungary, Slovakia, Croatia and other former socialist states, but not necessarily such European Union partners as France, Britain, Italy, Ireland, Spain and Portugal.

As with other post-1989 developments, the 'new Germany' did not come out of a clear blue sky. The gathering strength of Germany was already starting to push against the structures of world and European politics, some of which had been evolved in the years after World War II for the express purpose of a benign containment of Germany as a rival at the same time as maintaining it in place as a powerful bulwark against the Soviet Union. This balancing act was already in danger of tipping over before the Berlin Wall came down, as Germany emerged as the dominant state in western Europe and a powerful force within the G7 club of major powers.

Germany's history throughout the twentieth century is dramatic enough. However, the very scale of the changes which have swept Germany – from Kaiserism to Weimar democracy, and from fascism to the Federal Republic – masks the essential continuity in the ruling class of the country and its policies.[1] The expansion of German business into the lands to the east in search of raw materials, cheap labour and easily dominated markets; projects of European unity under German monopoly domination; the power within Germany of a closely knit network of industrialists and bankers – these basic characteristics have remained constant. Defeat in World War II concealed some of these elements for a while, whilst others were at one time or another hard to pursue, but today what would seem to be the basic interests of Germany's rulers are once more reasserting themselves most evidently.

Some politicians in rival powers purport to see in this some working out of an ineluctable national character. British Conservatives are particularly prone to this psychological reductionism, taking their cue from Margaret Thatcher, who enlivened the dying months of her premiership by convening a seminar of advisers to debate the German character. The leaked memorandum of the meeting caused a diplomatic fluster, since it in large part consisted of a list of various vices which could be attributed to the Germans, including 'angst, aggressiveness, assertiveness, bullying, egotism, inferiority complex, sentimentality . . . a capacity for excess, to overdo things, to kick over the traces . . . a tendency to over-estimate their own strengths and capabilities'.[2]

How much use this comprehensive and contradictory litany was to British diplomats is unclear; nevertheless a typically unrepentant Thatcher was still asserting five years later that 'Germany's national character is to dominate'[3] while the Thatcherite weekly, the *Spectator*, warned of a 'certain tendency to political Messianism'.[4] Setting aside the incongruity of a proud inheritor of the traditions of an empire which saw British business (presumably overcoming a national characteristic aversion to domination) bring a quarter of the world under its control lecturing others thus, the question of Germany's policy cannot be reduced to pretending that Kaiser Wilhelm, Adolf Hitler, Konrad Adenauer, Helmut Schmidt, Josef Goebbels, Helmut Kohl, General Luddendorf and Hermann Goering all share the same characteristics.

The roots of German policy must be found in the structure and position of German capitalism and its tendency, found in all such powers, towards expansion. Whilst the allied victory in World War II went a certain way towards uprooting Nazism and implanting the norms of a parliamentary democracy, no moves were made in the larger, western, sector to tackle the big-business concerns which had placed Hitler in power and whose interests the latter had endeavoured to meet through his aggressive policies. On the contrary, those interests were entrenched by the US and Britain in the Federal Republic after the war, precisely because they seemed much the lesser threat than a socialist Germany.

Thus the forces which had driven German expansionism for the previous 70 years were swiftly restored to the saddle, albeit in a much weakened position *vis-à-vis* American and British capital, after 1945. It should be of little surprise that, as internal and external constraints have gradually fallen away, the same tendencies should once more assert themselves.

The German economy is dominated by very large monopolies in engineering, the motor industry, energy, chemicals and other basic industrial sectors, the result of an uninterrupted process of capital concentration throughout the years of West Germany's post-war reconstruction, building on the pre-war position. Manufacturing accounted for 31 per cent of West Germany's GDP in 1989, as against 19 per cent in the US, 19 per cent in Britain and 21 per cent in France.[5] Having dominated its domestic market at the expense of external interests, this industrial colossus extended its sphere of operations throughout the territory of the then EEC, providing German companies with a large enough 'home base' to confront competition from external rivals, mainly in the US or Japan. By 1974, German car companies were exporting 46.5 per cent of the value of their output, the engineering industry 44.1 per cent and the chemical industry 36.2 per cent.[6] The export of capital has since emerged as a more decisive element in German business, although it is still relatively small compared to the proportion of capital exported from Britain or the US. Direct investment by German companies abroad totalled 42 billion DM in 1992–3 alone. The share of this investment going to other countries in Europe has been rising, at the expense of the share going to the US.[7]

Even while the socialist system prevailed in the lands to the east of the FRG, German companies were trading heavily there, accounting for over a third of all western exports to Hungary and Czechoslovakia,[8] and around a quarter to Bulgaria and Poland.[9] This industrial strength, and a high domestic savings rate, underpinned a policy aimed at maintaining the internal value of the Deutschmark and promoting its progressive appreciation against the currencies of other powers. Taken together, these developments constituted the 'German miracle' which restored Germany to the top table of the world economy.

As in the US, however, working people in Germany are learning that competition at that level is an exercise largely carried out at their expense. The drive outward and eastwards by big business is paralleled by a drive downwards as far as wage rates and welfare services are concerned, and by rapidly rising unemployment. The famous 'social consensus' which incorporated the working class into the post-war reconstruction of capitalism is now deemed superfluous to requirements, the more so since the high labour costs which it entailed can increasingly be avoided by the simple expedient of moving production to neighbouring ex-socialist countries.[10] The result is that while German corporate profits rose 40 per cent in 1994, this boom at the top co-existed with real wage cuts for German workers (of about 1 per cent in 1993) and continued moves to reduce welfare spending.[11]

This, together with the rise of a neo-fascist far right on the streets, has led to a great deal of angst in Germany. Its competitive position has been gently declining relative to other countries and there has been a great deal of speculation about the German 'model' running out of steam and of German society sliding into crisis.[12]

By any reasonable calculation, this is overblown. Germany remains the third economic power in the world, with a commanding position in Europe, the world's largest single trading bloc. It controls the evolution of the EU, dictating the pace and scope of integration at the same time as it is fast incorporating eastern Europe and some of the ex-Soviet republics into its zone of influence.

To the east, Germany's influence is almost unopposed at present. While US interests are involved in the region, Germany has grabbed most of the pie, accounting for more than half of total trade with eastern Europe. It has out-invested the US by four to one in Poland, five to one in the Czech Republic and twenty to one in the former GDR.[13] In 1995 alone, German businesses invested $1.9 billion in central Europe, as much as went to the vast US market.[14] When newly 'independent' Estonia withdrew from the rouble zone it was only to peg its new currency to the Deutschmark. More and more German industrialists are moving east in the search for cheaper skilled labour – at the cost of jobs in Germany. Car giant Audi has invested $475 million in plant in Hungary, replacing German factories. Siemens has invested $50 million in a Czech electric-motor plant, while Volkswagen has bought 25 per cent of the Czech car company Skoda. Clothing company Hugo Boss has shifted much of its production from Germany to Slovakia and Slovenia. General Motors is assembling Opel cars in Poland.[15] Small wonder that US business magazine *Fortune* wrote that Germany has 'extended its economic dominance to eastern Europe and the former Soviet Union'.[16]

The importance of eastern Europe to German business has sometimes been dismissed, since total investments there are, as yet, small compared to those German companies have made in western Europe. This, however, misses the *rising* strategic importance of the region. From a more-or-less standing start six years ago, German companies have invested billions of dollars. As it ties the economies of Poland, the Czech Republic, Hungary and the rest more closely to itself, these countries, rich in skilled labour and resources, will undoubtedly become more and more important to the profitability of German firms, seeking to put more pressure on the German working class. 'Germany will increasingly focus its efforts not on the European community but in turning east. German companies can benefit from low labour rates there and from supplying these countries capital goods', a strategist for the US merchant bankers Morgan Stanley observed.[17] The tightening grip of Germany on eastern Europe also greatly extends its sphere of influence, its possibilities for independent action and its economic strength *vis-à-vis* Russia, Japan or the US. To consolidate this, Germany is pushing hard for the extension of EU membership to Poland, the Czech Republic and Hungary, which would cement its grip on the region behind suitable disguises. Even the agricultural and industrial riches of the Ukraine are in Germany's sights further down the road. These moves are, to say the least, fraught with complications for Germany's relations with Russia, despite Kohl's wooing of Boris Yeltsin.

Nor does this renewed *'drang nach osten'* contradict a continuing German hegemony in much of western Europe. Belgium, the Netherlands, Denmark, Sweden and Austria, at least, are fast becoming economic satellites of Germany and would be certain to be included in any Deutschmark zone. If, in the east, the consequence of the 'end of communism' was to open up virtually virgin territory to the capital of the continent's greatest economic power, then in the west the result was to open the door to new and more assertive methods for the imposition of German domination on its neighbours.

The EU, of course, grew out of Franco-German post-war arrangements to provide the big business of both countries with a larger 'home market' and to develop a bloc in Europe to confront the menace of socialism. Germany's gradual pre-eminence within the steadily expanding 'common market' was a function of the size and productivity of its economy. It did not, however, amount to political domination, because West Germany still needed the military support and diplomatic sympathy of Britain, France and the US in the struggle against communism. European integration offered the possibility of strengthening German hegemony in western Europe, as the Deutschmark would have to be the foundation of any monetary union. However, this hegemony had its limits, since Britain and France, at least, were easily strong enough to prevent the pre-1989 FRG from imposing its will. Lacking any alternative, Germany was forced to compromise with London and

Paris, whilst shelling out mightily to underwrite the whole process
of integration, which had to include a measure of subsidy to such
weaker economies as Italy, Spain and Portugal.

This policy first began to change with German re-unification.
The strain this placed on the value of the mighty Deutschmark
(exchanged at par with the GDR's Ostmark) meant that continued
additional supply of Deutschmarks to the sickly brethren of the
EC could only be maintained at the price of raising interest rates,
despite the negative impact this would have on the recession-
wracked states trying to maintain their own currencies at fixed,
European exchange-rate mechanism parities with the Deutschmark. Along with Germany's diplomatic assertiveness over Yugoslavia, discussed below, this interest-rate aggression was the herald
of the new 'Germany first' policy which accompanied German
unification and the withdrawal of Soviet power from eastern and
central Europe, dramatically confirming the scarcely concealed
opinion of Thatcher and Mitterrand that two Germanies was about
right whilst one would be too much of a good thing for everyone
else in the neighbourhood.

With new opportunities opening to the east and flushed with its
own united strength, Germany did not lose interest in the EU, of
course. It merely found its negotiating position within the counsels of western Europe strengthened, to the point where it could
say to France, Britain and the rest of the world – European union
on our terms, or German domination of much of Europe in any
case. A federal Europe would be built in the German image, and if
some European nations could not get along with that, then they
could find themselves left outside the emerging Deutschmark
zone which would come to dominate the continent. No more
concessions were made to weaker countries and currencies, with
the strength of the Deutschmark being brandished like a club to
force other EU states to adapt their economies – at whatever cost –
to German monetary and economic policy. Some, like Denmark or
the Netherlands, had long been in the orbit of the Bundesbank.
Belgium, for many years a satellite of France, has shifted orbit over
the last generation to Germany. Italy's rulers look to Bonn to save
them from themselves (and the militant Italian working-class
movement). And German big business is taking the lead in trying
to create Europe-wide conglomerates and cartels in diverse sectors
from telecommunications and defence to vehicle building and
banking.

This has created the position in which Morgan Stanley foresees
Germany 'at the centre of a new grouping' including the Czech
Republic, Slovakia, Hungary, Poland, Belgium, the Netherlands,
Luxembourg, Switzerland, Austria and Sweden – to which
Slovenia, the Baltic Republics and Finland could possibly be

added.[18] This would, in Morgan Stanley's assessment, mean the end of the Franco-German axis in Europe. A Bundesbank official sketched out the same scenario, seeing European monetary union as including a EU core, the European Free Trade Area states and Poland, Hungary and the Czech Republic.[19]

Faced with the possibility of gathering half the continent around them in a bloc straightforwardly controlled by German business interests, politicians in Bonn (and, indeed, German public opinion) have noticeably cooled on the project of monetary union, which would mean sacrificing the Deutschmark for a new European currency – a 'Euro' unlikely to enjoy as strong a reputation for being a stable store of value. The German government and the Bundesbank have declared that there can be no weakening of the hairshirt criteria for monetary union, which in itself puts the project off until such time as sufficient countries can cut their budget deficit and debt levels considerably; while the opposition Social Democratic Party has begun to campaign against the whole idea. These stiffer criteria for monetary union can only slow down the process of 'European integration'. To try to recover momentum lost on the monetary front by purely political means, German leaders from Chancellor Kohl downwards have taken to warning of war if Europe is not integrated on their harsh terms. The other states of the EU are therefore being confronted with the demand for budget cuts at the point of a gun. History demands that this should be taken seriously.

Perhaps German business has noted former Chancellor Helmut Schmidt's case *for* monetary union:

> unless the D-Mark was replaced by a single European currency . . . the German currency by the year 2000 would be 'overwhelmingly strong'. This would make the Germans the 'masters' of the EC, a position which would eventually rebound on Germany by making it vulnerable to coalitions of European states joining forces to curb its strength.[20]

But it has drawn the opposite conclusion from his analysis.

Schmidt has been still more explicit: 'If the common currency does not come about within the next 15 years or so you will see the Deutschmark domineering banks, insurers and other institutions across Europe, and it would inevitably lead to a repetition of what one has already seen twice in this twentieth century.'[21]

Clearly, 'we are the masters now' does not sound so bad to Schmidt's successors, confident that no imposing 'coalition' can be assembled against them, as twice before. This has certainly been the tone of the new German foreign policy, which has carried a clear menace towards all and sundry. The *Wall Street Journal* noted that the German attitude towards the Czech Republic,

Hungary and Slovakia 'at times adopts the tone of a modern Monroe doctrine', referring to the US policy which excluded all other powers from an interest in Latin America. Chancellor Kohl behaved as if Warsaw and Prague 'must settle with him as their protector whatever his manner towards them'.[22] The ruling Christian Democratic Union's parliamentary foreign affairs committee adopted the same tone towards the West, warning France to end its obsession with 'the empty shell of the nation-state', adding: 'Never again must there be a destabilizing vacuum of power in central Europe. If European integration were not to progress, Germany might be called upon, or tempted by its own security constraints, to try to effect the stabilisation on its own and in the traditional way.'[23] The last phrase, apparently, needed no elaboration.

Likewise, Germany has appeared to identify the British government as the main obstruction to the integration of the EU on its own terms. Doubtless alarmed by the signs of growing closeness between London and Paris, there is little doubt that Britain was the main intended target of Chancellor Kohl's warnings of war if Germany's plans for the continent were not acceded to.

And, of course, the world has caught a glimpse of the new German policy in relation to the Yugoslav crisis, for which Bonn bears a large measure of responsibility, forcing the pace on the recognition of Slovenia and Croatia, hitherto elements of the Yugoslav federation, as independent states. This encouragement to anti-Serb nationalism had its foreseeable (and, indeed, by Britain and France foreseen) consequences in bloody strife. A BBC correspondent in the region identified this move as part of a German move 'to establish itself as *primus inter pares* in Europe', expanding its economic influence in the Czech Republic, Hungary and Poland, 'particularly in those areas in the west that once belonged to the Reich ... In Yugoslavia, the Germans ... have, not surprisingly, been most interested in the economic potential of Slovenia and Croatia. This offers exceptional value to the economies of Austria and Bavaria both as a new market and because it affords German industry an easy outlet to the Adriatic.'[24]

It might be added that the extension of German influence throughout the Balkans and eastern/central Europe depends on all political resistance, be it nationalist or communist, being broken down, whether or not there is a compelling short-term economic interest in a particular country. Turning the region into a patchwork of dwarf-states lacking much legitimacy or any independent means of action can only help draw the whole of the area under Germany's umbrella. The only potential rivals are the US, whose policy is largely in step with Bonn's at present (indeed acknowledging the latter's leadership in European matters in a new 'special relationship'), and Russia.

It is with the latter that the greatest potential for conflict could arise, as has been seen in Yugoslavia already. No doubt for this reason, Moscow has not been neglected in the general hectoring coming from German leaders. Karl Lamers, the president of the parliamentary committee whose report, full of threats, was cited above, gave his own warning to Moscow: 'our tolerance is limited'. Showing a deep moral obtuseness, he allowed that both the Russian and German peoples 'have inflicted great suffering on one another', as if the Soviet Union had invaded Germany and killed 25 million human beings, but now said that it was 'high time' for the West 'to show Russia its limits' and 'draw a line' against Russian behaviour deemed aggressive.[25] As Germany's interests push eastwards, even into the Ukraine, that 'line' moves closer and closer to Russia's state frontier, and well within the area regarded by almost every Russian politician as their own sphere of interest.

Turkey, on the other hand, is favoured as, according to Defence Minister Volker Ruehe, 'a strategic cornerstone [which] can serve as a stabilizing influence for the whole region. Turkey thus deserves the greatest possible degree of political and material support from the west',[26] an attitude which could again bring German interests into conflict with the Russian across a broad swathe of territory from the Balkans to the Chinese border, as well as embroiling Germany in an anti-Greek position, given the latter's frictions with Turkey over Cyprus and the Aegean Sea.

If both economic and foreign policy display a new tone from Germany, it only remains to bring military policy into line. The size of Germany's military has been somewhat reduced following the end of the Cold War. However, its orientation has shifted towards the possibility of more frequent interventions further from home. To this end, the German constitution, which banned the deployment of German troops, except under NATO control, outside their own homeland was reinterpreted by the judiciary to allow such interventions. The reason was instructive: to allow Germany to do its bit in 'new world order'-type United Nations humanitarian and peace-keeping operations. However, once this excuse had been used, and limited German military participation in Somalia was accomplished, then the Bonn Defence Ministry, pocketing the new constitutional freedom, declared itself disillusioned with such operations and would decide for itself where German troops might be used in future.

It is scarcely too much to see in all this a determination by Germany to establish its hegemony over most of Europe by one means or another even if it is expressed, as it was by the Nazis from time to time, in the rhetoric of pan-Europeanism. The great power for which this poses the most immediate and most serious problem is, as in 1914 and 1939, France.

France and Franco-German Relations

The French Foreign Minister, perhaps unwittingly, made the fundamental foreign policy concerns of his country abundantly clear when he was called upon to defend France's resumption of nuclear weapons testing in the South Pacific in 1995. The tests were needed, he said, because 'France had to protect itself after being invaded three times in the past century'.[27]

What he omitted to mention was that on all three occasions the invader had been the same, and that we are not talking about Islamic fundamentalists, Third World 'rogue states' or any of the other post-Cold War bogeys foreign ministers have been driven to inflate in order to justify continued high levels of military spending. But the fact is that Herve de Charette's words could only be understood in one way – France needed to maintain its famous *force de frappe* to deter the German invader of 1871, 1914 and 1940 from trying once more.

In a way, this seems far-fetched. France and Germany have been allied for nearly all the half century since World War II. The partnership of big business in the two states has been the foundation of European integration, from the Coal and Steel Community of the early 1950s through to the European Union forty years later. However, the conditions which underpinned that partnership have eroded. A divided Germany was a more manageable one for France, but Germany is now united, increasing the imbalance between the two countrys' economic potential. The security needs which locked the two countries into a military alliance under US hegemony have disappeared as well. Instead, there are two powerful states (one significantly more powerful than the other) with divergent and often competing interests.

For, despite its new empire emerging to the east, Germany cannot ignore France. Only if France is brought under Germany's wing can the latter truly stand as a world power alongside the US or Japan. An alliance with France, with Berlin in the saddle, offers two big advantages for Germany. Firstly, it would enhance the latter's military potential without having to go to the expense of paying for it from the German taxpayers' pockets. Secondly, it provides a politically respectable cover, particularly if mediated through EU institutions, for the pursuit of 'German-first' policies throughout eastern Europe.

Before 1991, the price of the alliance appeared to be affording France a measure of co-leadership in the emerging European Union. The mightier Germany of the 1990s is offering fewer concessions. So Paris is faced with the dilemma familiar to generations of French policy-makers – how to avoid subordination to the greater power to the east and assert French interests without colliding head on, and alone, with Germany.

Gaullism was one expression of this. But the pursuit of a 'French first' policy was, in the end, safe enough in a world dominated by the US and the Soviet Union, and with Germany divided. It could not be more than marginal in the world politics of the Cold War era. The reversion to an aggressive Gaullism by Jacques Chirac (building, it must be said, on rather similar policies pursued by François Mitterrand) has far wider ramifications.

The other expression of French policy towards Germany was the welcome most of the French ruling class gave to the invader in June 1940 and to the Vichy regime installed on German bayonets, as being better by far than rule by the French working class – an attitude which itself recalled the Prussian army standing guard over Paris while the French bourgeoisie butchered the commune of 1871. The same dichotomy presents itself today, when millions of French working people demonstrate against deflationary policies (as they did in December 1995) imposed by a government for no other reason than meeting the German-scripted criteria for monetary union. In fighting against the austerity politics of Chirac and Juppé, the French people were fundamentally opposing the price they were being asked to pay for the alliance of the ruling classes of the two countries. A French former President of the European Commission, François Furet, summed up France's dilemma thus:

> France today has two main problems – the first is that of budget deficits . . . the other, that of Europe . . . But these two problems have the same face: Germany . . . 120 years after Bismarck and two world wars, we find ourselves facing the very same question that was posed at the end of the last century: how can Europe be made to live when it has such a German preponderance?[28]

The furore over Chirac's nuclear testing programme in the South Pacific can also be understood in this setting. The fact that France has been condemned by states normally regarded as friendly to it underlines the truth of the assessment, made by John Laughland, a Brussels-based lobbyist and regular contributor to English-language newspapers on French affairs, that the nuclear decision 'should be understood within the logic of internal power-play between the big states in the European Union . . . [the tests] are intended mainly to send a message to Bonn . . . that France intends to be in charge of Europe's future defence policy just as Germany will be in charge of her monetary policy'.[29]

There is, indeed, evidence of Franco-German co-operation as well as of divergence in military questions. The 35,000-strong joint corps, based in Germany and operating outside NATO structures, is the most advanced expression of this. But to envisage a united Europe in which France takes charge of defence and Germany the economy, presumably leaving the cooking to Britain and the jokes to Belgium while they are at it, is to believe in the fundamental honesty of most Italian politicians. What philanthropic urge will inspire the French to defend a German-dominated economy? Presumably the same one as will lead the Germans to fund the French military. In fact, the nuclear-testing programme was designed to underline the military independence and self-sufficiency of France, not its dependence on another power.

France is far from putting all its eggs in the German basket in any case. Witness Chirac's conspicuous cozying up to the British Conservative government following the former's election in 1995. 'The President and I have concluded that the vital interests of one country cannot be threatened without the vital interests of the other being at risk' said British Prime Minister John Major after one Anglo-French summit, to Chirac's evident satisfaction.[30] Such a community of interest was underlined by Major's support for the French resumption of nuclear testing, by France inching towards a more sceptical position on European monetary union and by the establishment of a joint Anglo-French air-force command.

France and Britain do, indeed, have a lot of common interests to defend. Their status as nuclear powers, their permanent membership of the UN Security Council, their continuing neo-colonial role in Africa and the Middle East. The new joint air unit's military brief defines this community of interest. It would operate in another Gulf war, in a 'humanitarian crisis' in Africa (using the now-conventional 1990s cover for self-interested intervention in that continent and elsewhere) or in operations in the Channel. In Yugoslavia the two have followed the same approach, broadly opposed to that of Germany and the US. While the two powers have sometimes antagonistic interests in the Third World, both face the problem (which Germany does not) of trying to be a global, rather than just a European, power while living within very much reduced means in the shadow of Germany's new power. Traditional French fears of Anglo-Saxon conspiracies, driven by close US–British links, are also likely to diminish as the 'special relationship' hitherto enjoyed by Washington and London dwindles and is replaced by a US–German axis.

France's decision to rejoin the NATO military command, from which de Gaulle had withdrawn it in protest at US hegemony in the 1960s, is a further sign of changed times. Rather than being an indicator of France's desire for increased co-operation with its 'allies', it represents an attempt by Paris to take advantage of the vacuum created by the withdrawal of US troops from Europe and assert its own military leadership anew. With France inside (as well as independent of) NATO's military counsels in the post-US hegemony era, it will have greater scope to impose its own priorities in the Balkans and the Mediterranean, in particular – making what is left of the alliance work for French interests.

Of all the big powers, France is perhaps the least stable internally (Russia aside), as events at the end of 1995 showed. Its unemployment rate is highest, the activities of neo-fascists the most extensive. Under Mitterrand's governments, real wages fell (particularly for industrial workers) while income inequality grew more pronounced.[31] Violence against people of North African origin has grown under these dismal economic conditions. Through it all, the French elite is firmly putting its own imperial interests first. In early 1996 Chirac followed the German example of cutting back the size of its armed forces whilst orienting them more towards rapid interventions over a wide area (while ordering a renewed drive to make French companies the world's top arms exporters as well).[32]

This policy is a hard-headed recognition of the nature of the problems pressing in on France today. The broadening of the European Union has already brought in countries firmly in the German sphere of influence, like Austria, and will bring in more if membership is extended, as planned, to several of the former socialist countries of eastern Europe where French interests are limited (indeed, French trade with the region has hardly increased through the 1990s). The possibility of France in the future directing European affairs to the extent that it did before 1989 is very small. According to Dominic Moisi of the French Institute for International Relations, France is the great loser of the end of the Cold War. 'France benefited from the Yalta order more than anyone else', with its division of Germany, while the collapse of the USSR and European socialism 'weren't necessarily good news for France'.[33]

Hence the tilt towards London, which has traditionally been the response of the diplomats of the Quai d'Orsay to German resurgence. Hence also the almost desperate assertion of a 'France-first' attitude on every conceivable occasion. Paris all but wrecked the talks aimed at setting up the World Trade Organisation because of its determination to maintain agricultural protectionism. French commitment to cultural protectionism in the face of Hollywood is scarcely less. The celebrated expulsion of CIA operatives from Paris on charges of economic espionage and the attempts to build up the West European Union as a military alternative to NATO are all further indications of a policy increasingly directed against the US.

France has its own specific concerns and zones of interest

outside Europe, of which the most pressing is North Africa, and Algeria in particular. The civil war in France's former colony has already spilled over into France itself, since the Islamic opposition in Algeria correctly regards Paris as the main international support for the military-based government. There is no doubt that France would regard an Islamic government in Algiers as a disaster, likely to work against French interests throughout the region and possibly send a further wave of immigrants over the Mediterranean. It has already given the regime in Algiers $7.5 billion in direct and indirect aid.[34]

As part of its strategy for dealing with this problem on its southern flank, Paris has sought to establish freer trading relationships with all the countries of North Africa on a similar logic to that which impelled the creation of the North American Free Trade Area – unless investment and jobs head south, people will move north. France has also sought to impart a 'southern dimension' to EU and NATO strategy as a counter to German's determination to drive both organisations, and its own influence, resolutely eastwards. To this end, France, Spain and Italy formed a joint rapid-reaction military unit, based in Florence for the proverbial 'peacekeeping' in the region. The 12,000-strong force has no German or British participation, and will be effectively a Frenchled intervention force in North Africa and the Middle East. NATO's then Secretary-General Willy Claes also held meetings with ambassadors from several North African states to warn them that 'Islamic fundamentalism' posed as great a threat as the Soviet Union had once done. This attempt to get the organisations of capitalist collaboration to focus on North Africa has gone alongside clear statements that France will follow its own policy in a region it considers to be vital to its security.[35]

French policy towards North Africa is not driven solely by fear of the consequences of unrest, however. Oil-rich Algeria is a major export market for France and parts of the region's economy are now home to substantial inward investment. Cities like Casablanca in Morocco are developing as low-cost industrial centres similar to parts of Mexico and south-east Asia, oriented towards serving the European markets. Indeed, *Business Week* magazine announced in 1993 that 'Morocco wants to be Europe's Mexico',[36] based on cheap labour and agricultural exports, an aspiration the Moroccans have presumably abandoned in the light of Mexico's subsequent bankruptcy and economic annexation by the US. If France can keep these states in its own zone of influence (something which the US, for one, is contesting), then French business could have a useful outlet for surplus capital and source of raw materials. North Africa could play the same sort of role for France, albeit on a smaller scale, as eastern Europe may do for Germany.

Neo-colonial policy emerges still more sharply in relation to the 'Communaute Financiere Africaine' (CFA), the network of former French colonies which Paris still regards as its own backyard. France has long played a much more active role in Africa than other former colonial powers – certainly a more overt one. French paratroopers have intervened in Zaire, the Central African Republic, Chad and Rwanda in recent years, on each occasion to preserve or extend French influence, whatever pretext may have been offered. The relations between Paris and its former colonies has altered little as a result of the granting of formal independence. Currencies within the CFA are pegged to the French franc, and participating countries lodge most of their foreign exchange with the Finance Ministry in Paris, ensuring effective economic control by France and the primacy of French companies in the markets. France imports 33 per cent of its oil, 33 per cent of its copper, 25 per cent of its iron ore, 48 per cent of its uranium and 86 per cent of its aluminium from Africa, mainly from former colonies.[37]

This economic control was brutally asserted in 1994, when France devalued the CFA zone currencies against the franc by 50 per cent in an attempt to boost exports hit by falling commodity prices and cut imports like medicine, slashing living standards for millions of the world's poorest people (per capita income had already fallen 40 per cent over the previous ten years in the CFA zone). 'This is a collective murder of Africans by the IMF and France', said a civil servant in Mali, one of the affected countries.[38] Strikes and riots greeted the devaluation in Senegal and Gabon while primary school attendance in Cameroon has fallen by 500,000 since the cut, as children can no longer afford to enrol or buy text-books.[39]

An aggressive African policy has also succeeded in establishing a large French business presence elsewhere in the continent, including in former British preserves like Nigeria, where France has displaced the UK as the main trading partner.

Now, no one is likely to fight France for its African interests. However, their existence and importance establish the fact that France is an imperialist power with its own perspectives outside a strictly European context. Its global role is less pronounced than the British, but definitely forms a major part of its foreign policy. This is part of the background to the mounting strains in the Franco-German relationship, which exploded dramatically in the summer of 1993, when German refusal to adapt its interest rate policy to French needs precipitated the virtual collapse of the European exchange rate mechanism on which Paris had pinned such hopes. Given a choice between a policy in its own expansionist interests and one oriented towards France's European Union dreams, Bonn made it brutally clear where its preferences lay.[40]

As the German Foreign Minister Klaus Kinkel remarked, 'the time has come when German interests and those of France do not necessarily coincide'.[41] British strategist Jonathan Eyal observed that 'the Paris–Bonn axis is a phenomenon whose time has passed' and 'an ephemeral product of the Cold War, an arrangement which did not and could not outlive the end of Communism'.[42] On GATT, Yugoslavia, eastern Europe and the European exchange rate mechanism, the interests of the two countries have indeed diverged, with Germany usually finding an ally in the US and France one in Britain. French premier Balladur appealed for the ratification of the Maastricht treaty by the French people (something only accomplished by the narrowest of margins) because rejection 'would simply permit Germany to act as it wants, without caring about its neighbours and partners, not restrained by any single common European rule in its role as the dominant military, economic, financial and monetary power at the centre of the continent'.[43]

Alas for France, there is little evidence that Maastricht has had the restraining effect on Germany which Balladur hoped for. With the project of European monetary union faltering by the day, France faces the possibility of being confronted by a mighty Germany at the heart of a Deutschmark zone stretching from the Belgian coast to the Baltic Sea and the Balkans and then having to address once again the question on which its rulers divided in 1940: submit or rebel? Perhaps this time around the circumstances may be less dramatic – but those bombs did not destroy the coral beauty of the Mururoa Atoll for nothing.

Britain

One of the central causes of the first two world wars was the desire of other powers to knock Britain off the privileged and protected position atop the world economy which it had acquired in the nineteenth century. This was often as true of Britain's allies like the US as it was for its German and Japanese antagonists. The vast markets held captive for British manufactures, the endless tribute rolling in to the City of London from all parts of the globe, the raw material supplies secured by the British navy and an army of colonial officials could not but make the German or American capitalist drool with envy once their own domestic markets began to feel constricted and unfit for further super-profitable exploitation.

The objective of dislodging Britain's world pre-eminence has now, of course, been accomplished and there is a large body of literature dealing with Britain's relative decline and the failures of governments from Attlee to Thatcher to reverse it. Yet often this overstates the marginalisation of Britain in world affairs. By any reasonable account Britain remains a major force in the global economy and politics, with its own special interests which are playing a part in shaping the new alignments between the great powers.

British strength is most obvious in its continued status as an 'official' nuclear power and its permanent membership of the United Nations Security Council, attributes it shares with France. It is also apparent in the important (if secondary) military role Britain played in the Gulf War and, on a more modest scale, in former Yugoslavia. And, in an era of increased interference by big powers in the Third World, the Malvinas/Falklands War deserves to be seen as the mother of all interventions.

This reflects not just an imperial past, as is often assumed, but the global spread of economic and strategic interests which Britain maintains to this day, together with more than sufficient military strength to intervene, when required, in support of those interests. Overshadowed, at least from the decolonisation of the 1950s onwards, by the overarching contradictions of the Cold War, in which London was Washington's most loyal helper, the real nature of British businesses' worldwide scope is once more becoming visible. Even today, Britain's external involvement is often seen as only an extension of the European Union question. In fact, Britain's long-standing debate over its place in Europe, and the intensifying divisions in the ruling class which that debate is causing, can only be understood against the background of a wider appreciation of British capitalism's specific aspects.

This has several features which set it apart, in kind or in extent, from German or French capitalism. There is the global role of the City of London as a pre-eminent centre of world finance, and the importance of financial institutions within the structure of the economy. There is the high degree of capital concentration in British industry, and the correspondingly large role played by British trans-national corporations. There is the exceptionally high rate of the export of capital from Britain.

On all these criteria, Britain's economy stands apart, not because of its exceptional strength but because of its exceptionally parasitic nature. Thus, by some indicators, Britain ranks third in the world of great powers, even if by the most basic accounting of gross domestic product per capita, it would not merit a place in the top ten. For example, the total market capitalisation of firms traded on the London Stock Exchange is $892 billion, a much lesser figure than for the US and Japanese bourses, but more than that of Germany and France put together. And in *Business Week* magazine's ranking of the 1,000 largest corporations in the world (by market value) 101 British firms were listed, compared to 45 from

France and 37 from Germany. Only the US, with 396 monopolies listed, and Japan with 246, out-ranked British business in the league table of the goliaths of the world economy.[44] Fully 179 of the top 500 European companies by market capitalisation and 49 of the top 200 by turnover are British.[45] British big business is very big indeed, and depends relatively little on its domestic market for the scale of its operations. And the big will get still bigger. More than £66 billion worth of mergers and takeovers took place in Britain in 1995,[46] confirming the country as the takeover capital of Europe, where vast sums are spent on the concentration of capital, rather than in investment in new plant or technology.

Sweeping international orientation is the second striking feature of the British economy. Between 1979 and 1990 the proportion of gross profits earned by British banks and companies overseas rose from around 14 per cent to 20 per cent. In the same period the external assets of British business rose from £199 billion to £950 billion, with income from interest, profits and dividends increasing from just under £17 billion to £76 billion – two-thirds of it earned by banks.[47] The investments underlying this profit surge are mainly portfolio rather than direct: throughout the 1980s the former rose from £887 million to £35,486 million, while the latter increased less dramatically from £5,889 million to £21,515 million.[48] This investment is not building factories abroad; rather it is speculating in stocks, shares and bonds throughout the world system.

The City's role is pre-eminently a global one. For example, British insurance firms derive 35 per cent of their premium revenue from abroad, compared with just under 4 per cent for German companies;[49] while 20 per cent of transactions in publicly traded Japanese company shares were carried out on the London stock exchange.[50] And the City is the world's currency trading centre. Foreign exchange turnover in 1995 amounted to $465 billion, as compared with $244 billion in the second-placed US, or $76 billion in Germany.[51] This is not a reflection of the strength of the pound; rather, it highlights the way in which British speculators have cornered the market for 'Eurodollars' (dollars held outside the US for purposes of speculation or trading) and other 'eurocurrencies'.[52]

The massive haemorrhaging of capital abroad in the 1980s coincided, of course, with the dramatic contraction of Britain's industrial base to the point where the once workshop of the world became a net importer of manufactured goods – Britain now earns more from overseas assets than from the export of manufactures. Throughout the 1980s, the gross capital stock of British manufacturing industry (at 1985 replacement cost prices) increased marginally from £253 billion to £278 billion, while that of the banking sector nearly doubled, from £71 billion to £138 billion.[53] This would have been of little concern to the shareholders in British business, who have seen the dividend payout share of corporate profits rise from less than 7 per cent when Thatcher was elected Prime Minister in 1979 to over 20 per cent today.[54]

This all presents a picture of a Britain in which a few big companies and banks play a large global role despite a relatively small domestic market, and in which the commanding heights of the economy are held by interests with a far more pronounced external orientation than could be found in any other of the great powers except the US. British economists Jonathan Michie and Seumas Milne aptly summarised the position:

> Britain's economy is by far the most parasitic in the indus-trialised world: its net overseas assets represented 20 per cent of national income in 1987, compared with Japan's 8 per cent, West Germany's 12 per cent and a figure of minus 8 per cent for the US. Its international interests are based on the import of materials, semi-manufactures and components, and the ex-port of commodities; the export of financial and industrial capital and the repatriation or re-accumulation of profits; the pivotal role of the City of London in global financial markets . . . and the far-reaching transnational operations of British-based companies.'[55]

This scenario explains two of the most important elements of British foreign policy today. Firstly, while there may be more or less a consensus within the ruling class over the desirability of being part of a European free trade zone for business, there is much less enthusiasm for incorporation in a federal Europe which would circumscribe, in the German interest, the *global* role of the City of London and limit the international trading and specula-tion role of British finance. Secondly, more than any other power except the US, there is a British interest in a 'new world order' – that is, a stable worldwide system for profit-making, in which the powers acting in concert order the affairs of the globe. While Germany's vital interests are overwhelmingly concentrated within Europe, Japan's mainly centered in Asia, and Russia's limited to its contiguous regions, the profits and power of British capitalism come from all parts of the world, and therefore demand order and stability everywhere. 'Globalism is Britain's natural and logical style and . . . the world as a whole, including the Commonwealth, is Britain's natural economic territory', according to a recent paper written by an Australian economist for the Royal Institute of International Affairs.[56]

Since the days are long gone when the British navy and British diplomacy could guarantee such order themselves, London is now in the front rank of those seeking to form a united great power coalition to ensure that those who today dominate the world economy continue to do so. Leading right-wing journalist Peregrine Worsthorne was quite explicit when he advanced Britain's case for playing a leading military role in the new world order's main project: '. . . to help build and sustain a world order stable enough to allow the advanced economies of the world to function without constant interruption and threat from the third world'.[57]

However, every episode in world politics only highlights the near-impossibility of such a consensus being formed on anything more than the most temporary and *ad hoc* basis (as against Iraq, and even then the coalition was a fragile one). In the absence of such a united great-power approach, Britain, like the other powers, is forced to fashion a new policy which meets its own particular needs.

Throughout the post-war period, British foreign policy took as its starting point the 'special relationship' with the US, above all in the anti-Soviet bloc organised by Washington. The UK was the US's first partner in world affairs from the founding of NATO down to the bombing of Libya in 1986 and the war in the Gulf in 1991. That relationship is now visibly crumbling. The US sees Germany as its natural partner in Europe, and the Clinton administration has gone out of its way to snub the British government on a number of occasions. On the other hand, the then British Defence Secretary Malcolm Rifkind poured unprecedented scorn on US diplomacy in former Yugoslavia in 1995, in the clearest sign yet that Britain no longer puts all its diplomatic eggs in the transatlantic basket.

The second, if more controversial, pillar of British diplomacy over the last 30 years was support for the development of the European 'common market', throughout a period in which there was a reasonable balance of power within the evolving 'community' and there were, above all, the Soviets still to be faced down. All that, too, has changed. John Major made it clear in 1994 that in his view the ending of the Cold War had rendered the integration process redundant. 'The European Community was born to end divisions in western Europe. It has succeeded . . . the determination of the founding fathers has succeeded far beyond the estimations of most people in their time . . . But it is outdated. It will not do now.'[58] This, of course, reflects the fact that the European operations of British big businesses are now only one-third as profitable as those in Asia and Pacific, and that 40 per cent of the top 100 companies on the London Stock Exchange now earn most of their profits outside the EU (including Britain itself).

In the place of the Euro-centred policy, powerful voices are being heard arguing for an assertive new 'Britain-first' view of the world. One of the most consistent has been the chairman of the House of Commons Foreign Affairs Select Committee, Conservative MP David Howell. In a series of articles in the *Wall Street Journal Europe* and in the *Daily Telegraph* of London over the last two years, he has called 'for a less submissive approach to foreign policy'.[59]

'Now (more than ever before) is the age of the nation-state', Howell argues, stressing that Britain 'has vast reserves of energy and experience with which to carve out a global role, and it is this role which promotes Britain's interest as a trading and business nation in the European single market, the Commonwealth and the booming markets of Asia and Latin America'.[60]

Howell points out that British business is far from having an exclusively European orientation. Exports to other EU states as a share of the British total have fallen from 60 per cent in the 1980s to 45 per cent in 1993, while 80 per cent of Britain's vast overseas investment went outside Western Europe. For example, Britain accounts for 25 per cent of all foreign investment in Australia (which in return sends 35 per cent off its outward investment back to the old mother country), and is its third largest trading partner as well as being well placed in the booming markets of the Asia-Pacific region generally. Britain is 'in the super-league as a global investor' with a particular stake in the booming markets of many Commonwealth states and should make a 'strategic adjustment' to its foreign policy accordingly.[61]

The foreign policy demanded by the business community, according to Howell, should project Britain as 'a business-first trading nation' that 'punched its way into new markets worldwide'. This would involve not 'following every twist and turn of American policy', opposition to a single European currency, which would 'divide Europe' and be 'useless for a global financial centre such as London', taking a firm line with Russia and building stronger links with the Commonwealth.[62]

Howell is not a voice in the wilderness. The Director-General of the powerful Institute of Directors, noting that Germany's economic interests were far from being the same as Britain's, wrote that 'the net effect of the lie down and let it happen approach to the European Community is like economic unilateral nuclear disarmament. It is about time it was recognised that Britain does have real economic interests to defend and that they need to be defended as our partners defend theirs.' The Diplomatic Editor of the BBC pointed out that

> international influence depends on a country's range and scope, and Germany and Japan are restricted in both. It is reach as well as weight which counts, and our interests in so

many different parts of the world provides us with a considerable potential advantage, both in terms of political influence
and trade. The Major government . . . has already shown signs
of wanting to run a vigorous foreign policy which is more
independent of the United States than the 'me too-ism' of the
Thatcher years . . . the accelerating decline in American power
can only continue, and it seems fair to assume . . . there will be
a political weakening of the European Community itself. In
these circumstances the old assumptions about Britain's position in the world will need some swift rethinking.[63]

Of course, this does not, in most respects, amount to a 'new
policy'. In most particulars it is a reversion, on a more modest
scale, to pre-1939 or even pre-1914 British diplomacy. As the Tory
minister Nicholas Ridley observed in the remarks which led to his
dismissal from government: 'we've always played the balance of
power in Europe. It has always been Britain's role to keep these
various powers balanced, and never has it been more necessary
than now, with the Germans so uppity.'[64]

Unsurprisingly, 'uppity' Germans and their friends do not like
this policy. Former US National Security Council chief Zbigniew
Brzezinski has described it as a menace to European stability and
global security,[65] while Karl Lamers, Kohl's top foreign policy
adviser, has accused London of running an 'irresponsible propaganda campaign' against a common currency, destabilising the
continent.[66]

In essence, however, it is only the British variation on the
policies outlined by the Pentagon as meeting the needs of the
post-Cold War US, of the threatening ruminations of the Foreign
Affairs Committee of the German Bundestag, or the new assertiveness of leading Japanese politicians.

And, as with these other powers, Britain appears willing to
support its position with judicious amounts of menace. In its first
major post-1991 military policy review, the British Ministry of
Defence had this to say: 'The government may decide to require
defence provision to help serve other ends – national prestige,
showing the flag, international political influence, supporting
industry, helping science or humanitarian relief, easing regional
problems.'[67] It would be hard to compile a more comprehensive
list of reasons for intervention than that, drawn up by the most
experienced imperialists of all.

This policy can be supported by a far-flung military network.
Alongside the US, the British armed forces, although reduced in
size, are represented on every continent. There are bases in the
Falklands (Malvinas) and Belize, in Cyprus and Australia. Oman
in the Middle East is virtually a British military protectorate.

Defence agreements still bind the UK to Australia and New Zealand, while African armies are formed under the supervision of British soldiers. And this military machine is getting, like its counterparts elsewhere, technically re-equipped to meet new tasks. In fact, British defence procurement spending has *risen* by almost 10 per cent since the end of the Cold War.[68] This was exemplified by the recent decision to spend £200 million on non-nuclear cruise missiles which, according to the *Daily Telegraph* 'would give Britain the ability to deter a threatening nation almost anywhere' and would 'against some third world countries ... be more effective than its nuclear deterrent'.[69]

Alongside, and deeply intertwined with, defence policy is Britain's foreign-aid programme, recently exposed as a ramp for arms sales and political influence in the notorious affair of Malaysia's Pergau Dam. Even a blue-ribbon Independent Group on British Aid was forced to conclude more than ten years ago that 'what should be its primary aim, to help the people of the receiving countries to help themselves by raising their productive capacity, was often subordinated to the aim of promoting purely British interests: the securing of contracts for British firms and the protection of jobs for British workers'.[70] Indeed, every year Britain transfers billions of pounds *net* out of the world's poorest countries more than it puts it in terms of investment, loans and aids.

The continuing vitality of British big business is written in the misery of much of the globe and there can be no doubt that, in the new world order, Britain's rulers will pursue all means possible to maintain their privileged position as the pawnshop of the world and London's role as the 'capital of capital'.

Russia

Chapter 3 described the collapse of the USSR and its consequences for world politics, the stark realities of the restoration of capitalism across the formerly socialist territories, and the struggles developing between various powers for influence and control over the economic resources of the ex-Soviet republics.

One of the competing powers is, of course, Russia itself – a Russia in which the new ruling class is hardly secure in the saddle and where the main lines of its policy are only gradually becoming clear and are being fiercely contested within the country itself at every stage.

Beneath all the confusion, however, the most important fact is the simplest – capitalism has essentially been restored in Russia, even if the capitalist class has yet to consolidate itself politically and banish the possibility of a socialist restoration. Most Russian industry has been privatised, and it is the laws of commodity production and the private accumulation of capital which are shaping its economic future. It is therefore necessary to assess the policy course likely to be followed by the new rulers of Russia, where their vital interests lie, what foreign policy goals they set themselves and where they might collide with those of other powers. Internal developments may render such an analysis wholly or partially redundant; nevertheless, the likely re-emergence of Russia as a classic great power has such an enormous bearing on the prospects for war and peace that its implications cannot be avoided.

Just as there were no models for the Soviet endeavour – the creation of a socialist society – so also the present course Russia is following is unprecedented. A capitalist system is being re-created on an economic basis developed over 70 years of socialism. This is reflected in the composition of the emerging Russian capitalist class. Much of it is rooted in the industrial managers who ran Soviet industry, 'bosses' up to ministerial level who shed their 'communist' skin rapidly when it seemed prudent – the 'nomen-klatura capitalists'. President Yeltsin himself and his Prime Minister, Chernomyrdin, are typical of this element. To them can be added out-and-out criminals, who control much of the trade sector, as well as a smattering of flashy young entrepreneurs, the 'new millionaires', who are by no means a large or politically decisive element in the new set-up.

Capitalist Russia has been from birth not a 'free enterprise' economy, however much some of the its architects may have pored over the works of Adam Smith, but a *monopoly* capitalism, based on the privatisation of the vast factories, associations and combines which characterised the Soviet economy. It is estimated that Russia's largest company by revenue, United Energy System of Russia, ought to rank at number 85 in the world listing of industrial giants, with the second largest, Gazprom, at number 96 (though both rankings could be much higher to reflect the real relative size of these concerns, which are deflated by the vagaries of the rouble exchange rate). United Energy System employs 216,298 workers, while manufacturing giants AutoVAZ and GAZ employ nearly 100,000 each. The list of Russia's major companies is a list of giant conglomerates in the energy, manufacturing, metallurgy and construction sectors, with the most profitable of them being very profitable indeed – Gazprom turned a profit of over $2 billion in 1994.[71] This is not a Third World economy subordinated to Western interests (the direct involvement of which in Russia is still small, with only $2 billion invested in 1995 and a per capita foreign direct investment of $7, as compared with $214 per head in Hungary and $59 in the Czech Republic),[72] but a fast emerging competitor to the trans-national corporations of the West and Japan.

As elsewhere, the industrial monopolies are closely fused with the banking sector. For example, Russia's banks (many of which are affiliated to particular enterprises), flushed with cash accumulated in the last few years of feverish currency speculation and high-interest, short-term loans, recently offered to loan the government $2 billion, with shares in 7,000 enterprises on the threshold of privatisation to be used as collateral, as clear an expression of the development of a form of state monopoly capitalism as one could wish for. One bank, newly created out of the old Soviet foreign-trade organisation, has secured control of the state nickel monopoly, for example, which in turn controls world nickel production. The banks are also stimulating the further growth of conglomerates and the formation of what are called 'finance-industrial groups', which on their own control about 5 per cent of Russia's GDP.[73] The big private banks also, according to the *Wall Street Journal*, directly control many of Russia's parliamentarians.[74]

One Western official, sent to Moscow to help build parliamentary organisations, described this as an emerging 'corporate fascism',[75] while the *Financial Times* alluded to 'the emergence of a mildly authoritarian Russia, in which big business and government are locked in a mutually beneficial and somewhat corrupt relationship and the state ruthlessly cracks down on dissenting voices'.[76] A US diplomat in Moscow analysed the new ruling class as being based around 'clans' tied to industrial sectors or big cities, each with their own people in government.[77] These clans compete for influence and profits, but increasingly unite in pushing an aggressive nationalistic line. A growing element in this policy has been the introduction of tariff barriers to preserve the profit margins of domestic industry from the possibility of foreign competition. Quotas and tariffs are now being imposed on a range of goods, including oil-industry equipment, textiles and poultry, while across-the-board import taxes are under consideration.[78]

Business Week painted a vivid picture of the new lords of Russia's economy in 1996. It described a rising generation of bankers who have

> scooped up formerly state-owned oil, mining, forest products and real-estate assets to create sprawling financial-industrial conglomerates that resemble Japan's prewar *zubatsus* or today's South Korean *chaebol*. About 32 of these giants have already taken shape, linking more than 500 factories and 72 banks employing more than 2.5 million people. Dozens more are being formed. The top six already control Russia's oil, gas and metals industries and bring in the bulk of the country's hard currency . . . each has political 'uncles' . . . in the government to grease the bureaucratic wheels.[79]

This is the picture of an emerging ruling class which does not simply do the bidding of foreign interests, as it may have appeared in the immediate aftermath of the destruction of the Soviet Union. There are those who have argued that a capitalist Russia must inevitably be subordinate, that Russia's choices boil down to either a return to socialism or neo-colonial status, completely under the thumb of Western governments and monopolies. The G7 cannot afford to let Russia become a competitor, the argument runs.

The other great powers may, indeed, not want to see the emergence of another competitor and would surely rather Russia became little more than a source of raw materials and market for finished goods. Alas for them, there is little they can do about it if a new competing power arises. Russia is not nineteenth-century Africa, but a powerful, industrially developed state of a size, and with resources and armed forces, which make its emergence as an independent great power almost inevitable.

Of course, during the phase of anti-communist agitation, many of the pro-capitalist leaders like Yeltsin and Foreign Minister Andrei Kozyrev sounded enthusiastically pro-Western. Indeed, they even went to the point of destroying the Soviet Union to ensure their own control over Russia. However, since 1991 all leading Soviet politicians have adopted nationalistic aims with varying degrees of fervour. All of them talk of the restoration of Russia as a 'great power', of standing up to the US and NATO and the restoration of a Russian domination over former Soviet territories by one means or another.

Kozyrev, long the liberal darling of the West, told his US counterpart early in 1995 that 'the honeymoon is over', adding that 'Russia will never bow to arbitrary political pressure – not even to please the US'.[80] A 'moderate' party led by Deputy Prime Minister Sergei Sakhrai warned that 'Russia is destined by her geopolitical position to be a great power, and it does not befit her to engage in self-reproach'.[81]

While at the fringes, much Russian political rhetoric may appear as extreme talk and the manifestation of a backward-looking militant nationalism which shades into forms of Nazism in the case of Liberal Democratic Party leader Vladimir Zhirinovksy, it actually corresponds to the needs of Russia's nascent capitalist class, most graphically expressed in the war against Chechnya to secure the oil pipeline route from the Caspian Sea (see Chapter 3). This war was fought under the slogan of defending the integrity of the Russian Federation, of course, just as the extension of Russian influence in ex-Soviet republics has been dressed up as concern for Russians living in the 'near abroad'. However, the nationalist rhetoric, although it may express the anger of a humiliated and frustrated people, is tailored to meet the need of Russian industry to reintegrate, under its domination, as much as possible of the economies into which the former Soviet Union has splintered.

The Soviet economy was, famously, centrally planned. Although this bedrock practice of the socialist economy was increasingly honoured in the breach in the USSR's latter years, enterprises and industries were built up in the closest possible connection with each other for one five-year plan after another, in relationships that often had little to do with commodity–money relations. Often component supplies for an industry throughout the whole territory of the union came from a single source and raw materials were allocated through the control of a single centre. The location of industries and supplies reflected the fact that the USSR had been treated as a single economic entity by generations of planners, who attached no overriding significance to whether a particular factory was built in Kazakhstan, the Ukraine, Russia or Latvia. It was inconceivable that the boundaries between these republics could one day become international borders, with each state under a separate government.

The dislocation caused, first by the Gorbachev reforms which undermined the central planning system, and then by the disintegration of the USSR itself, was a major factor in the vast drop in industrial production across all the ex-Soviet republics (and, to a lesser but still dramatic extent, the ex-Comecon states of eastern Europe). The reconstruction of the Russian economy under its new (or politically transformed) masters demands renewed control over the oil of Azerbaijan, the coal and steel of the eastern Ukraine, the cotton of Central Asia. This drive to expand economically into other former Soviet territories performs a dual political function as well – it helps legitimise the Russian rulers in the minds of millions of nationally minded (or even Soviet-minded) Russians, and it helps the new ruling class integrate and form itself by creating possibilities, through expansion, to overcome the bitter rivalries between energy, banking, military and farming sectors which presently bedevil it.

Alongside the war in Chechnya, Russia has stimulated, or involved itself in, conflicts in South Ossetia and Abkhazia (both regions of Georgia), Moldva, Tadjikistan and between Armenia and Azerbaijan. In each case, the objective was to reassert Russian control. In the case of Georgia, this meant successfully destabilising the government of former Soviet Foreign Minister Eduard Shevardnadze, who was lent strong support by the CIA, no doubt in return for services rendered. After two civil wars, Shevardnadze came to heel, and the CIA's top man in the Georgian capital of Tiblisi was discreetly shot dead by one of Shevardnadze's bodyguards.

Elsewhere, the process has gone more smoothly. Belarus has

more or less given up the ghost of the unwanted sovereignty thrust upon it by Yeltsin and Kravchuk in their haste to bury the USSR in 1991, and collapsed back into economic union with Russia. Kazakhstan has even agreed to merge its military with the Russian. Almost every external border of a former Soviet republic, other than those in the Baltic and the Ukraine, is now protected by Russian troops. In the economic sphere, it is in many cases only the fragility of Russia's own finances which have held back still closer integration. But the republics of Central Asia have been bluntly told by Russian deputy premier Sakhrai that they must choose between trading relationships with Russia, Belarus and the Ukraine on the one hand, and Turkey, Iran and Pakistan on the other.

The Ukraine remains the main outstanding problem from Russia's perspective. The two governments have fought over the division of the Soviet Black Sea fleet, over 500 ships based primarily at Sevastapol in the Crimea, and over the future of the Crimea itself, a largely Russian-populated region gifted by the Soviet government from Russia to the Ukraine at a time when such a shift did not seem to matter very much. The Ukraine enjoys strong political support for its independence from Germany and the US, and is too big to be cowed by the methods used against Georgia. A large Russian population, mainly working in heavy industry in the east of the country, favours closer ties with Russia. As Russia grows stronger, attempts to settle the 'Ukrainian question' are likely to become more assertive, since the economic and historical imperative (the Russian state was originally based around the Ukrainian capital of Kiev) is stronger here than elsewhere. Indeed, some form of Russian–Ukrainian union is a *sine qua non* for Russia regarding itself, and being regarded by others, as a real 'great power'.

Many of these moves have been supported by the Left in Russia, anxious to see a restoration of the Soviet Union, as far as is possible. Such a reintegration would command a great deal of popular support not only in Russia, but in many other republics as well. The main issue, however, is who is pursuing such a line, what their purpose is and how they are pursuing it. The Russian Left does not stand for force, for example, and has not supported Yeltsin's war in Chechnya (unlike Zhirinovsky). The re-creation of a Russian Empire and the re-creation of a Soviet Union are actually dramatically different projects: the one is the project of the nationalists and big businessmen taking control of the Russian economy, the latter is the hope of those who have suffered as a result of that takeover. For example, Russian Communist leader Zyuganov went to Kiev to call for the peaceful integration of the Ukraine and

Russia, while Zhirinovsky threatened the Ukraine with 'ceasing to exist' if it did not come to heel.

The rising imperialist trend in Russian foreign policy was codified in a decree issued by President Yeltsin in September 1995 concerning Russia's relations with the former Soviet republics. This spelt out clearly the Russian government's priorities: a renunciation of the orientation towards the West; a rejection of the military, economic and political independence of the former republics; and a desire to create a new, smaller, Warsaw Pact to meet the threat from the US.

The same document also urges an economic and monetary union of the ex-Soviet republics – a 'rouble zone' controlled from Moscow. While none of these plans apply to the Baltic republics – Latvia, Lithuania and Estonia – which are not part of the 'Commonwealth of Independent States', the USSR's nebulous successor, they are instead earmarked in a separate, and leaked document, for military occupation in the event of Poland joining NATO.[82]

Opposition to the eastward expansion of NATO forms the second main plank of Russian foreign policy and is connected to the first, gathering up its own sphere of influence to the west and south once more. It is this proposal – to bring Poland, Hungary and the Czech Republic, as a first step – into NATO which has done more than anything else to cause a deterioration in relations between Moscow and Washington. NATO expansion would leave Russia isolated in Europe and would bring Western, probably US or German, troops and nuclear weapons into Poland and the Czech Republic. (The latter has said it would welcome even NATO nuclear arms on its territory.)

Boris Yeltsin said that moving NATO eastwards would 'plunge Europe into the flames of war' and his former nationalist rival and now deputy General Alexander Lebed (an admirer of Chile's General Pinochet) has said still more explicitly that 'it would mark the beginning of world war three'.[83]

Naturally, Russia's leaders are motivated by a hope that they might some day extend their own sphere of influence from the 'near abroad' of the ex-Soviet republics into eastern Europe, building on the economic connections established under Comecon. Yeltsin was clear about this, telling Western journalists in 1995 that relations were particularly good with Hungary, for example, because 'Hungary is orienting itself more to Russia because its entire economy is built on Russian technology'.[84] This policy clearly collides with German ambitions in the region.

Similarly, Russia's new assertiveness has caused friction with the US as the main hegemonic power in the Middle East, through its attempts to rebuild economic relations with Iraq and Iran.[85]

These are only the first tremors of what the *Financial Times* has described as a 'pragmatic imperialism' on the part of Russia, and one carried out by the same politicians, by and large, as appeared so 'pro-western' in 1990 and 1991. The ruling class in the West has, however, not been slow to get the point. The influential magazine *The Economist* backed Yeltsin to the hilt in his 1993 confrontation with the nationalists running the Russian parliament, accepting 'the view that this was nothing less than a fight between light and darkness'.[86] Yet by the start of 1995 the same magazine ran an editorial with the heading 'The Wrong Man for Russia' next to a picture of the Russian president.[87] By the start of 1996, they had turned again, backing Yeltsin as the only plausible alternative to the election of Communist leader Gennady Zyuganov as president. Such flip-flopping illustrates the difficulties Western interests have in grasping Russian politics – do they want the emergence of a nationalistic and authoritarian rival, or a return to the political threat represented by the word 'soviet'? In many ways, it is similar to their dilemma over Hitler in the 1930s – build up a ruthless rival to meet the Soviet 'menace' to civilisation and risk finding that he turns on his rivals' interests first. Millions paid for that miscalculation with their lives.

In fact, any president in Moscow in the near future is likely to be the 'wrong man' for the other great powers. Even the growing influence of Russia's Communists, whilst an expression of the desire for a return to socialism among Russia's suffering people and of tremendous symbolic significance in a world which was told that 'communism is dead', may not halt the emergence of a new Russian imperialism fighting for its place in the sun and for its part in a new redivision of the world.

CHAPTER 6

The Great Powers – the Far East

On the surface, the relations of the powers in Asia have changed less as a result of the collapse of the USSR than they have in Europe. However, the present situation in the region reflects both the long-term development of new rivalries combined with the consequences of the shock to the world system caused by the ending of Soviet power.

Broadly, the 'new Asia' is based on the following elements:

- The decline of Soviet military power in the region, and the start of a US military withdrawal alongside it.
- The rise of Japan as the dominant economic power in Asia and the Pacific, with growing signs of a new military role to match.
- The integration of China into the world economy, with again the potential for a major military presence as well.

All of this is happening in what has become the only really dynamically developing region of the world economy left. Asia is, of course, home to the famous 'four tigers' which have led the world in economic growth over the last 15 years – the merchant cities of Singapore and Hong Kong and the half-states of Taiwan and South Korea. Real countries, too, have displayed impressive growth, including, of course, China and Vietnam. Since this dynamism is unique in the capitalist world of the last generation, the region has attracted the interests of all major powers, each seeking a bigger slice of the only pie which is expanding. Japan aims for a yen bloc, the US for a 'free trade' regime to give it an 'in', Britain to manipulate its Commonwealth connections – and all in a power vacuum explicitly overlain with the shadow of war.

In Asia as elsewhere, the US is trying to protect its historic hegemony with reduced means which are nevertheless, not negligible. Its basic strategy, as outlined in Chapter 4, is to prevent the creation of a bloc excluding US interests, or the emergence of a regional hegemonic power. Two powers represent, in different ways, threats to the US position – threats so substantial that Washington's position is more obviously disadvantaged than it is anywhere else in the world. These are, of course, Japan and China.

Japan

Even while the Soviet Union was still amongst us, Americans had decided where the main threat to their way of life came from. As early as 1989 opinion polls showed most voters considered Japan's economic strength more of a threat to the security of the US than Soviet military power – the product, in the words of one commentator, of 'Japan's inability or unwillingness to restrain the one-sided and destructive expansion of its economic power'.[1]

Certainly, the expansion of that power has been the most dramatic single shift in relationships within the world economy since the end of World War II, dwarfing even the advance of the German economy. Japan's share of world GNP has increased from 6 per cent in 1970 to 16 per cent by 1991. Its trade surplus (much of it with the US) has risen from under $7 billion as recently as 1982 to over $106 billion ten years later and external net assets have increased from $180 billion in 1986 to over $513 billion by 1992.[2]

This economic behemoth is in the control of a small number of giant companies. Of Business Week's list of the 1,000 most valuable companies in the world, 246 are Japanese, while Japanese banks are well established as the world's largest.[3] In 1992, the ten biggest firms were responsible for over a third of Japan's exports, and the 30 biggest accounted for over half.[4]

These are the Keiretsus, the closely interlocked groups of corporations which also enjoy the most intimate relations with the banks and, for that matter, the key ministries in the Japanese state bureaucracy, the Ministry of Finance and the Ministry of International Trade and Industry. The cross-ownerships, long-term commercial relationships with suppliers and distributors, state direction of industrial organisation and close ties with banks that characterise the Keiretsu system have underpinned Japanese business's ability to conquer one world market after another at the expense of American, British and other rivals. They have enabled Japanese business to take a 'longer-term' perspective towards getting a return on capital, in contrast to the short-termism which characterises the stock-market-driven capitalism of New York and London. For example, Japanese industry only requires an 8.7 per cent rate of return on a research and development project with a ten-year pay off period, as against 14.8 per cent in Germany, 20.3 per cent in the US and 23.7 per cent in Britain. Throughout the 1980s, the share of the Japanese GDP devoted to investment exceeded the share of the US GDP so used by between two and three to one.[5] These Keiretsu relationships, all but unbreakable to the outside interest, have survived even the sharp and protracted recession and banking crisis which hit Japan over the last few years.

Exploitation of the Japanese worker, technology and trade are the three factors which have driven Japanese capitalism's rise. The first factor is often neglected in considerations of the Japanese 'economic miracle', but it needs to be remembered that this is the land of *Karoshi*, literally, death from over-work. The average Japanese worker works 500 hours a year more than the German, and wages average (in terms of purchasing power parity) around 50 per cent less. This is indeed a 'miracle' raised from the dead – the dead Japanese worker in particular. The Japanese trade unions march under the slogan 'We Want to Live and Work as Humans',[6] a demand which might be more normally associated with labour in the less developed nations of the world.

If this intense exploitation of the Japanese worker is largely hidden from the world, foreigners are invited to revel in the achievements of Japanese technology. It would be more accurate, however, to credit Japanese capitalism with achievements in the *application* of technology, rather than its development. As one Japanese economics professor confessed: 'Rapid technological progress stemmed mainly from "borrowed technology" from the US, the UK, Germany etc.'[7] Indeed, Japan has only won four Nobel Prizes for science since the war, compared with 158 for American scientists. Yet Japanese industry claims to have 275,000 robots deployed in its factories, as against just 37,000 in the US.[8] This is the result of an irony of international politics which has not been lost on the American public. The US lead in basic science is largely due to the huge military research programmes sponsored by the Pentagon, consistent with the US's strategic 'responsibilities'. Yet the Japanese lead in civilian industrial application of new technologies is due in part to the relatively low levels of military spending in a country which for 50 years has sheltered under the US umbrella. The sweated Japanese labour has been united with this borrowed technology in order to produce goods which seemed, at one point, to be overrunning the backyards of almost every other big power on earth.

This, of course, was the result of the success of Japanese industrial giants, purposefully backed by the Japanese state, in international trade. While the quality and cost of Japanese-made goods may account for the success of the Sonys, Toshibas, Toyotas and Mitsubishis in world markets, the soaring Japanese trade surplus owes as much to the dogged protectionism which excludes foreign goods from the domestic market. The world turned a blind eye to this whilst Japan was recovering from World War II, but the measures designed to allow Japanese businesses to secure their home base in the 1950s and 1960s remain in place to this day in many cases.

British historian Michael Montgomery summarised some of the

measures by which Japanese officialdom has kept imports at bay:

> Every imported car has to be individually tested on landing for compliance with local exhaust-emission requirements; all foreign drugs have to be tested either in Japanese laboratories or on Japanese living in their country of origin; a leading British drink was rejected on the grounds that the glue on the bottle label did not conform to Japanese standards . . . a new non-international set of standards has recently been imposed on skis, one of the few markets in which foreign imports predominate, on the grounds that Japanese snow is 'wetter' than that in Europe or North America.[9]

To which list one can only add the wisdom of the Japanese minister who recently explained the impossibility of importing foreign rice into Japan on account of Japanese intestines being shorter.

Unsurprisingly, the extent of the Japanese use of trade as a weapon in international politics has caused one row after another. Japan and the US have fallen out over Japan's expensive refusal to buy US fighters, building its own in preference, over the difficulties US construction firms have had in bidding for public contracts and over auto parts, the latter dispute almost leading to full-blown trade war.

However, perhaps the most striking example – and the most significant, on account of its strategic importance – was the semi-conductors dispute of the 1980s. This unites trade, technology and military-strategic implications in a critical fashion. If control of the high seas was once the key to a leading position in the world economy, control of the micro-chip plays much the same role today.

Semiconductors are small chips of etched silicon which channel electricity along microscopic pathways. According to the US Defence Science Board, they are the 'industrial rice of the information age',[10] while *Time* magazine calls them the 'indispensable heart of the techtronic age, raw material for everything from talking teddy bears to personal computers to intercontinental missiles'.[11]

Japanese conquest of the market in this strategically critical component proceeded in the usual way. US Pentagon-sponsored scientists developed most of the basic technology. US semiconductor firms then sold the licenses and know-hows to lower-cost Japanese manufacturers for production for the protected Japanese home market. The Japanese firms – NEC, Hitachi, Toshiba amongst them – then slashed prices for export to the US to a level way below that at which the US manufacturers could profitably compete. The Japanese firms were taking a loss on their US sales as well, of course (perhaps as much as $4 billion overall), but cushioned by their arm-lock on their own home market and fortified by the long-term *keiretsu* relationship with banks and shareholders, they could sustain this for longer than their US rivals, answerable to Wall Street every Monday morning.

Thus it was that by the mid-1980s, with the Cold War still in full swing, the US found itself staring in the face the prospect of technological dependency for a key part of its war-fighting capacity – dependency on an ally, to be sure, but Washington was unsurprisingly unwilling to bet its last talking teddy bear or intercontinental missile on the durability of its alliance with Tokyo. The problem was particularly acute since semiconductors were used in the Cray supercomputers which formed a critical part of Ronald Reagan's 'star wars' Strategic Defence Initiative, then its main lever in trying to bankrupt and/or intimidate the USSR.

So when Japan overtook the US in world market share, the Pentagon launched a 'defence semiconductor initiative' to reestablish the leadership of US monopolies in this field, setting aside 50 million dollars for the purpose. 'Foreign domination of the computer, communications and control industries would obviously have very profound implications for the Department of Defence . . . such domination could be a threat of non-trivial magnitude to the overall economic health of the US in the decades ahead', the Pentagon warned.[12]

The Pentagon's logic was impeccable, even if every line of it contradicted the official view that the future of humanity lay in free trade between democratic capitalist states in eternal alliance. It ran as follows:

- The US military depends on technology to win.
- Electronics are the key to most military technology.
- Semiconductors are the key to leadership in electronics.
- Volume production is the key to sustaining leadership in semiconductors.
- Volume production can only be supported by the commercial market.
- US leadership in the commercial market was being lost.
- Leadership will therefore move abroad.
- US defence will then depend on foreign sources.

This is not just Pentagon paranoia. Their logic was backed up from the other side of the Pacific by Shintaro Ishihara, a member of the Japanese diet (parliament), and Akio Morita, the legendary chairman of Sony, the giant consumer electronics monopoly. In a famous book, *The Japan That Can Say No*, the duo bluntly staked out the possibilities open to a newly assertive Japan, and they addressed the implications of Japan's lead in semiconductor technology head on:

> The increasing sophistication of defensive missiles means . . . they need ever more powerful computers to process information instantaneously. These weapons systems use fourth-generation computers; the so-called fifth generation, presently under development will require multimegabit semiconductors. While US companies may already have the technological know-how for the advanced chips, only Japanese electronics firms have the mass-production and quality control capability to supply the multimegabit semiconductors for the weapons systems and other equipment. In short, without using new-generation computer chips made in Japan, the US Department of Defence cannot guarantee the precision of its nuclear weapons. If Japan told Washington it would no longer sell computer chips to the United States, the Pentagon would be totally helpless.[13]

'Non-trivial magnitude' indeed.

Ishihara and Morita also pointed out that a lead in this field becomes self-perpetuating. 'It takes a highly advanced computer to create an even more advanced computer. Technology is so structured that once a gap opens, it keeps widening.'[14]

Little wonder that the Reagan administration sent its trade diplomats into battle to force open the Japanese microchip market, and end 'dumping' in the US market, armed with the threat of sanctions against such household names in the consumer-capitalist world as Toshiba. The story of those trade negotiations is a story of one agreement after another dishonoured, one promise after another unkept. At the end of it all, one of the leading US negotiators, Clyde Prestowitz, simply concluded that the Japanese Ministry of International Trade and Industry

> is now the arbiter of the world semiconductor industry. By controlling Japanese production, it determines world prices and the availability of critical devices . . . The Japanese said the semiconductor industry is a strategic one in which they intend to remain, regardless of profit or losses. They had little regard for their US competitors who, they claimed, are now behind in technology as well as in financial staying power.[15]

In other words, the Japanese state was taking control of the world's ability to wage high-tech war. Japanese dominance in the sector has continued into the 1990s, despite ever-more alarmist reports from US business. By 1991 over 80 per cent of 4 megabit microchips were produced in Japan.[16] Only the onset of recession forced Japanese semiconductor manufacturers to start searching for international partners to help develop the next generation of chips. Control of this market, however, basically rests with the Japanese trans-national corporations and their government in Tokyo, and US and Japanese negotiators were still, in 1996, haggling over market share.

Japan's commanding position in trade and technology has, over the last ten years, been complemented by the growing export of capital. Foreign direct investment by Japanese companies outstripped that of the US in the late 1980s, and has totalled around $200 billion since 1988.[17]

This development is closely linked with Japan's earlier trade triumphs, which caused foreign countries to erect barriers to protect local industry from Japanese competition. Japan's monopolies were thereby compelled to invest directly in order to retain their market share. Direct investment was needed to preserve the export market, a development referred to as 'tariff factories', a feature of Japanese investment both in Asia and the EU. Japanese monopolies, however, went a stage further in their investments elsewhere in Asia, in a striking development of imperialist policy. 'Tariffs themselves were often raised by the local governments at the urging of *investing* (emphasis in original) Japanese companies. In some instances, a given investment was implemented only on the condition that competing imports would be curbed or completely prohibited once the local venture started production', a Japanese economics professor has explained.[18]

The extent of Japanese investments around the world, including in Europe and the US, are sometimes used to suggest that Japan would have no interest in creating an economic bloc around itself in East Asia and the Pacific. This neglects, however, the different nature of Japanese investments around the world. Investments by Japanese firms in Asia have generally been in manufacturing, mining and raw-material production. On the other hand, nearly half of Japanese money invested in Europe has gone into the banking sector, while in North America it has been put primarily in real estate, banking, entertainment and other services, despite the establishment of some highly publicised production plants. The profile of Japan's investments outside Asia is therefore one of short-term gain, relatively easily withdrawn, while that in its 'home zone' is more long-lasting, more integrated with the domestic economy and of greater strategic significance.[19]

In fact, the dominant trend in Japanese economic development throughout these last few years of crisis has been precisely the creation of an Asian economic bloc under its own hegemony with, to the greatest extent possible, the exclusion of all others, all buttressed by a resurgence in pan-Asian, anti-Western rhetoric and ideology which last did a turn during World War II. At the same time, many Japanese businesses have seen major investments in the US entertainment, property and finance sectors turn spectacularly sour in the mid-1990s.

The re-establishment of the leading position of Japanese business in Asia, after the disastrous failure of 1945, began long ago. Japanese reparations and aid in the 1950s and 1960s to the countries it invaded was closely tied to winning new markets for Japanese companies.[20] As early as the late 1960s, Japan started replacing US influence in Australia (the US having displaced Britain a generation earlier), becoming its leading trading partner, a fact Australia acknowledged by becoming the first 'Western' nation to hold joint naval manoeuvres with the Japanese.[21]

Since then, Japan has become the leading economic force throughout the region. In exports of manufactured goods to east Asia (including China) it out-performs the US and all the countries of the EU combined, and its trade surplus with the region tripled to reach over $62 billion in 1994, exceeding Japan's surplus with the US.[22]

In terms of direct investment in the region, Japan's stock of $75 billion is roughly twice the US level. Sony, to take just one example, now operates 17 manufacturing plants (some as joint ventures) in east Asia outside Japan itself. From 1986 to 1990, Japan's corporations made 956 direct investments in Asia, 467 in the US and 264 in the EU.[23]

By every measure, Japan's external economic orientation is becoming more Asian, and the Asian economy is becoming more oriented on Japan, as well as becoming more integrated overall. The creation of the Asia-Pacific Economic Cooperation forum (which includes the US) is the overt signal of this, but the real mechanisms of Japanese domination are not expressed in institutional form. They reside in the control over the bulk of the region's capital and high technology in the hands of Japan's monopoly corporations and banks, and is symbolised in the increasing use of the yen for transactions throughout Asia. Japanese transnational corporations are careful to keep the closest control over the operation of their overseas holdings, and the manufacture of key items of technology are retained in Japan itself.

Asia has every possible attraction for Japanese industrial corporations and their bankers, low wages being chief among them. Wages in the Philippines are 4.7 per cent of those in Japan, those in Indonesia, 3.6 per cent, in Malaysia 7 per cent and in Thailand 4.8 per cent.[24] These Asian countries clearly play the same role as a low-wage hinterland for the Japanese imperialist centre, to which manufacturing jobs can be exported, as Mexico does for the US and the former socialist countries of eastern Europe do for Germany.

This new emphasis on the development of a pan-Asian bloc is given a suitable ideological gloss by Japanese leaders. The chief executive of Fuji Xerox Co. has described it as a 're-Asianisation', while Shintaro Ishihara, the apostle of anti-Americanism, says that 'this is a nation of Asian people with Asian blood. It seems natural that we recognise that we exist first for Asia.'[25] Such talk chimes with ideas of 'Asian values' and an 'Asian way', counterposed to the materialistic individualism of the US, increasingly popular amongst the region's political leaders. Since they preside over rapidly growing economies, the leaders of the Western capitalist powers are bound to hear them out in respectful silence. For a number of Japanese politicians this is only a continuation of the 'liberate Asia from Western colonialists' crusade which provided a justification for Japanese imperialism's attempt to create a 'Greater East Asia Co-Prosperity Sphere' through war and conquest in the 1930s and 1940s.

Hand in hand with the drive to dominate in Asia, Tokyo has increasingly asserted its independence from Washington. Japan now has both the capacity and the necessity to emerge from under the US umbrella and follow a 'Japan-first' policy. Ishihara and Morita were explicit on the need for this in *The Japan That Can Say No*. Japan should 'get rid of our servile attitude toward the United States. We should no longer be at Washington's beck and call.' In particular, the 'security treaty [with the US] is no longer indispensable. We have sufficient resources to maintain the present level of defence capability on our own.'[26]

Not only is the security treaty, which governs the large US military presence in Japan, no longer indispensable, it is not in the least popular either. Hundreds of thousands of Japanese, particularly in Okinawa, where most of the US bases are sited, marched in late1995 to demand the departure of US forces in demonstrations triggered by the rape of a twelve-year-old Okinawan girl by three American servicemen, but expressing longer-standing discontent. The Japanese unsurprisingly resent paying 70 per cent of the cost of the US occupation forces when the threat against which they were supposed to guard is officially non-existent.

Since public opinion has already forced a US military withdrawal from the Philippines, a retreat from Japan would mark the definitive waning of the Pentagon's power in the Pacific rim.

Using old Cold War logic, this might seem eminently reasonable, since the 'Soviet threat' can no more now be conjured up in the Far East than in Europe. However, it is increasingly clear that the reasons for the projection of US military power in Asia is not to protect Japan but to protect *against* Japan. The abiding fear, both in Washington and amongst Japan's neighbours which have a rich experience of an unshackled Japanese imperialism, is that, in reaching 'the present level of defence capability on our own', in Ishihara and Morita's words, Japan would embark on a major military build-up, including the acquisition of nuclear weapons – something which is obviously well within Japan's technological reach.

Again, this might not alarm the US so much were it not for the multiplying number of conflicts arising between the two powers. There have been the highly publicised trade disputes over fighter aircraft, computer parts and, most recently, the car industry. The factors which made for restraint in pursuing such trade rows have evaporated with the USSR, so the American public has been edified by the sight of US congressmen smashing up imported Japanese cars on the steps of the Capitol. There have been problems caused by CIA spying against Japanese trade negotiators and companies – 'this will be a matter of grave concern that will badly affect our diplomatic negotiations in the near future', said Japan's deputy-chief cabinet secretary.[27] There were the frictions aroused by Japan's lukewarm support for the Gulf War – 'nationalism erupted as pacifism', in the words of US business magazine *Fortune*.[28] Similarly, Japan was reluctant indeed to become embroiled in the US's sabre-rattling against North Korea over the nuclear issue, probably suspecting that it was fear of Japan's nuclear potential which was Washington's real target.

But above all, there is the struggle for pride of place in the Asian economy, at a time when both Japan and the US are mired in economic difficulties of their own. The Japanese 'economic miracle' has hit the buffers most spectacularly in the 1990s, with the collapse in property prices and the failure of a number of financial institutions, dispelling any notion that Japan had found a way to suspend or supersede the crises which beset every other capitalist system. Asset price inflation (land prices rose by an average 22 per cent a year from 1985 to 1990)[29] and reckless speculation in real estate were followed by a stock market slump and the worst post-war recession in the Japanese economy, which in turn has led to pressure on the mighty banks at the heart of the system. The rate of growth of gross domestic product has fallen since 1991, and the economy actually shrank in 1995. Unemployment has started to inch upwards (from a low base) as the high yen has forced plant closures, including the first in the car industry for 50 years.[30]

However, this crisis is further stimulating Japanese capital's push outward into the rest of Asia in search of new markets and easier profits. And Japan's massive capital investment programme, even if funded from unsustainable borrowing, will help ensure the domination of Japanese companies in the region far into the future.

If Japan has the motive and the opportunity for regional hegemony already, it is also now acquiring the means. For all the talk of 'pacifism' and 'free riding' at US expense in military matters, Japan has always had a formidable military, which has been built up in the aftermath of the Cold War (rising by a staggering 58 per cent in real terms over the last ten years),[31] suggesting that the Japanese government, at least, did not take the 'Soviet threat' too seriously. Japan has now the third-largest military budget in the world.[32] As long ago as 1969, Japanese officials speculated (secretly, in a country where the particular aversion to nuclear weapons needs little explanation) on the need to some day acquire nuclear arms. A foreign office document leaked 25 years later said: 'For the time being Japan's policy will be to not possess nuclear weapons, but it will always maintain the economic and technical potential to manufacture nuclear weapons, and will see to it that [Japan] won't accept outside interference on this matter.'[33]

As in Germany, constitutional provisions against the deployment of Japanese forces outside their home territory have been set aside in practice – again, participation in UN 'humanitarian' missions (this time in Cambodia) was the thin end of the wedge. A growing assertion of Japanese military power in Asia and the Pacific – perhaps using the spectre of a 'Chinese threat' as justification – seems almost inevitable as US power starts to fade. An analyst at the Deutsche Bank said in 1992: 'The trump card Japan will play in the second half of the 1990s will be its strategic control of a 600 million-person megamarket stretching from Tokyo to Jakarta, the fastest-growing consumer market in the world.'[34] Will this control be left unchallenged? Strobe Talbott, then a *Time* magazine columnist, now the United States' Deputy Secretary of State, wrote in 1992: 'The Japanese attack on Pearl Harbor was motivated largely by the desire to prevent the US navy from interfering in Japan's mercantile scheme for East Asia. That episode stands as a reminder of what can happen when economic anxieties and commercial quarrels get out of hand.'[35] Talbott could also have pointed out that a US embargo on the export of key materials to Japan in 1941 also played a part in causing 'the episode'. And high-tech exports today are as critical to Japan as iron ore and manganese were in the 1940s.

Today, as then, trade war is the ante-room to shooting war, and the frictions between the US and Japan form two sides of a Far Eastern triangle of tension, with no easy resolution in sight.

China

China differs in two important ways from the other great powers in the world today – in the nature of its social system and in its general level of economic development.

Despite its accelerating integration into the world economy and the growth of a private sector in agriculture and trade, it must be doubted whether China can be fully regarded as a capitalist economy. Its leaders still speak of building 'Socialism with Chinese characteristics', roughly half of the economy remains state-directed and the social 'safety net', although increasingly straining under the consequences of the reforms of the last 15 years in terms of mass unemployment and destitution, remains far in advance of that in India, south-east Asia or, for that matter, anywhere in the Third World. There is no doubt that the momentum of development is towards a full return to capitalism, and that conditions in some coastal parts of China already appear no different to those in neighbouring countries; however, that destination has not yet been reached. It meets resistance from within the Communist Party of China and big sections of the population at large, albeit often in the name of the Party's emerging nationalist ideology rather than socialism.

It is still clearer that China cannot in any sense be described as an 'imperialist power'. None of the features which mark out such powers exist in China. The role of big private companies remains small (albeit growing) and the banking sector has not fused with industry in a way comparable to developments in Russia; despite a growing external trade orientation, there is very little capital exported from China; China maintains no military presence outside its national territory and takes part in no blocs or alliances.

Rather, China has been a victim of neo-colonial exploitation in this century, and it has emerged from the ranks of the world's oppressed nations with what is still a very low level of economic development. Despite the sustained high levels of growth the economy has enjoyed since 1978, China's per capita gross domestic product remains far behind those of the other major powers. While the sheer size of the population makes China's economic bulk loom large, it could not become more productive than even the most backward of the 'developed' countries until well into the next century. China remains an overwhelmingly agrarian nation and displays many symptoms of social backwardness which the intermittent best efforts of the Communist government's erratic leadership have failed to completely uproot.

Despite these factors, there is no disputing that China is a major power in the world which, as it integrates more closely with the world economy, is playing a decisive part in the politics of Asia and an important part more generally.

Taking 1978, the year Deng Xiaoping's reforms started, as the baseline, China's share of the world's GDP has risen from around 3 per cent to over 6 per cent (in purchasing power parity terms), while industrial production has grown nearly six times over.[36]

The share of world trade has more than doubled (although only to around 2 per cent), and foreign direct investment has risen from zero in 1978 to $19 billion in 1993. China runs a huge trade surplus with most capitalist countries, and its surpluses with the US alone amounted to $30 billion in 1994 and around $38 billion in 1995.[37]

There is little sign of China's economic boom abating. When the government wants to cool things down a bit, it tightens credit to the point where annual growth rates drop below 10 per cent! This great accretion in Chinese economic strength, when allied to its established status as a nuclear power and a permanent member of the UN Security Council, and to its vast size, has ensured that China's increasingly assertive engagement with the wider world has had many repercussions.

Even before Deng's economic opening to the outside world, China had alarmed its neighbours on account of a frequently hegemonistic policy, most clearly expressed in its attitudes towards south-east Asia, where support for Pol Pot's regime in Cambodia was followed by an invasion of Vietnam in 1979. China has, at least on paper, border disputes with almost every country it could, and several of these have led to armed clashes over the years, most importantly with India in 1964 and the Soviet Union in 1969. Today, the most frequent military engagements are with the Philippines over disputed reefs. There is also conflict with Vietnam over the Spratley Islands, which may prove to be near substantial oil and gas fields, coveted by US monopolies amongst others. The rapid development of China's navy, which is bigger than those of all its neighbours put together, is widely seen as laying the basis for a stronger geo-political role in the region.

The growing urbanisation of China, with the correspondingly greater demand for food and fuel (China became a net oil importer in 1993), raises new problems for Chinese economic management. While it runs large trade surpluses, these issues can be resolved commercially, but a move towards protectionism or anti-Chinese tariffs in the US would obviously alter the equation radically.

China's bigger role will, inevitably, lead to friction with both the declining dominant regional power, the US, and its most likely replacement, Japan. Unlike the other states of the region, China cannot possibly be subordinated to either. Any potential for dispute with the US was contained for 20 years by Beijing's *de facto* anti-Soviet alliance with Washington, under which both powers co-ordinated strategy closely underneath 'anti-communist' and 'anti-imperialist' rhetoric. The collapse of the USSR, an alarming development in any case for the leadership of the Communist Party of China, removed the strategic rationale for the alliance. Since then, Chinese–US relations have gone into a tailspin to the extent that 'there is an eventual risk of military confrontation' in the words of a *Financial Times* commentator.[38]

The immediate causes of such a clash could clearly be a Chinese military action to reintegrate the rebel province (and economic 'tiger') of Taiwan under the central government in Beijing. Taiwan is too big an economic prize for Washington to let it go lightly (it is the world's second largest holder of foreign currency reserves, to take just one issue), and it is, furthermore, a popular anti-communist cause with the Republican right-wingers now running Congress. In 1995, Clinton's decision to let Taiwan's president pay a 'private visit' to the US sparked an icy stand-off between the two countries and to China test-firing missiles in the seas around the rebel island. In 1996, Washington dispatched an aircraft carrier with escorts to patrol the seas between the mainland and Taiwan in response to Chinese military exercises. The Taiwanese government may yet be tempted to declare its 'independence' from China. US support for such an act on behalf of Taiwan would almost certainly provoke a broader armed conflict.

Yet could the US stand idly by? It has carefully avoided saying. However, China will regain control of one of the 'four tigers' in 1997 when the flag of British colonialism is finally lowered over Hong Kong and sovereignty reverts to the government of the People's Republic. To lose a second 'tiger' would seem like more carelessness than Washington could easily bear.

A Chinese move, with less political justification, to annexe the Spratleys and assert its claim to control all the wealth of the surrounding seas (some of them over 2,000 kilometres from the Chinese mainland), could also spark a confrontation. Chinese publications openly talked of war after the Philippines military blew up border markings erected by the Chinese on reefs off the Philippine coast and subsequently arrested some Chinese fishermen.[39]

In the face of this development of China's national agenda, many voices have been raised calling for a 'containment' of China and the establishment of an alliance of Asian capitalist powers, co-ordinated by the US, to impose 'good behaviour' on the Chinese,[40] raise the stakes in the event of any Chinese military activity and undermine 'its aggressively dictatorial regime', in the words of *Time* magazine.[41]

However, holding the line on such a policy may prove to be beyond Washington or anyone else. Even milder measures directed against Beijing have met resistance from big business in the US, anxious not to miss out on its slice of the booming Chinese market. One option for the US is to strive to set aside its differences with Japan in order to present a common front on regional issues. Henry Kissinger has re-emerged as an advocate of this policy.

Japan and China certainly have their own rivalries – in an ironic inversion of Japanese–American frictions, Tokyo is investigating Chinese 'dumping' of textile products in the Japanese market; and Japan's recent defence white paper expressed alarm at the growth in China's navy and air force. Each accuses the other of seeking regional military hegemony in the wake of the decline of American power.[42]

However, Japanese business will be still more reluctant than their American counterparts to jeopardise its burgeoning investments in China for the sake of an alliance with a declining power, rather than a rising one. Indeed, the dream of Japanese business must surely remain to harness China's vast, cheap, labour force to Japanese capital and (borrowed) technology in a new 'co-prosperity sphere'. The major snag for the Japanese, however, is that this is not the China of the 1930s, weak and divided, but the China which has 'stood up' and will never accept a subordinate place in anybody's scheme of things.

The new Chinese military is the most potent symbol of this. In 1995, China tested its first mobile intercontinental ballistic missile, which has a range sufficient to reach both Europe and California.[43] Advanced attack aircraft have been purchased from Russia, amphibious assault and rapid-deployment forces have been organised and a major fleet developed.[44] While China's armed forces are technologically inferior to those of the US or Japan, they are quite sufficient for achieving limited regional objectives.

As a commentator in the London *Spectator* wrote: 'Today China is a problem for GATT negotiators, tomorrow it may be a problem for NATO. Military conflicts generally begin as either ideological or economic conflicts, and we in the west, and America in particular, have both with China.'[45]

So the scene is set for a three-way struggle for influence (and perhaps a fourth, if Russia revives as an eastern power). Each power may try to play the other two off against each other for their own advantage. The smaller states of the region, including an increasingly economically strong South Korea, cannot avoid getting caught up in the competition. They are unlikely to align themselves with the US, the power of which grows remoter by the year, and they fear an extension of rivalry between the two great powers on the doorstep into the military sphere.

Asia therefore moves towards the twenty-first century with two antagonistic nuclear-armed powers involved in the region and the prospect of the leading economic power, increasingly aligned with neither, joining them in the military super-power category. The power which emerges on top in booming Asia will be set fair to extend its domination to the rest of the world as well.

CHAPTER 7

The New World Order

Hitler's thousand-year Reich expired after 13 years. Winston Churchill's dream of the British Empire lasting a thousand years had more or less evaporated by the time of his death just over 30 years later. Even American publisher Henry Luce's 'American Century' had the shine taken off it in less than half that time. But even by the standards of grandiose imperial rhetoric, the end of the 'new world order' as the hope of humanity was unusually rapid.

Launched in the wake of the fall of the Berlin Wall in 1989, the new order survived just long enough to perform the rather old practical function of sanctifying a neo-colonial war (against Iraq in 1991) before collapsing under the weight of worldwide public ridicule. Whatever hopes the world's peoples entertained of a secure, stable and peaceful future arising out of the defeat of communism, the world's powers could not have disabused them faster.

The general miseries of the Gulf War, the series of wars in the ex-Soviet republics in the Caucuses region, the intervention in Somalia, the civil strife in Rwanda, the power politics around Haiti and, of course, the civil war in the former Yugoslavia do not need retelling here. Conventional analysis offers a discrete explanation for each, ascribing them to particular factors (usually non-existent 'deep rooted ethnic animosities') to prevent the common features of each conflict – their roots in the actual world order – becoming apparent. The aim here is to explain how all of these wars, with the endless suffering they have brought down on the heads of millions of people, are rooted not only in general great-power policy and its opposition to the desire for independent development on the part of most of the world, but particularly in the rising conflicts between the big powers in their scramble for position in the real 'new world order'.

Gulf War

George Bush's war against Iraq to hoist the Emir of Kuwait back onto the throne of his British-created oil company protectorate is usually hailed as the one (and only) great example of the new world order inpractice. Of course, there is nothing at all new about the US trying to bomb an independent Third World country back to the Stone Age in order to secure the power and profits of giant corporations through the medium of a preposterous puppet ruler.

What was hailed as a breakthrough, however, was the supposed unity of the 'world community' around the attack on Iraq following the latter's invasion of Kuwait. George Bush assembled a coalition of active military collaborators, including such unlikely defenders of freedom as the princes of Saudi Arabia, shook down other powers to pay for the enterprise and secured the acquiescence, for the first time, of the dying Soviet government in a major attack on a Third World country – one in the sensitive Middle East, near the USSR's own borders, to boot.

However, behind this appearance of harmony there was clear evidence of different policies being followed, which make the repetition of such a united front by the great powers unlikely. The leading role was, of course, played by the US. It is now easier to see that this was less the harbinger of a 'new world order' directed from Washington than it was the last gasp of the truncated 'American Century'. The hypocrisies attending the US military action have been well canvassed. American scholar Michael Parenti wrote that Bush

> claimed he was concerned with protecting human rights in Kuwait and elsewhere in the Middle East. But there was precious little democracy in any of the region's feudal emirates and autocracies. In Saudi Arabia, women were still stoned to death on charges of adultery, citizens were denied basic rights and millions of foreign workers were treated little better than slaves. In Kuwait, democratic councils and other organised political groupings were regularly crushed.[1]

Likewise, US claims to be upholding national independence could not be taken seriously from a government which, in the preceding ten years alone, had invaded Panama and Grenada to overthrow their leaders, bombed Libya and sponsored and directed a terrorist war against the government of Nicaragua. Nor were the US military being sent to uphold international law – were that the case they could have been deployed far earlier against Israel for its illegal occupation of the West Bank, or against Turkey for its seizure of nearly half of Cyprus. Both, of course, are US allies which received every encouragement and even subsidy and military material to underpin their violations of international law.

In fact, the US action in the Gulf was all of a piece with the policy this litany suggests. It is directed towards making the world safe for big business – stable for a system in which the latter meets no obstruction to its profit-making anywhere in the world. Iraq had to be attacked not because it was undemocratic and aggressive, but because its policy was directed towards tilting the economic balance of power away from the vested interests of the great powers and towards the nations of the Third World. Whether or not Saddam Hussein entertained such idealistic motives is hardly the point – given his position he could do no other if he was not to see his country ground down by the established order and distribution of power in the Middle East.

In this respect, the US administration was indeed acting on behalf of all the big powers – all those whose economic interests prospered from the status quo, and stood to prosper still further from the collapse of the Soviet Union and its allies. It was, moreover, the only power which could play that role, which commanded the military strength to make plausible threats against Iraq and the diplomatic muscle to lever everyone else into line for the great crusade on behalf of the Emir (who did his own bit for human rights, international law, national independence, etc. from a London hotel). The US was the only power aspiring to, or able to, play the role of 'globo-cop'.

But behind that apparent unity of purpose of the powers, different considerations were already at work. A further motive for the 'Desert Storm' project, and scarcely a secondary one, was the need of the US to maintain hegemony over the politics of oil production. The US economy is a vast consumer of energy resources, and access to cheap oil is deeply embedded in the workings of American capitalism and, for that matter, popular car culture. The OPEC cartel, which has managed to increase the share of oil wealth going to the producing countries over the last 25 years (often, alas, only to the benefit of their ruling plutocracies), has always appeared as a menace to the US. If it cannot be broken up, it must be controlled, in part through the good offices of sundry emirs, princes and sultans, for whose grandparents the colonial powers obligingly created countries in order to meet just such a purpose.

Yet such considerations do not exercise all the powers equally. Some have different sources of energy supply, much less dependent on the state of the world oil market, while others, like Japan, are better able (or at least willing) to pay a higher price in that market if they have to. There was, indeed, little enthusiasm in Tokyo for waging war to knock a few dollars off the price of a barrel of oil, despite Japan's dependency on imported energy supplies. Along with Germany, Japan was quite unwilling to make a contribution to the great fight for 'human rights, national independence, etc.' which went beyond rhetoric and convertible currency. George Bush bludgeoned them into stumping up the cash for the crusade, an exercise he was so effective in that he managed to turn a profit even on current account for the war.

This may well have been a first in the history of war (more generally the victors have accepted short-term cash losses in expectation of dividends down the road), but it was also an admission
that crusades, even for great ideals, were now beyond the budget
of the US Treasury alone.

This sponsorship of the US war effort by Germany and Japan –
the former gave $3.4 billion, the latter $5.3 billion[2] – was not
achieved without a great deal of public humiliation of the reluctant
allies, who had to endure Congressional taunts about the 'wimps
of Weimar' and the 'jittery Japs'.[3] It is scarcely surprising that, at
around this time, both Tokyo and Bonn seem to have set themselves on a course towards greater national self-assertiveness and a
determination to set their own political and diplomatic agendas,
rather than forking out to pay for someone else's.

So Washington had two tiers of allies in the Gulf War: those who
palmed Washington off with a cheque to fight a war they had little
interest in, and those who took part in 'Desert Storm' alongside
the US military. Britain and France were prominent in the latter
category, a fact which was not accidental but reflected both the
different histories of these two powers, heirs to an inglorious
tradition of colonialism in the Middle East, and also their different
contemporary interests.

Britain and France shared the US interest in the general
stability of the Middle East, in keeping the whole region safe for
capitalism. Both countries have themselves intervened readily
throughout the region in the past, and retain big economic interests. Britain, in particular, is a major arms supplier to many Arab
countries, while British oil companies are long established there.
London's role as a financial centre also makes Britain home to a lot
of Arab capital, a point underlined by the choice of London as
home-in-exile for the Emir of Kuwait and his family after the
Iraqi invasion. British banks have profited handsomely through
'recycling' the oil riches of the sheikhs in loans to underdeveloped
countries, from which vast interest has been exacted. Small wonder that Britain's rulers rushed to the side of the US – all in the
interests of 'human rights, democracy, etc.' of course.

The parasitic rulers of the Gulf embrace this protection, sometimes finding it less politically difficult than direct patronage by
Washington, on account of the latter's unyielding support for its
Israeli client state. One statelet, Oman, is virtually run as a subsidiary of the British Ministry of Defence. His Sandhurst-educa-
ted[4] Highness the Sultan forks out for the services of no less than
six British generals, 1,500 other British officers and a number of
the Metropolitan Police's finest to help keep him on the throne.[5]

The French and British establishments clearly found a community of interest with the US in relation to the Gulf war.

However, it did not last long. No sooner had the 'Desert Storm' abated than it was back to business as usual. The *Guardian* reported:

> Nothing could better illustrate the transition from economic competition to economic warfare among western nations than the American decision to cut the British out of the re-arming of the Gulf states ... what is emerging in the Middle East is a single, huge near-monopoly market for the American arms industry ... in the main it is coming about as a result of a ruthless cashing in of the chips that the US won during the Gulf War.

The *Guardian* detailed the measures Washington was using to ensure that Kuwait rebuilt its army (a pointless exercise for any but arms manufacturers, since when it comes to fighting the Emir has to contract out the operation anyway) with exclusively American material, to the exclusion of the British, whose role as 'gallant ally' during the actual war now counted for nothing, concluding:

> Every episode of Anglo-American cooperation in the Middle East has concealed a powerful element of rivalry, albeit of a despairing nature on the British side, and has usually been followed by a significant further accretion of power and economic influence to the United States. It seems the Gulf War will prove no exception to the rule.

Military warfare with the enemy, economic warfare with the ally – the American way in the Middle East.[6]

Nevertheless, the backing of Britain and France helped George Bush win the critical mass of political support in the 'international community' to press ahead with the war to smash Iraq (but not Saddam Hussein, who was carefully allowed to retain power to forestall the possibility of a democratic revolution in Iraq – what would the Saudi princes have made of that?). However, the whole 'Desert Storm' episode showed up the fault lines in the alliance which were to take on still greater significance in subsequent episodes.

Yugoslavia

The civil war across the territory of the former Socialist Federative Republic of Yugoslavia illustrates still more starkly both the general nature of the new world system developing after the end of the Cold War and the way in which the great powers pursue different interests, at present fought out by proxy but in the end capable of provoking direct clashes. It is small surprise, but of little comfort to the peoples involved, that the Balkans should once again provide the testing-ground for the contradictions in great-power politics.

While all the powers welcomed the downfall of socialism in Yugoslavia, since support for Tito and his dissenting line from the Soviet Union had only been of value during the Cold War confrontation with Moscow, their separate plans for the region shaped the emerging conflicts at every stage – Slovenia against Yugoslavia, Croatia against Yugoslavia and then Serbia, the three-way struggle over Bosnia, the separation of Macedonia from Yugoslavia and on into the future.

That is not to set aside the internal factors involved. There were forces within Yugoslavia as well as outside working for the federation's destruction in order to advance a nationalist position. However, most analysis of the situation has gone no further than conjuring up age-old animosities between Croat, Serb and Muslim as the causes of the civil war. This not only overlooks the fact that two generations of Yugoslavs of different nationalities did more than coexist peaceably – they took the first steps towards building a new society together – but also the active role of great power policy in producing the present conflict. Certainly, no outside power has taken as its diplomatic starting point the by now obvious fact that the only solution to the problems of Yugoslavia is . . . Yugoslavia, a socialist federation based on the equality of the nations in the region. Instead, each power has sought a post-Yugoslav outcome which might strengthen its own hand. The *Wall Street Journal* admitted that 'the war in Bosnia has as much to do with divisions among the world powers as it does with the ethnic furies of Serbs, Muslims and Croats',[7] and a Serb correspondent writing to the same paper observed that 'the New World Order was, on the one hand, violating Yugoslavia's external borders and, on the other, decreeing that the internal administrative lines were henceforth external and inviolable.'[8]

The leading part here was played by Germany, which marked its reunification by immediately readopting the traditional policies of Germany in Europe – looking eastwards, breaking up strong states, subordinating weak ones and establishing its own sphere of influence. Certainly, the map of Europe now boasts states which last appeared during Hitler's 'new order' of the early 1940s – Slovakia, Ukraine and Croatia amongst them. It was Germany which pushed the EU into the recognition of the independence of Slovenia and Croatia, thereby setting in motion the Yugoslav civil war. This was the precise policy followed by Germany in World War II – pro-Croat and anti-Serb; a policy which, first time around, produced atrocities on the part of the Croatian fascist Utashe which reputedly shocked even the German SS representatives on the scene. The US ambassador to Yugoslavia at the time

clearly blames Slovenian 'selfishness' for provoking the civil war
by its unilateral and unjustified secession from the federation[9] –
he omits to mention which power inspired the Slovene move.
Likewise, apologists for the German government present its determination to sustain a Croat state as springing from a genuine
humanitarianism and from a desire to avoid appeasing aggression,
as if there were any evidence of such concerns actuating German
policy anywhere else in the world, either now or in the past.[10]

The US initially followed a pan-Yugoslav foreign policy, similar
to the policy for the formal preservation of the Soviet Union
proclaimed by George Bush – a policy for orderly transition
to capitalism. However, Washington has since shifted sides
dramatically, joining Germany in all-out support for the Croatian
regime, having obstructed any number of peace proposals because
they were insufficiently anti-Serb. This reached the point where
Croatia's attack on the Krajina Serbs within Croatia in August
1995 was blessed by the US government in advance and directed
by 'retired' US officers, and the large staff attached to the US
military attaché in Croatia. This policy, like many others, reflects
the emerging strategic alliance between the US and Germany,
which as Washington's main European ally is the other half of the
new 'special relationship'.

This line – of breaking up Yugoslavia and leaving the Serbian
state, with its traditional alignment with Russia, in the weakest
possible position – has been opposed, after a fashion, by Britain
and France. The former has described the US ambassador to
Croatia as 'extreme' in his support for Croatian behaviour, and
both have been dismissive of German–US policy. France and
Britain have, paradoxically, intervened in the former Yugoslavia
in order to prevent anything very much happening to disturb the
balance of power there. The presence of British and French troops
has served no practical purpose – nor was intended to – beyond
allowing a measure of control over NATO diplomacy to pass out of
the hands of Washington and Bonn. Holding a sort of moral
advantage by virtue of deploying troops 'on the ground' allowed
the west European powers to stall, at least for a long time, any
moves to put the bellicose anti-Serb rhetoric of the US into practice. Indeed, it has recently been revealed that the CIA intercepted
communications of the British crack SAS troops operating in
Bosnia, which revealed that the latter were refusing to identify
Serb 'targets' on the ground for US warplanes to bomb, much to
the fury of the US embassy in the Croat capital of Zagreb.[11]

Certainly, Britain and France had no interest in seeing the
Balkans reduced to a collection of pitiful statelets utterly dependent on Germany, and they would be reluctant to see Serbia disappear as a factor in the Balkans balance of power, which would be

the certain consequence of the triumph of German policy. This would tilt the balance of power on the European continent still more sharply against the victors of World War II. A *New York Times* reporter described US policy as assuming that 'two local powers will dominate this part of the world – one in Zagreb, one in Belgrade; one tied to Washington, the other locked into a Slavic bloc extending to Moscow'.[12] London and Paris are working to try to obstruct such a polarisation by maintaining Serbia, for whom they officially went to war in 1914, as a force in the region.[13]

This has, of course, been camouflaged behind the usual sugary talk of a united NATO front on the issue. But in reality, Britain and France have followed a policy much more closely aligned with Russia, Greece and Serbia than with the US, Germany, Turkey and Croatia. There has been no common UN position of any efficacy, because there has been no common interest among the decisive powers. Indeed, almost all the institutions of international co-operation controlled by the great powers have had their unity shaken and their pretensions exposed by the Yugoslav conflict. *Financial Times* commentator Ian Davidson observed that the fiasco of UN peace-keeping was due to the fact 'that Europe and the US have from the start had diametrically opposed aims ... it is difficult to discount the thought that this is a symptom of an underlying disengagement between Europe and the US, and that we may be in the early phase of the unravelling of the Atlantic alliance'.[14] However, Davidson errs in appearing to suggest that there is even a common 'European' position, as against the American. In reality, the EU has had its diplomatic inadequacies just as ruthlessly exposed. 'There is no common policy. What we are seeing is a renationalisation of Bosnia policy', observed a German diplomatic expert; while a French authority observed that 'Europe doesn't exist from a security point of view'.[15] The UN, NATO and the EU alike have 'failed' in the face of the conflict, not because they lack the means to impose their collective will, but because they do not have such a collective will, and any attempt at a decisive move by one power is checked not merely on the ground in Yugoslavia but also in the chancelleries of the power's own allies.

The 'peace settlement' concluded under US auspices towards the end of 1995 reflects all these contradictions in a way which makes it improbable that it will be a basis for a lasting settlement. The US needed a peace agreement, and needed to be seen as the author of it, in order to keep the rhetoric of a 'new world order' under American supervision still faintly flickering. But the agreement was immediately repudiated by the French military leader on the ground in Sarajevo and embraced as its own by the French government in Paris – a difference reflecting uncertainty as to whether the agreement could be used to extend French influence in the Balkans, or marked the end of it by causing France to lose credibility with the Serbs. The US Right immediately began calling for the re-arming of Bosnian government forces to commence, ready for the next round in the anti-Serb crusade, while Germany made ready to despatch troops to the region for the first time since 1945. The settlement embodies not only the limits of the military option amongst the warring parties, but a compromise among the various external interests. The latter will surely come unglued sooner or later.

The lines thus drawn in the Yugoslav civil war may have claimed the people of Bosnia-Hercegovina, Serbia and Croatia as their first victims, but imperial power blocs have always taken the Balkans as the starting point of their conflicts, never as the conclusion.

Rwanda

In terms of human suffering, the civil war in Rwanda in 1994 has probably been the most ghastly feature of world politics since the dawn of the 'new order'. The hundreds of thousands of deaths have been almost universally ascribed to ancient tribal animosities between the Tutsis and Hutus, the two main groups in Rwanda's population.

It has sometimes been noted that this animosity, far from being ancient, is a product of this century, and of the reactionary and racist policies followed by the Belgian colonial power, in association with the Catholic Church, when it had control of the territory. What has, however, attracted less attention is the role of French imperialism in the contemporary crisis, and its manipulation of events in Rwanda to advance its own interests as against those of rival powers in Africa. Behind the familiar rhetoric of humanitarianism Paris followed a policy as anti-human as any in the whole history of the involvement of the European powers in Africa.

Naturally, it was under the banner of saving lives that France dispatched 2,500 marines in 'Operation Turquoise' to Rwanda after the collapsing government unleashed a reign of terror against the peoples of the country, trying to exterminate the Rwandese Patriotic Front (RPF) and, indeed, any citizen who might oppose the ousted regime, particularly Tutsis. However, it immediately became clear that the French role was to protect the murderers and prevent the RPF from establishing a new government. So-called 'safe havens' were established, in which only the killers were safe. On top of this, the French government worked might and main to prevent the new government receiving any EU aid, routeing it instead to refugee camps in Zaire under the control of the defeated government.

This was all of a piece with long-standing French foreign policy towards Rwanda, with which it signed a military assistance pact in 1975. As a result, France 'inherited' Belgium's neo-colonial mantle, and maintained the same divide-and-rule policies as its predecessor – as, indeed, Paris has done elsewhere in Africa. In 1990, Paris sent forces to Rwanda to prop up the reactionary Hutu-dominated government in the face of the advance of the RPF, which is supported by both Hutus and Tutsis. Despite clear evidence of the Rwandan government's genocidal intentions, France continued supplying arms to the rulers in the capital, Kigali[16] – indeed, this carried on even after the massacre of hundreds of thousands had started.[17]

A statement issued by the Rwandan community in France said that

> when one knows that ... it is France which has furnished the killers of Kigali with their arms; that it is French military instructors who have formed and trained those criminals over years; that France has never for a single moment stinted its support for all the apparatus of the Rwandan genocide, from the summit of the state to the last militiaman ... that finally the genocide was practically completed before Operation Turquoise was launched, one can well understand the real reasons for and particular nature of this new French military intervention in Rwanda ...
>
> The first objective was to prevent the total defeat and moral collapse of the political administrative and military apparatus of the power responsible for the genocide ... The second objective was to create the conditions for a future destabilisation of Rwanda [from behind the secured 'safe humanitarian zones' and refugee camps] ... France has put everything in place to assure a base for the reconquest of power by those responsible for the Rwandan genocide.[18]

Undoubtedly, France was inspired in this excess of imperialist humanitarianism by its desire to keep the closest control over all its neo-colonial apparatus in Africa, and to prevent any one part of it slipping out of orbit, lest all of it start to do so. The RPF was therefore the enemy. But behind that enemy lurked another, as was explained to British parliamentarians by the secretary-general of the RPF, Dr Theogene Ruchasinga:

> One of the problems we have had is that the French government has lobbied intensely in the European Union to stop us from receiving multilateral or bilateral aid. That is because they supported the previous regime. *They accuse us of*

trying to anglify the country [my emphasis] – when in fact only three members of the cabinet are English speakers. In any case, the real problem in Rwanda is that 80 per cent of the people cannot read or write in any language.[19]

So it is perfidious Albion and a new struggle for Africa which lies behind the French marines' summer outing. Better genocide in French than reconciliation in English. The victims of the greatest massacre of the 1990s are, in part, the victims of great-power rivalry, of the determination of France to keep rivals out of its African enclaves.

Somalia

The UN-sanctioned intervention in Somalia started off on an improbable basis – George Bush dispatching US marines to Africa on a 'humanitarian mission'. With this logic, the next time a US president requires armed intervention, he will send for Mother Teresa of Calcutta or the Red Cross. Certainly an organisation as rooted in a history of aggression and violence and as saturated in the most bovine machismo and extreme chauvinism as the US Marines was an unlikely instrument of humanitarianism.

And so it proved. After barely a show of handing out grain, the US Marines reverted to the more congenial task of scouring Somalia to round up what the tame media was pleased to describe as 'warlords', although had the latter been American they would most likely have been known more respectfully as 'senators'. In fact, the Marines were carrying out a task for which they are in principle much better suited (although singularly inept at executing on this occasion) – tracking down any political leader and his/her followers who might stand in the way of US objectives.

In the case of Somalia, as with others, the US objectives were a mixture of a general reassertion of great-power hegemony in the Third World (from which the US has most to gain) alongside the pursuit of specific objectives for US corporations – an activity which straightaway creates the potential for conflict with other powers, who might be persuaded to stand shoulder to shoulder with Washington in support of 'rule of law, democracy, humanitarianism' and so on, but do not see why they should stand shoulder to shoulder with Exxon rather than BP, with Ford rather than Volkswagen or Toyota.

The general purpose of the US intervention in Somalia (carried out under UN auspices) was brazenly stated almost from the outset – it proved that there was a need for a new colonialism, to be exercised by the great powers under the fig-leaf of the UN. It was, of course, to be exercised in the name of humanitarianism, in much the same way as nineteenth-century colonialism was all done in the name of Christian civilisation. Reactionary British historian Paul Johnson urged that the UN Security Council 'using one or more advanced powers as its agents, move into the business of government, taking countries into trusteeship for varying periods', adding that this was what was needed in 'Somaliland', using Somalia's colonial name in case anyone had missed the point.[20] Hoover Institution fellow Angelo Codevilla described colonialism as 'an act of generosity and idealism' which was the only alternative to leaving Somalia to its misery.[21] The *Wall Street Journal* even illustrated its editorial on the subject with a drawing of British colonialist Lord Kitchener. An article in the same newspaper urged a US 'form of colonialism' which should 'restrain its moralistic and improving impulses'.[22]

Somalia was, in short, to be a test case for a US takeover of an independent country (but which had until a few years previously been a US satellite) establishing a precedent for the UN sanctifying a new colonialism. The issue of food distribution was no more than a smokescreen – the US Marines did little in that direction and, it transpired, hunger and starvation was overcome faster in those parts of Somalia where local leaders negotiated their own arrangements for food supply without the intervention of foreign military.

The marines were also there, however, to advance very specific US interests – most of all, to ensure that US companies secured the rights to Somalia's large oil reserves. The *Los Angeles Times* reported that 'four major US oil companies are quietly sitting on a prospective fortune in exclusive concessions to explore and exploit tens of millions of acres of the Somali countryside . . . nearly two-thirds of Somalia was allocated to the American oil giants Conoco, Amoco, Chevron and Phillips in the final years before Somalia's pro-US President Mohammed Siad Barre was overthrown'. The suspicion that the US intervention was really aimed at humanitarian assistance to the stockholders of US oil companies can only have been reinforced by the fact that the invasion force was headquartered in Conoco's offices in the Somali capital of Mogadishu – rented from the company, of course.[23]

If that sounds somewhat grotesque, worse was in store for the Somalis struggling to rebuild their country under the auspices of Pentagon humanitarianism. The US fruit monopoly Dole Food Co. took advantage of the US presence to take over the country's banana export trade, which had for the previous 60 years been a profitable Italian concession and the country's main earner of hard currency. However, the Italian company Somalifruit then returned and tried to reassert its rights over the plantations. Matters quickly

degenerated into a literal banana war, with private armies of
Somalis being hired by each company to slug it out for control of
the plantations and ports. Several have been killed in a struggle
which involves blockades, mortar attacks and hit-men. Naturally,
those doing the killing and dying are Somalis, while only foreign
interests stand to gain. So a 'humanitarian intervention' ostensibly
to help secure the free movement of food supplies ends up in a
blockading of the country's main food export as part of an inter-
capitalist struggle.[24]

Like Rwanda, Somalia was a victim of 'humanitarian assistance'
from the West, not a beneficiary of it. Africa is once more being
tormented by the great powers in their struggle to control its
resources and advance their own interests in opposition to those of
their rivals, waging 'little wars', by proxy if possible, in the interests of the giant corporations.

Much the same is the case in relation to the one 'success' the
proponents of the 'new world order' still boast of – the US restoration of Jean-Bertrand Aristide to the presidency of Haiti, to which
he had been elected before being deposed by the military. It is true
that the course of events in Haiti ran relatively smoothly. No
power other than the US had any great strategic or commercial
interest in the island; indeed, as an international question Haiti
was largely an extension of US domestic politics. The Clinton
administration was motivated by the need to try to provide a cover
for its broken election promise to give shelter to refugees from
Haiti. It therefore accomplished the feat of restoring Aristide to
office while leaving him with little or no power with which to
implement his original programme, which had meant challenging
the vested interests on the island, all of them closely associated
with US business.

From all the foregoing, it is fairly easy to draw some conclusions
about the 'new world order', the world political situation into
which we have been impelled since the end of the Cold War.

Firstly, it is based on a naked reassertion of the unfettered
pursuit by the big powers of their common interests, where they
have them. All the dreamy rhetoric of a world order based on
'universal human values' and policed by an impartial UN has been
shown to be just that. The world community has only ever been
brought into play as a device to disguise the pursuit of the policy
interests of Washington and the other major powers. As *Time*
magazine put it:

> If the 'international community' means anything, it denotes
> the US, Britain, France and Germany, and especially the
> first three. Russia must be consulted, Japan writes occasional
> checks, and China's non-obstruction is sometimes needed.

Largely, though, Washington, London, Paris and Bonn are the governments that count.[25]

The same magazine, writing earlier about the Yugoslav crisis, stated that 'the UN comes to life only when animated – manipulated by the US'.[26]

This is the case because there is no abstract 'global interest' and one is only conceivable in the event of, perhaps, intergalactic invasion. Policy is determined by the leading powers, each of which have their own national interests. Sometimes these may overlap and sometimes, even where there is friction, it is possible to make enough effort to avoid that leading to conflict. Under such conditions, the UN may act with some sense of purpose, although even then it does not act for humanity as a whole, but rather for the big powers.

The proposed restructuring of the UN by bringing Japan and Germany into the Security Council will only strengthen both these negative tendencies – it will be still more exclusively a club dominated by the great powers, and the clash of different interests will be still more pronounced. For each of the episodes which have marked world politics over the last five years – the Gulf War, the Yugoslav civil war, the interventions in Somalia and Rwanda – show the reality of divergent great power interests and the potential for still sharper divisions.

NATO, too, is having difficulty in adapting to the new age, although it does not pretend to do more than speak for the Western capitalist powers. Talk of its eastward expansion against Russia does little to mask its lack of internal cohesion without a plausible 'communist threat' to make the rulers of the North Atlantic huddle together. The European powers – Britain, France and Germany – are unlikely to continue to accord US leadership the same pride of place it had during the Cold War. Germany's own ambassador to NATO, Baron Hermann von Richthofen, warned that 'cracks are appearing in the alliance's cohesion', citing divisions over Bosnia, different regional priorities on the part of NATO powers and 'unilateral changes in US policies' as causes.[27]

The process of decay in NATO is slow, but the withdrawal of the US from Europe, parallel to the growth of exclusively European bodies like the West European Union and bilateral Anglo-French and German-French military structures point the way into the future. There is, as Ian Davidson wrote in the *Financial Times*, 'a structural deterioration in transatlantic relations' leading to the point where 'NATO is a hollow shell'.[28] This is as true of the US–Japanese security relationship as it is in Europe.

So there are no international structures which will be capable of mediating and reconciling the different interests of Europe and the US, Japan and China, Britain and France, France and Germany, Germany and Russia, the US and Russia, Russia and the Ukraine. They must do it for themselves, as in the nineteenth century, or not at all, as in the first half of the twentieth.

CHAPTER 8

Currency Conflict

Money may not be the root of all evil, but it has certainly been at the bottom of a good few conflicts. Indeed, if you want to see the shape of tomorrow's wars, you could do worse than looking at the state of today's money. Like the conflicts which have followed the announcement of a 'new world order', the situation in the currency markets is replete with indicators of the rising contradictions in the world.

Throughout the modern capitalist era, currencies have acted as a barometer of economic power and of a nation-state's place in the sun. Currency instability has been a reflection of systemic problems, and the decline (or rise) of the relative value of currencies mirrors the changing fortunes of states.

There is nothing terribly complicated about money. It is the universal medium of exchange within the sphere of its circulation, a general claim on the wealth produced by the society issuing the particular currency. The greater the productive power of a country, the more of its money there is to go around (expressed in a common form). In classical economic theory, this should not give anyone sleepless nights. If country A enjoys strong economic growth, then the value of its currency relative to that of country B, which is developing its economy more slowly, should grow painlessly.

However, things do not go so smoothly. One obvious problem is that currencies are issued by nation-states, which control the supply of their own dollars, Deutschmarks, pounds, yen, francs, etc. Yet the sphere of circulation of each is, in fact, almost universal. Of course, if you wanted to buy an American car in downtown Osaka (which would be difficult enough in the first place, for reasons of Japanese protectionism) you could not do it with dollars. But if you had the dollars you could easily go to any bank or exchange bureau and buy enough yen to get the car. Since all the main currencies of the capitalist world are now 'freely convertible' they are as interchangeable as you want them to be. Yet the currencies remain national currencies. In the end, a franc is only good if you want to go shopping in France and to the extent that you want to do so. It is a claim on the wealth of French society alone.

This gives governments the means to manipulate the value of their currencies for advantage. Inflation, for example, was developed as a means of cutting the real value of wages without putting less cash money in the workers' pockets. A fall in the value of country A's currency would be bad news for any of its citizens fancying a holiday in country B, but good news for a manufacturer in country A seeking to expand market share over the border with B.

On top of this, currencies provide a fertile field for outright speculation, for gambling on the movements of currencies against each other as a result of factors ranging from changes in the interest rate to the weather. The vast volume of this activity can drive the value of money as against other money up and down quite regardless of the will of governments, at least in the short term.

These speculators, however, do not live on some other planet but are found amongst us, mostly New York and London, making money for themselves. If it annoyed the British government to see the speculators in the City of London making a fortune out of the pound's crisis in the European exchange rate mechanism (ERM) in 1992, it was still more galling for the French government to watch Anglo-Saxon speculators across the Channel and the Atlantic rake in the cash out of the franc's ERM dénouement a year later.

A currency can also start to lose its value if the volume of it in circulation ceases to be connected to the actual wealth of the country issuing it – if a government pursues policies which create an enhanced demand for their currency, to meet certain economic or political goals, which is not driven by a desire to invest (or go shopping) in that particular country.

In that sense the relative values of the main exchangeable currencies of the world (those issued by the G7 powers in the first place) are not merely expressions of the economic might of the respective issuing powers, but are also instruments of struggle between them – weapons in the battles for markets and hegemony.

The world has known two hegemonic currencies since the rise of capitalism: the British pound sterling before 1914 (and to a diminishing extent for some years thereafter) and the dollar from 1945 to 1971, lingering on until the present. The years between the end of the pound's hegemony and the rise of the dollar's were, of course, years of crisis, instability and ultimately war. Likewise, the years since 1971, while not yet comparable to the inter-war period, have been years of mounting instability and dislocation in international economic relations, a fact which continues to prompt forlorn calls for some sort of global return to the gold standard or to the post-war dollar-dominated Bretton Woods system.

Both the pound and the dollar in their heyday provided stability because their value was, ultimately, fixed in that a given quantity of the currency could be exchanged for a given quantity of gold. This was not meant to be taken literally and it was regarded as a hostile act if anyone ever did so, as General de Gaulle pretended to in the mid-1960s when he tried to trade in France's stock of dollars for the contents of Fort Knox. But the idea that it could be done was comforting and stabilising, not because anyone could do anything with the gold, which was perfectly useless, but because via gold one could always buy something more amenable.

This worked not because of the moral probity of the governors of the Bank of England or the chairmen of the Federal Reserve but because, in the end, it corresponded to some extent to the real economic strength of the country issuing the currency. Britain enjoyed a near-monopoly of world trade in its mid-Victorian peak, while the US turned out an astonishing 50 per cent of the industrial production of the planet at the end of World War II. Both states were, for a time, the economic sun around which other countries orbited. When that ceased to be the case, the value of the currency inexorably came under pressure. Wars certainly exacerbated the problem by making huge demands on the state's finances – World War I in Britain's case, the Vietnam War in that of the United States. But the underlying pressures were there in any case. What economists call 'the fundamentals' – growth and productivity – were turning sour.

So the currency crisis which gripped the world in the first half of 1995 was not an act of God, an isolated event or the result of pure gambling and speculation. It was an expression of the real shifts in power which are causing turbulence throughout every aspect of economic and political life. The decline in the dollar, the rise in the Deutschmark (DM) and the yen are not only telling us something about what has happened, but also about what is going to happen.

The dollar's weakness has immediately been caused by the huge trade and budget deficits which are part of the legacy of Ronald Reagan's administration, a regime far more geared towards winning the Cold War than it was to the health of Washington's finances. He threw open the national cheque book to finance the enormous arms build-up of the 1980s aimed at intimidating and ultimately bankrupting the Soviet Union. This was quite beyond the resources of the US government, the more so since Reagan's anti-communist zeal was matched only by his religious conviction that the rich and the big corporations ought to pay a good deal less in tax. The enormous budget deficits which predictably resulted from this exercise in what his Vice-President George Bush once famously described as 'voodoo economics' (but might more accurately be called a sort of artillery Keynsianism) were only sustainable to the extent that foreigners were prepared to buy up the US government's debt. This they did, buying US Treasury bonds in the mid-1980s and then US companies and property later on.

Now the Soviet Union is gone but the huge budget deficit remains, standing alongside its twin tower, the trade deficit. This latter is itself a sign of the anaemia in the US economy and the loss of markets suffered both at home and abroad by many leading US corporations.

The bottom line is that the US has gone from being the world's biggest lender to being its biggest debtor in a period of 15 years or so. This starts to become a problem when foreign investors begin to doubt that the value of the billions of dollars sloshing around the world is going to be maintained, that they will still represent the same claim on the wealth of the US as they did when they were bought.

This confidence has been ebbing away for the last 15 years. The DM is now worth twice as much in dollar terms as in 1985, and the yen is worth three times as much. This reflects both the growth in the economic power of Germany and Japan and the dramatically low savings rate in the US and its low rate of capital formation. Since the mid-1970s the increase in the stock of productive capital per worker in the US economy has declined from an average 2.5 per cent per year to around 1 per cent. Net national savings have fallen to 2 per cent of gross national product, as against over 7 per cent throughout the three decades after World War II.[1] This leaves little for investment in the domestic economy and its technological renewal.

The sneaking feeling that the greenback is not going to get you what it promised also emerges in the figures for worldwide holdings of foreign currency (money that is not the national medium of the institution or individual holding it). Twenty years ago, 80 per cent of foreign currency was held in dollars. Ten years ago this had fallen to 70 per cent. Today it is down to 60 per cent.[2]

The main beneficiary has been the DM, which has seen its value appreciate internationally because it has maintained its stability internally as German business has extended its power – it has increasingly become a refuge for those battered in other currencies. The yen has also profited, since east Asian central banks have shifted their reserve holdings into the Japanese national currency. Since these East Asian countries have the fastest-growing economies in the world, this signifies no good for the dollar's world role. In early 1995, for example, the central bank of China boosted the non-dollar share of its reserves from 10 to 25 per cent of the total.

The different fortunes of the dollar and the DM are also determined by the different policies pursued by the US and Germany.
The problems besetting the dollar are partly the problems of being
a world policeman. Washington was able to shake-down its 'allies'
to pay for the Gulf War of 1991, but that was by way of being an
exception. The money for the Reagan arms build-up was only lent
and must be repaid. The hegemonic policy expressed in the economic annexation of Mexico through the North American Free
Trade Area has also proved expensive. The economic crisis this
unleashed in Mexico less than a year after the treaty came into
effect in 1994 resulted in the need for a bail-out by Washington at
the cost of sending another 20 billion or so dollars out into the
wide world. The effect of these policies is to gradually undermine
the dollar as a store of value.

The Bundesbank, stalwart defender of the value of the DM
against all comers (not least the Bonn government at times), has,
on the other hand, ensured that Germany has landed itself with
no such entanglements. As soon as the progress towards European integration looked like placing a strain on Germany's
financial position, the brakes were applied. And even as German
big business has spread its wings in eastern Europe, Bonn has
entered into no commitments to Poland or Russia as yet ana-
logous to those the US has contracted into with Mexico. The
annexation of the German Democratic Republic (at parity of the
DM and the GDR's ostmark) has been the sole deviation from
this prudent policy, and that was the price of the conversion of
Germany into a world power once more. The DM goes abroad
as a conqueror, not as an ambulance; and Germany's rulers are
determined that European monetary union, if it happens, should
not alter this position at all.

For Japan, the rise in the value of the yen against the dollar
comes despite the recession in the Japanese economy over recent
years. It is also deeply unwelcome to the leading circles of the
Japanese establishment, which see the yen's rise as a threat to their
established policy of export-led growth, seizing a dominant position in one market after another. Further, it increases the trade
frictions with the US, which in turn drives speculators towards the
DM as a reserve currency unaffected by the mounting tensions
between Tokyo and Washington.

This situation is starting to cause alarm in the US, where it is
now beginning to be grasped that their whole position of world
leadership is under threat along with the value of the dollar and its
status as number one reserve currency. Wall Street *éminence grise*
Felix Rohatyn, a senior partner at Lazard Freres, was quite clear
when he told Congress: 'We are gradually losing control of our
own destiny . . . the dollar's decline is perhaps the single most

dangerous economic threat we will face in the long term because it puts us at the mercy of other countries.'[3]

It is, after all, only the dollar's reserve currency status which has permitted Washington to sustain its huge deficits. Were the dollar to become just one tradeable currency amongst many then the US Treasury secretary could one day be faced with the humiliations confronted in 1976 by British Chancellor of the Exchequer Denis Healey, forced to dash home from Heathrow Airport to deal with the IMF, imposing (at US direction) strict conditions on a loan to bail out an apparently bankrupt government. The willingness of foreigners to hold dollars allows the US to continue to spend, spend, spend without any loss of sovereignty. Nevertheless, 'the dollar is, in a sense, the price of a share of America. When it is devalued, the dollar cheapens not just US exports, but the entire economy', according to one expert.[4]

The implications were spelt out by another commentator thus:

> As long as the dollar remains the international medium of exchange, the United States can import cars with the oil to run them and satisfy its foreign debts, as it has in times past, by printing more dollars. Should a competing currency arise, which could only be the European Currency Unit, Americans would have to buy ecus to pay their import bills, thereby finding themselves in the same position as Brazil or Mexico or Poland.[5]

The 'competing currency' is unlikely to be the ecu, unless that is a convenient diplomatic cover name given to a Deutschmark with an extended area of circulation, but the effect would be the same – the dollar could only be defended by measures (trade or exchange controls) which would spell the end of its worldwide hegemony.

The immediate consequence of the dollar's slide is not, of course, to turn the US into anyone's colony. It is to unravel the international economic order which the US hoped to maintain under its hegemony, the ending of the Cold War which had provided the geo-political glue notwithstanding.

For one thing, it unleashes Germany from the restraints which had been carefully placed around it for the last 50 years. The strong DM has, as we have seen, increased divergences within the EU, as Germany will be still less able and willing to pay the costs of economic integration, which would involve aiding the economies of much weaker states like Spain and Italy. Instead of the cheque book, integration is now being forced along by threats and intimidation. Out of the ashes of the 'federal Europe' dream, a differently configured DM bloc is being shaped.

On the other side of the world, the strength of the yen will similarly stimulate the drive to create a 'yen bloc' around the

Japanese economy. The rise in the yen can only further damage Japanese exports of goods, and promote as a result the increased export of capital throughout the east Asian economies which are increasingly becoming a focus of rival ambitions on the part of the powers.

So every tremor on the world currency markets both expresses and exacerbates the basic rivalries between the centres of world capitalism. The triangular movements of dollar, DM and yen are the centre of this tangled web. Second-rank currencies like the pound and the franc suffer in the crossfire. Those which are weaker still, like the peso, can collapse completely.

The larger part of the problem is that it is insoluble. The conditions do not exist for a return to the happy days when the pound or the dollar or anything at all could be 'as good as gold'. The US can no longer hope to maintain that role, but neither are Germany or Japan yet able to take it up. Until they have formed larger currency blocs around their core economies, they lack the critical economic mass necessary – their markets could not absorb the demands which reserve currency status would make on them. As the ultra-conservative US economic pundit Paul Craig Roberts observed:

> Flight from the reserve currency when there is nowhere to go means a breakdown in the international monetary system. When British sterling failed in its reserve-currency role, the dollar was there to assume the mantle. Unless the dollar can last until, for example, the 1.2 billion Chinese build a capitalist economy that can take on the role of reserve currency, a big crisis is somewhere in our future.[6]

The contours of that big crisis are now taking shape. Japan sees no point in propping up the US's profligate ways now that it no longer needs the Pentagon's protection. Germany seeks the power to match its economic advance, which the need for the US military umbrella long prevented it from achieving. Washington looks for new ways of maintaining the dominant position of US business in the world. And all of this works its way through into the value of the money these states underwrite.

The possibility of the three powers concerting their monetary policies can be dismissed. The *Financial Times* wrote that Japan and Germany would contemplate the idea of accepting the US leadership which such a harmony would require 'with fear and loathing . . . that would be a miracle of the same order as in biblical prophecies about lions lying down with lambs'.[7] Or, as one US historian put it, 'without a pronounced shift in Washington's policy, the decline of the dollar could resurrect the ghosts of the

1930s'.[8] Not the worst part of the 1930s was that they ended in 1939, a date forever connected with the outbreak of war.

So the US tourist in Europe moaning at how little the dollar fetches in the bars and restaurants of Berlin is standing at one end of a chain, the other end of which is the third round of world war between the great powers. Currency is one side of the life of the nation-state; on the other is the general staff.

The US Treasury Secretary speaking to the famous Bretton Woods conference in 1945 spelt out the connection clearly:

> We saw the worldwide depression of the 1930s. We saw currency disorders develop and spread from land to land, destroying the basis for international trade and international investment . . . In their wake, we saw unemployment and wretchedness – idle tools, wasted wealth. We saw their victims fall prey, in places, to demagogues and dictators. We saw bewilderment and bitterness become the breeders of fascism, and finally, of war.[9]

Unthinkable nowadays? When a German Bundesbank official was asked why Germany was, in effect, bending the rules to help the French franc during its moment of crisis in 1992, he replied that had they done otherwise 'the sky would be dark with the squadrons of Mirages coming across the Rhine to bomb us'.[10]

CHAPTER 9

The Division of the World

In his extraordinary novel of wish-fulfilment, *Hadrian the VII*, Frederick Rolfe, a Catholic frustrated in his ambition to become a priest, has himself (thinly disguised as the hero of the tale) elected pope, from which pulpit he sets about reordering the world to his liking. Perhaps unconsciously, Rolfe then turns his novel (first published in the early years of the century) into a sort of collective wish-fulfilment for the ruling classes of his time. Pope Hadrian first sets about undermining and discrediting socialism, then to averting the gathering crisis in relations between the great powers which was, well before 1914, becoming obvious. Invited to mediate their differences, Hadrian imposes an organised, if not entirely peaceful, division of the world as follows:

> He dwelled upon the essential differences which divided Germany from America, and both from England . . . Three such enormous powers must have each its own separate and singular existence and sphere of action. Three such spheres must be found, in which the three nations independently might thrive . . .
> Hence the Pope proclaimed the instauration of the Roman Empire, under Two Emperors, a Northern Emperor and a Southern Emperor, and confirmed the same to the King of Prussia and the King of Italy . . . The Northern Emperor would nominate sovereign dynasties for Belgium and Holland. He might replace the present exiled monarchs on their respective thrones; or he might depose them and substitute members of his Imperial family. He would then extend the borders of Germany, eastward to the Ural Mountains by the inclusion of Russia, westward to the English Channel and the Bay of Biscay by the inclusion of France, southward to the Danube by the inclusion of Austria. At the same time he would federate the constitutional monarchies of Norway and Sweden, Denmark, Holland, Belgium, Hungary, Bohemia, Poland, Roumania and the Republic of Switzerland with the other sovereign states already under his suzerainty: while the Southern Emperor Victor Emanuel would federate the constitutional monarchies of Portugal, Spain, the extended

kingdom of Greece, the principalities of Montenegro and Albania and the republic of San Marino, with the kingdom of
Italy . . .

The United States were to be increased by the inclusion
of all the states and republics of the two Americas from the
present northern frontier of the United States to Cape Horn.

The Japanese Empire was authorised to annex Siberia.

All Asia (except Siberia), Africa, Canada, Australia, New
Zealand and All Islands, were erected into five constitutional
kingdoms, and added to the dominions of the King of England, Ireland, Wales and Scotland . . .

. . . the armies and navies of the signatories instantly set
about the pacification of France and Russia by martial law.[1]

As simple as that. The whole world re-divided in favour of the
strong powers, with the weaker subject to 'martial law'. Living
space for the Germans, an empire for the English, a continent for
the Americans and the riches of Siberia for the Japanese. Even the
Italian king got more under Hadrian's scheme than he was ever
likely to do any other way. Every corner of the globe neatly handed
over to one 'great power' or another.

Rolfe's Pope was surely the expression of the longing of the pre-
1914 ruling classes for a straightforward reordering of the world
with only the minimum unavoidable conflict. Hadrian's division
was not only a logical one for the time; it was also, with
some modifications, the sort of division which has insistently re-
appeared in one form or another throughout the century.

For example, is not the list of states he places under German
control the Deutschmark bloc of the Bundesbank's dreams in the
1990s, while the lands of the 'southern Emperor' those which
could not easily fit into a German-led Europe? The North American Free Trade Area is very much in line with Rolfe's papal
dispositions, and there is more than a glimmer of the 'Greater East
Asia Co-Prosperity Sphere' in his plans for Japan and Siberia.
Only Britain's allocation appears as the wildest fantasy at the end
of the twentieth century. Even the holiest pope could not re-
establish the British Empire here on earth.

Rolfe was mainly wrong, in fact, only in his hope that such a
settlement could be settled with no more violence than a swift
imposition of martial law on Russia and France would require.
Kaiser Wilhelm did indeed send his armies east and west in 1914,
but the upshot was anything but that anticipated by Rolfe.

If, in the words of the Internationale, 'no saviour from on high
delivers' the proletariat from wage slavery, neither will a saviour
from on high effect the organised redistribution of land, markets
and power which the great capitalist powers from time to time

require. Rolfe's Pope symbolises what does not and cannot exist, a universally acknowledged, neutral arbiter of the common affairs of the ruling classes of all lands, who can act in all their interests because he represents none. Such an institution (never mind individual) seems further away than ever. Even Hadrian VII might have found sorting out the complexities of trade in auto parts or soya beans beyond him.

Everywhere, the old blocs fade away and, in their wake, the stronger powers strive to assert the primacy of their commercial interests at the expense of the weaker. Ten years ago the division of the world seemed a clear, fixed and simple thing. There was the socialist bloc centred on the USSR, and the capitalist world under the general hegemony of the US. The largest Third World states, India and China, were not entirely one or the other (in political terms capitalist India being more aligned with the USSR, while socialist China was informally allied with the US), but most of the nations of the world could be placed in one of the two columns. Sometimes states shifted sides and back again (Somalia, for example) but the end of the British and French colonial empires in the 1950s and 1960s removed anything that could be called a serious 'sphere of influence' within the capitalist world which was not ultimately controlled from Washington.

Today, blocs are emerging which mark the start, rather than the conclusion, of a new process of redivision of the world. The EU, the 'yen bloc' in the Far East around Japan and the NAFTA bloc (which may ultimately include the whole Western hemisphere) headed by the US, are the most developed expression of this. However, these groupings do not cover all the possibilities for a new division of the world (were it so, such a division might be smoothly and peacefully accomplished), nor are they in themselves finished and friction-free processes.

In fact, the endeavour to accomplish this redivision is already becoming a determining factor in the domestic politics of states around the globe. Creating an EU under German auspices is the main motivating factor behind the attack on the 'welfare state' throughout western Europe, an attack which has already brought millions out onto the streets of France and Germany itself in protest. The formation of NAFTA has stimulated armed uprising in the Chiapas region of Mexico. Russia's loss of power and influence was one of the main elements causing a resurgence in support for the Communist Party.

If we consider the stage of redivision of the world reached so far, several general points are clear. It is rooted in the relative economic decline of the US and much greater decline of Russia, following the complete disappearance of the USSR. It corresponds to the rise of Germany and Japan to leading positions in the world economy –

both are, indeed, achieving already some of the objectives for which they took up arms under reactionary and chauvinist leadership in World War II. These developments mark the end of the 'American Century', even if the cultural lustre of Hollywood and Madonna affords an afterglow which may last awhile.

The three blocs defined above differ one from another in their present stage of development. The EU is buttressed by an elaborate network of treaties and agreements, supervised by a vast bureaucracy exercising detailed supervision over a range of economic and social affairs. It is now seeking to extend its competence into the fields of defence and foreign affairs, alongside the introduction of a common currency – in effect, the creation of a federal state. Each step taken in these directions increases the differences between the member states and pushes the whole union closer to fragmentation. The North American Free Trade Area covers only three states to date, and has no central institutions or regulatory functions outside monitoring trading provisions. The 'yen bloc' has no formal existence at all and is simply a trend, an emerging 'fact on the ground', at present. The Asia-Pacific Economic Co-operation (APEC) council, with its plans for an extremely gradual progress towards free trade in the region, is a first sign of this. The participation of the US in APEC would have to be downgraded or ended before this could serve as a satisfactory vehicle for Japanese ambitions, and before progress towards a single market within the bloc could be expedited.

These differences to some extent reflect the fact that the EU has emerged from an alliance of powers (Germany, France, Britain, Italy) which were approximately equivalent at the times of negotiation (early 1950s through to 1973). There could be no question then of one state annexing another economically, as the US has done to Mexico, and any institutions would have to be specially created supranational ones, since formal control from Bonn, Paris or London would have been unacceptable. Both the Far East and North America are far more clearly under the domination of a single power, around which the other countries must orbit. These blocs are built, to the extent that they are built, according to the prescription of Washington and Tokyo alone.

All three blocs are based on the geographically contiguous expansion of the economic power of the dominant country, or countries, a fact which again highlights the retreat from 'globalism' which these developments represent. None of the blocs could yet be described as autarchic, yet the EU's rules, Japan's existing trade practices and Clinton's 'managed trade' policies are all steps down that road. The drawbridges are starting to move up.

Each bloc includes a core of rich powers (or power), from where capital and technology are controlled, and a large periphery of low-wage economies, carrying out a range of manufacturing operations and supplying raw materials. Many types of job have moved from the 'core' (US, Germany, Japan) to the 'periphery' (Mexico, Eastern Europe, south-east Asia) in each case, something which is gathering momentum. Many Third World countries are vying to attach themselves to one bloc or another in the forlorn hope of being the next 'tiger' economy, and fearing that the price of exclusion will be the worse than the price of inclusion. The Mexican experience, which is examined below, seriously challenges this assumption.

Very large areas of the world are not yet clearly within any particular bloc, and many countries could be drawn into the orbit of one 'core' or another within the world economy. Furthermore, it is possible that a fourth grouping centred around Russia could emerge, while at least one of the blocs – the EU – may pass out of this world, at least in its present form, to be succeeded by a closely defined 'northern empire' around Germany, a looser 'southern empire' around the Mediterranean and a stand-alone Britain.

What is certain is that the existing state of affairs marks only the beginning of the redivision of the world, not its conclusion. The formation of three regional economic blocs could not provide a stable resting place for the dynamics of capital accumulation in the hands of trans-national corporations for long.

One reason for this is the evidence that each putative bloc is itself host to such competing interests and so divergent in their potential that dislocations *within* them are likely to provide the curtain-raiser to clashes *between* them.

Western Hemisphere

If nothing else, the incorporation of Mexico into the North American Free Trade Agreement created what must have been a first in the annals of popular protest. 'Hundreds of upper-middle-class women marched on the presidential residence with their cellular phones in hand and their maids alongside waving banners demanding TRUTH AND DEMOCRACY.'[2]

This improbable demonstration reflected the anger of prosperous Mexicans at the betrayal of the hopes their leaders had invested in the NAFTA agreement with their mighty northern neighbour. They had been told that NAFTA was the fast track out of the Third World for Mexico, and that their country could join the ranks of the developed nations, mobile phones and all, through signing away their economic sovereignty.

Disillusionment came in the form of the collapse in the value of the peso and the Mexican stock market due to foreign capital flight, followed by the mortgaging of the country's economy to the US in return for a bail-out loan.

The middle class of Mexico City was coming late to the reality grasped by the peasants of the southern province of Chiapas a year earlier. They had greeted the inauguration of NAFTA in January 1994 by launching an armed insurrection against the Mexican government and, explicitly, its backers on Wall Street and in Washington. Their struggle was the most graphic expression of the resistance of the peoples of the 'periphery' to their intensifying economic subordination to the metropolis of capital.

In this, they supplied an object lesson on the nature of the world economy to those in the Third World who put their faith in the World Bank and the International Monetary Fund, who believed that if the free-market, free-trade and budget austerity prescriptions of these Washington-based institutions were followed, the gates to prosperity and membership of the 'First World' would swing open.

The debacle in Mexico also highlighted the limitations of a hemispheric trade bloc as a panacea for the problems of the US economy. The whole process of the formation of NAFTA has, far from binding the member states closer together, ended up causing new complications in their relations.

Canada was the first country to be annexed to the US economy under the banner of free trade. The initial result was a sharp recession in Canada as the less efficient economy scrambled to stay up with the more efficient.[3] To make matters worse, the US then slapped tariffs on Canada's two principal exports southward – lumber and cars – on spurious grounds. The real reason was they damaged US commercial interests, for whom 'free trade' meant conquering other markets, not surrendering their own. US business wanted to get its hands on Canadian energy resources and open up their northern neighbour to the export of capital.[4]

Since tariffs had been not only an economic necessity for Canadian industry but had virtually been the only guarantee of Canada's nationhood for the preceding century, the one-sided 'free-trade' agreement proved extremely controversial, leading to the defeat of the government of Brian Mulroney which negotiated it and the unprecedented parliamentary annihilation of his Conservative Party.

For the US, however, the desire to extend the Canadian experiment to the rest of the continent proved unsurprisingly strong, at least amongst the establishment. President George Bush launched an Enterprise Initiative for the Americas, although 'Profit Initiative for US Business' might have been a more accurate designation. First, four South American countries – Brazil, Argentina, Paraguay and Uruguay – were prodded into a free-trade zone of their own dubbed Mercosur. Throughout Latin America, social spending was cut, industries handed over to private business, tariffs and subsidies abolished to meet US demands. In a continent already impoverished by the organised robbery of the 'debt crisis' of the 1980s, these measures further compromised any possibility of independent development and confirmed their peripheral status in the hemispheric economy (as well as inflicting still further miseries on their peoples). Even the World Bank acknowledged that there was very little benefit to Latin American countries in free trade with the US.[5] But for the ruling circles of Latin America, the fear of being shut out of the emerging US bloc, at a time when alternative paths of development appeared foreclosed, prevailed. 'If the world is dividing into blocs, we have to form a bloc or disappear', the *Wall Street Journal* quoted an Argentinian businessman as remarking.[6] As events were to show, US policy was to ensure that those like him formed a bloc *and* disappeared.

Mexico was the proving ground for the consequences of free trade with the US for the economies of Latin America which, of course, are much less developed and productive than Canada's. The proposal to extend the free-trade agreement to Mexico was deeply controversial in the US itself. Trade unions rightly feared manufacturing jobs would be moved south in search of wages only 10 per cent of the rate in the US, while environmental groups saw industries heading off to take advantage of laxer controls and regulations in Mexico. Mexican workers, on the other hand, drawing on the experience of the hundreds of foreign-owned (mainly by US concerns) factories established along the southern side of the border of the two countries in order to produce goods for tariff-free re-export to the US, saw NAFTA as a recipe for an extension of the ruthless exploitation and vile social conditions associated with this development. The 1980s, for example, saw a 400 per cent rise in foreign investment in Mexico, while at the same time the proportion of Mexico's GDP going to wage and salary earners fell from 40 per cent to 23 per cent.[7]

Nevertheless, the Clinton administration in Washington, in alliance with the only slightly more corrupt Salinas government in Mexico City, pushed through the agreement, amid promises that it would speed Mexico's industrial development and create new, higher-waged jobs in both countries.

As in Canada, trade barriers against US imports and controls on the scope of operations of foreign capital were a crucial element in Mexico's existence as a sovereign state. In Mexico's case, national control over the oil industry, the country's main resource, was particularly important.

Within a year of the NAFTA pact coming into force, Mexico was all but bankrupt, its oil industry had passed into the effective control of the US government, unemployment had soared by over a million, wages plunged still further and social turmoil was gripping the whole country.

By opening its markets, Mexico had become vulnerable to the volatile whims of the controllers of portfolio investment in New York, speculators well used to shifting sums the size of Mexico's GDP around the globe in a single day. To corner this money, the Salinas government raised interest rates, at the cost of bankrupting a number of indigenous businesses. Yet as discontent rose throughout the population, Mexico came to seem a risky place to have your funds parked, with an over-valued currency, huge foreign debts and an unstable government. When the government finally devalued the peso, confidence collapsed.

Almost overnight, the peso lost over 40 per cent of its value, and the Mexico City stock market dropped by half,[8] with knock-on falls in the bourses of Brazil and Argentina of 34 per cent and 29 per cent respectively.[9] This drama compelled the US government to ride to the 'rescue' of its neighbour before a complete economic and social collapse took hold. However, the terms of the bail-out of the peso imposed by Washington made the rescue worse than the original mugging. In return for $50 billion in loans and guarantees, the Mexican government pledged its oil revenues to the US Federal Reserve as collateral, began the privatisation of a number of companies and embarked on a programme of cutting wages by around 33 per cent[10] – a package which combined maximum affront to Mexican nationalism, maximum pain to the Mexican people and minimal inconvenience to the US investor. Small wonder that the matrons took to the streets with their maids and mobile phones.

With Canada irate and Mexico prostrate, the formation of a hemispheric bloc under US patronage has hardly got off to an auspicious start, and momentum towards expansion has slowed. However, the US will surely press it forward again. Already, Latin America is home to almost as much in the way of US exports as the EU, with trade growing at twice the rate. US exports to little Costa Rica are as great as those to the whole of eastern Europe. As President Clinton's special adviser Thomas McLarty wrote: '. . . if the US does not seize the opportunities now facing it, there is a real danger the nation will become a bystander in its own hemisphere . . . the game is on, and the US must compete'.[11]

The Mexican episode also helps highlight the limitations of any such bloc for US monopolies. The markets are simply not large enough or developed enough to go any way to compensating for the ground US industry has lost in much of the rest of the world, let alone the markets it would lose if protectionism is embraced in earnest in Asia or Europe. Withdrawing into a 'fortress Americas' can only form a part of the US game plan for redividing the world. Hence Washington's anxiety to play a part in APEC, and the floating of the idea of a Trans-Atlantic Free Trade Area (TAFTA) with the EU, to maintain the patina of a global role as it actually seeks to divide the world up. Too weak to be a global leader any more, too big to settle for regional hegemony, the US demands to be master in its own backyard (a policy asserted in blood in Panama, Nicaragua and Grenada) and consultant, at least, in everybody else's.

Asia

It is a fact of life that, when it comes to redividing the world, one bloc begets another. A Malaysian stockbroker put his finger on the problem when discussing developments in the Western hemisphere – important markets for many Asian exporters: 'What we don't want to see is that NAFTA comes to represent a closing in of the US.'[12]

His prime minister, Mahathir Mohamad, has already drawn the conclusion that it probably does, and wants to circle the wagons in Asia, too, as a result. Whilst participating in APEC, he has called for the creation of an East Asian Economic Caucus, which would exclude APEC members Canada, Australia, New Zealand and the US (a caucus without caucasians, as it is referred to locally); in effect, a 'yen bloc' in outline. 'We have to be united and have a trade and market pact of our own', Dr Mohamad said in words very similar to those of the disappearing Argentine businessman.[13]

The foundations of such a bloc are, as discussed earlier, the great shift in the Japanese economy towards an Asian orientation. Capital has flooded out of Japan into its neighbours since the mid-1980s, sustained by Japan's impressive savings ratio, in search of a much higher rate of return on sales than is available in either Europe or the US. In the words of the *Financial Times*, 'Japanese companies are building a commercial empire in East Asia'.[14] A Hong Kong banker puts it simply: 'Americans, British, French all make a lot of noise. But the Japanese are the real power in Asia.'[15]

The region's trade has adjusted. Intra-Asian business now accounts for around half of all exports, much of it denominated in yen. It is not surprising, then, that the dawn of protectionism in North America and in Europe should have led to calls for a Tokyo-led trade bloc in the Far East, a bloc which could control over one-fifth of total world output, twice the figure of 30 years ago. The formation of APEC is the first half-step in that direction. However, the inclusion of the North American and Australasian states in it have so far reduced its role to that of a talking shop promoting pious long-term objectives. Since Japan and the US are in combat for control of many of the markets in question, APEC in its present form may be heading towards becoming an economic version of the UN Security Council in the days of the Cold War. After APEC agreed to create a form of qualified free trade within 25 years, maybe, it became clear that it was, in the words of one Washington expert, 'about to talk itself into irrelevancy'. The *Wall Street Journal* reported that 'rather than have APEC serve as a tough negotiating forum . . . the Japanese want it to become a vague, touchy-feely process.[16] Japanese officials speak hopefully of miring the US in [the] process.' In other words, to the extent that APEC is anything, it is a vehicle for Asia-Pacific economic combat, not co-operation.

Hence Dr Mahathir's more practical – and threatening – proposal, an idea whose implications were underlined by his boycotting of the APEC summit hosted by President Clinton in Seattle in 1993. As a move towards the East Asian Economic Caucus, six nations in south-east Asia, including Malaysia and the Singapore 'tiger', have agreed to form a common market, a move paralleling the Mercosur development in South America.

Creating Dr Mahathir's bloc would, however, be even harder than giving birth to NAFTA has proved to be on the other side of the Pacific. Anti-Japanese feelings in a number of countries which suffered during World War II remains extremely high. An overt political leading role is something Japan would have to enforce – it could not expect to easily win assent to it. Then there is the growth of other economies around the Pacific rim, most notably that of South Korea. They have possibilities for independent action not easily available to Mexico or Chile. And there is the problem of relations with China and, to some extent, India. Even if an Asian bloc could be launched without the participation of the latter, the former can neither be excluded nor subordinated. As noted earlier, China's potential for emergence as a strategic rival to Japan is enormous.

How these issues are being dealt with illustrates the Japanese way of redividing the world, and indicates the nature of the 'commercial empire' Japanese corporations are erecting in the region.

For example, world capitalism has been hypnotised by the growth of Asia's 'four tigers': South Korea, Taiwan, Singapore and Hong Kong. They have been held up as models of how poor countries (half-countries or cities, in reality) can successfully break into the rich nations' club. However, examination of their actual position reveals an enduring economic subordination to the greater powers. In the case of the two largest 'tigers' – Taiwan and South Korea – they remain, despite the spectacular rise of some of their big corporations, firmly in Japan's orbit.

They are hooked on imports of Japanese technology. South

Korea imported over $21 billion-worth of technology in 1991 alone[17] – none of it cutting-edge material, however (Japan being anxious not to allow any Asian neighbour to repeat its own success in importing US technology). South Korea is incapable of bridging the huge trade deficit which this engenders by exports to Japan, because protectionism freezes its companies out of the Japanese market. South Korea and Taiwan have therefore demanded genuine technology transfer from Japan, more open Japanese markets and less dependence on Japanese capital goods. In short, they have learnt a lesson similar to Canada's *vis-à-vis* the US: 'free trade' means whatever the commanding power wants it to mean.

The President of the Daewoo Research Institute in Seoul summed up South Korea's difficulty: '. . . Korea cannot maintain its economic level without help from Japan. We must import technology, capital, equipment, and we do not have the core technology or even parts for assembly production.'[18]

So while the 'tiger economies' are certainly far wealthier than most Third World countries, and their industries are becoming increasingly competitive (even the famed Japanese semiconductor industry is facing a serious challenge from South Korean companies), their rise has not altered the basic power relations in the world economy. They remain largely dependent on foreign capital and technology, most of it Japanese. Indeed, the 'tigers' form something of an intermediate zone, between core and periphery, in the Asian economic zone. Japanese business long ago started transferring slower growth industries like textiles and steel out of Japan – initially to the 'tigers', which in turn, a generation later, have started re-exporting the industries to Thailand, Malaysia and Indonesia, where cheap labour is more plentiful. The 'tigers' now themselves supply around a third of all foreign investment in the latter countries.[19]

South Korea is the only Asian country (with the obvious exception of China) which might gain the potential to challenge this regional structure. For this reason, the Seoul military's new talk of '360-degree defence' is causing considerable disquiet in both Tokyo and Washington. The new South Korean doctrine was set out in a defence ministry white paper in 1992:

> The . . . US, Japan, China and Russia, not only have conflicting interests, but also are showing shaky signs as a result of power reorganisation to establish the new order. Given Washington's strategic retreat from the region, the military build-up of Russia, China and Japan remains a good reason to think the Korean peninsula's security situation isn't all that positive.[20]

Turning words into deeds, South Korea has purchased two Russian aircraft carriers, as well as submarines and spy planes, and is building its own destroyer fleet. Such an arsenal would be of little use if South Korean defence planners were really working on the assumption that they are preparing against a North Korean invasion. It would seem that the 'threat from the north' is a propaganda one only, and that the enemy Seoul really has in mind is to the south – hence '360-degree defence'. As a fellow at the Korea Institute for Defence Analysis said: 'History shows that the relationship between countries can change at any time. Relations between South Korea and Japan are OK now, but we have to do our best to protect ourselves.'[21]

Clearly, South Korea will not be easily integrated into a bloc on Japanese terms. And it is not the only country in the region with potentially frayed relations with Tokyo. The lively Dr Mahathir Mohamad, promoter of a Far East bloc with the Americans shut out, is also voluble in his denunciation of Japanese economic policy. His complaints include the impossibility of Malaysia exporting to Japan anything not made by the subsidiary of a Japanese monopoly, the unwillingness of Japanese companies in Malaya to appoint any Malaysian national to leading management positions in their local subsidiary (in contrast to the policy of US monopolies in the country), and the absence of any technology transfer from Japan to Malaysia. The high yen has applied a financial squeeze on a country with $4 billion-worth of yen-denominated debt and a dependence on yen-denominated Japanese parts imports. In the words of US magazine *Business Week*: 'the country is finding it extremely difficult to move beyond being a cheap-labour assembler of made-in-Japan components for Japanese companies. It finds itself locked inside a yen-dominated economic hegemony.'[22]

Malaya is not unique. A Foreign Ministry official in Thailand said recently: 'Economically, we are dependent on Japan . . . it would be next to impossible to restructure our economic relationship.'[23] Thailand's telecommunications network illustrates the way in which Japan links foreign aid with technological control to ensure big profits for Japanese businesses. Japanese aid financed the expansion of the system, which could only be sustained through the massive importation of Japanese equipment, leaving the new network entirely dependent on Japan.

These are difficulties which US and European businesses will no doubt strive to exploit in order to avoid being shut out of the region, although Malaysia and Thailand, like other Asian countries, will only be offered a choice as to which 'core' they would like to be a periphery to. Slipping out of a 'yen bloc' will be no easier than slipping into it on any terms other than Tokyo's.

India's position is a further complication in the region. Since the collapse of the USSR, the Indian government has increasingly opened up to Western capital and followed IMF-approved policies, integrating into the world economy. Henry Kissinger now sees India following

> policies like those of the British raj . . . India will seek an influential, if not a dominant role in the arc extending from Aden to Singapore. This attempt will produce potential conflicts with China in Tibet and Burma and with Indonesia, Vietnam and, to a lesser extent, China in Southeast Asia.[24]

India is increasingly planning on that basis. As long ago as 1974 it established that it could produce and detonate an atomic weapon. It has retained its option of developing as a nuclear military power primarily to oppose China, with which it has border disputes. China is additionally a strong ally of Pakistan, with which India also has a wide range of conflict points, and which also probably has the capacity to develop a nuclear arsenal. The security establishment in New Delhi has recently started calling on the government to adopt its own programme of nuclear testing because 'India cannot rely on its present defense posture if it wants to safeguard its security', in the words of one expert.[25]

However, India's economic subordination to Western big business remains intense, and its level of economic development impeded. Ninety per cent of Indian exports remain primary commodities, and one sector of the economy after another is falling under the control of trans-national corporations. It is mainly British and American companies, with substantial political and economic support from their respective governments, rather than Asian ones, which are competing for business in India's huge market at present. Britain, for example, is laying elaborate plans to woo away from the US the young Indian business people who presently complete their business education in American colleges.

Teasingly, Indian politicians have sometimes spoken of trying to join in any extension of NAFTA.[26] In any redivision of world economic power and influence, India will not be absorbed in any 'yen bloc', but may become a considerable source of friction between such a bloc and other big powers. At any event, far more clearly than in the case of China, India's integration into the world economy can only be on disadvantageous terms (particularly for the millions of people living in the direst poverty) and it will face great difficulties in even working its way up the Asian economic 'food chain' to a South Korean level.[27]

Finally, Japanese strategists will have to consider the Chinese question. China has never, of course, been subordinated to one single external power. It took a sort of condominium of Western interests to bring it to its knees in the nineteenth century. The big powers are clearly striving to follow a similar path today, with concessions, 'special zones' and so on. Whilst encouraging this development in the interests of economic growth, the Chinese government of today cannot, nevertheless, be compared with that of the dying days of the imperial dynasty.

Japan has, however, a head start in investment in China, following the usual foreign-aid 'wedge' put in the door by the Japanese government in the late 1970s. So eager have Japanese interests been to develop their position in China that the government was even induced to make Emperor Akihito, in the course of a visit, express his 'sorrow' for the 'great sufferings' Japan had inflicted on China in the course of an 'unfortunate period' which, given the reluctance of the Japanese establishment to refer to its activities during the 1930s and the World War II, was saying something.[28]

Competition between the two powers is now pervasive. If Japan dominates the Thai economy, then China is re-equipping the Thai military. If China still hankers after hegemony over Mongolia, it is Japan which is pumping in the economic 'aid' there. If Japan manages to prise open the door to investment in Myanmar (formerly Burma), they will find Chinese military advisers already working there.[29] The rivalry is even extending into the Middle East, with Japan offering cash and China weapons to Iran and Iraq.[30] Japanese officials like to speak of an 'interdependence' between the two countries. The Chinese are less sanguine – 'we will not tolerate Japan having a big military' is a sample statement from a Chinese official.

When China re-establishes its sovereignty over Hong Kong and Taiwan it will be well placed to impose its own priorities on any emerging 'yen bloc', or even to prevent it happening at all. The take-over of Hong Kong is, of course, alarming Britain – there are around 1,000 British companies controlling $108 billion-worth of assets in the colony, accounting for 28 per cent of the value of companies on the stock exchange there.[31] The British government is now fighting to protect those interests (in property, telecommunications, power and air transport) before the 1997 hand-over. But it seems as if China will enormously increase its strength in relation to Japan. As Newsweek put it: 'Greater China's rapid emergence probably means an end to the rapid growth of Greater Japan.'[32]

All this can only leave the smaller nations of Asia alarmed (the prospect of a China–Taiwan conflict has already affected stock markets and investment throughout the region). In no part of the world do the possibilities for a peaceful redivision of power look closer to zero than they do in the Far East.

European Union

The idea that the process of 'European integration' is leading to conflict and even war, rather than the promised gentle death of nationalism, is not just a warning from the margins. It is an opinion propounded by the senior Brussels official charged with making monetary union happen – Bernard Connolly, head of the European Commission unit organising the European Monetary System until his Euro-career came to an abrupt halt with the publication of his now celebrated book, *The Rotten Heart of Europe*, sub-titled 'The Dirty War for Europe's Money'.

Connolly shows at length how the whole project of European monetary union has been 'a fierce, ruthless struggle for *national* [his emphasis] interests', which he sees as reproducing the plans for a 'European Economic Community' adumbrated by Nazi strategists in 1941.

> Kohl, Mitterrand, Delors and their supporters and successors do not *intend* [his emphasis] the abominable, pagan barbarism of Nazism; they are not threatening recalcitrant countries with military annihilation; they do not intend to unleash racial pogroms or establish death camps. But their ambitions, if realized, would create the conditions of economic decline, political illegitimacy and resentment among 'regions' in Europe in which xenophobic, as opposed to liberal, nationalism would flourish, and military superpower status would, as in Wilhelmine Germany, produce a temptation to engage in 'adventurism' on the world stage as a distraction from intractable domestic problems.[33]

This view from the inside of the European integration process corresponds to what the whole world can see both of the frictions which attend every step, summit meeting and proposal leading towards European federalism, and of the state of the European continent today – the attack on the welfare state, the rise of far Right political parties, the unstable situation in much of central and eastern Europe, the near-universal discrediting of conventional political leadership, both Social Democratic and Christian Democratic/Conservative. These problems were crystallised in the strikes and demonstrations in France and Belgium in December 1995.

The bloc most advanced in the process of formation, the European Union, is also the one most likely to be the first to lose its wheels. In Chapter 5, the different policies of the three major powers in the EU, Germany, France and Britain, were analysed. Germany looks to expand eastwards and wants nothing to do with a monetary union on any terms other than its own, preferring the creation of an authentic Deutschmark bloc to a fudged 'common currency' throughout the EU. Britain is anxious to avoid getting bogged down in any form of monetary union or Euro-federalism more generally which would compromise the global financial and trading role of British interests, while retaining the advantages of a free-trading Europe. France remains desperate for any plausible financial and political procedures which might bring Germany, and the Bundesbank in particular, under some form of collective (i.e. French) control, yet is being forced to consider other neo-Gaullist schemes and alliances as a fall-back.

The other large state, Italy, remains in the hands of a ruling class which has long used 'Europe' as a device for making it do what it knows it should but cannot muster the internal political strength to impose – budget cutting and wage cutting. Italy's rulers have hitherto lacked the internal legitimacy and capacity for independent action which might allow their country to act as the 'great power' its economic size would indicate. The smaller countries orbit, somewhat erratically, around the larger powers, principally Germany.

Of course, the fact that 'the construction of Europe' has got as far as it has is proof that it serves some need. Indeed, its original purpose of constructing an integrated internal market suited the purpose of big European businesses anxious for a larger 'home base' to compete with US and, latterly, Japanese rivals, than could be provided by each nation-state on its own. However, that phase has now passed to a large extent, with the big businesses of different nation-states looking in different directions for future expansion. While, at present, they nearly all want to keep the 'free-trade' EU in business, they increasingly divide over the future of a 'federal' EU.

Currency has so far been the main weapon of choice of the big powers fighting to set the EU agenda, with the periodic Exchange Rate Mechanism crises being the set-piece battles. These saw Britain and Italy forced out of the ERM in September 1992, and when the French franc came under pressure a year later, the system was abandoned in all but name. This was not before immense damage had been done by the attempt to maintain a more-or-less set exchange rate against the Deutschmark. This had meant following German interest rates, which were relatively high throughout the early 1990s in order to finance the annexation of the former GDR without causing excessive inflation. The effect on less efficient economies was to prolong and deepen recessions.

The main casualties of 'European integration' to date have been Europe's unemployed and needy, as the struggle to meet the 'Maastricht criteria' for participating in monetary union imposes austerity and cut-backs, and prolongs recession, in one country after another.

These criteria call for budget deficits and overall national debt to be reduced broadly in line with the German figures (less than 3 per cent of GDP for the first, less than 60 per cent for the second). Hence the budget cuts and privatisations which are stirring up such opposition across the continent from Italy to Sweden. The choice in Europe has become simple: monetary union on German terms (the only ones possible) or the welfare state. There is no way of having both, since the people's welfare is the slice of the budget the bankers have their eye on.

Despite the austerity, many of the EU's 15 member states are not in reach of the criteria – and one of those which might be, Britain, is unlikely to sacrifice the pound to a single currency because of its opposition to a Euro-federalism which would be counter-productive to British commercial interests.

This has served to make monetary union deeply unpopular in Europe. It has also become rather unpopular in Germany itself, which sees itself sacrificing the stability of the DM for a weaker 'euro' currency which will be subject to the depredations of feckless Latin bankers and politicians. To try to appease this discontent, the German government has spoken of tightening up the criteria for entry to a single currency still further, something which would make progress into monetary union effectively impossible for all the states of southern Europe.

German Finance Minister Theo Waigel has already all but ruled out the possibility of Italian participation, despite the Rome government's heroic efforts to meet the Maastricht criteria at the expense of the Italian public. Some German conservative politicians did not hesitate to infer that Waigel's real target was the French government, then buckling in the face of mass working-class resistance to budget cuts and privatisation, rather than the hopeless Italians. Cutting the 'southerners' adrift, with or without France, would mean the end of European monetary union as originally conceived and open the way for the creation of a political Deutschmark bloc, admission to which would be determined by Germany alone.

All this has led to mounting doubts as to whether the whole European integration project will move any further. EU commissioners from Britain and Italy have publicly speculated that the original timetable, which calls for the 'euro' to be introduced in 1999, may be unfeasible or undesirable, wrecking the single market in the process. Business and government leaders in Italy (those not yet behind bars for corruption) openly doubt whether their country, one of the EU's 'big four', either could or should sign up for monetary union. The neo-fascist leader Fini, a rising

star of Italian politics, observed in early 1996, in the spirit of Pope
Hadrian, that there should be two Europes – a German-led
one oriented eastwards and another composed of south European
states.[34]

Germany has responded to this, not by loosening the Maastricht
criteria, but by bluntly warning that the alternative to integration
could be war. 'The policy of European integration is in reality a
question of war and peace in the 21st century . . . if there is no
momentum for continued integration, this will not only lead to a
standstill but also to retrogression . . . nationalism has brought
great suffering to our continent, just think of the first 50 years
of this century', Chancellor Kohl said in February 1996.[35] His
remarks, in effect a confirmation through inversion of Bernard
Connolly's thesis (that proceeding with integration could lead to
war), caused a storm of criticism, particularly in Britain, identified
as the recalcitrant 'slow ship' in the German-led European convoy.
He was generally derided as making 'wild threats' and 'distorting
the shape of things to come'. There were broadly two sets of
arguments against Kohl's position. The first, as we have already
seen, is that integration on Germany's terms would actually
exacerbate international tension still further. That line of argument simply points out a different route towards the same Armageddon. The second argument, advanced by leading British
commentator Andrew Marr, was that an absence of 'manic imperialism in London and Berlin', the existence of nuclear and
chemical weapons and the existence of the EU itself all made
things different to 1914, even though Marr himself acknowledges
the bankruptcy of the EU in terms of peace-keeping.[36] 'Manic
imperialism' can, of course, appear very rapidly, and there are signs
of its growth in a number of big powers at present.[37] As for nuclear
and chemical weapons, which are discussed in the next chapter,
they complicate the war-making perspective, rather than negate it.

At any event, Kohl was surely correct in asserting that failure to
move to a single currency would not simply leave the EU where it
is now. The present 'single market' free-trade zone would immediately come under pressure, since states outside the diminished
monetary union would be able to practise competitive devaluation,
in which their goods, cheapened along with their currency, could
displace those produced by companies within the monetary bloc.
Italian firms, for example, might be able to expand their market
share at the expense of the German, since single market rules
would make it impossible for the latter to prevent the Italian
companies reaping the benefit of the weak lira in the common
market place. Indeed, British market share in the EU has expanded since the pound was forced out of the Exchange Rate
Mechanism in 1992 (and immediately substantially devalued),

while the German share has contracted. This only deepens opposition to the whole project among export-oriented German industrialists.

Since institutionalising competitive devaluation is scarcely going to be tolerable to the countries in a Deutschmark bloc, Europe would most likely split into two rival blocs. One, with a common currency based around Germany and with tight federal institutions, would, in effect, be Pope Hadrian's 'Northern Empire', with much the same borders. This bloc would doubtless seek to expand eastwards, into states and markets which could be easily subordinated to German dictat. To the south another, much looser, bloc of European states would form, with little of the economic strength of the 'empire' to the north. Its main preoccupation would be the countries to the south of the Mediterranean Sea, with which some form of neo-colonial relationship would be created. Again, the beginnings of the military infrastructure and political outlines of such a bloc are already in place. As Connolly reveals in his book, the idea of a 'Latin Monetary Union' based around France, Spain, Portugal and Italy has been floated.[38] Since these countries draw a large part of their energy needs from Algeria, the logic of an extended trading zone is manifest. Such a scenario would perhaps prove the final blow to the fragile unity of Belgium, the state created as a buffer between France and Germany, divided as it is between a French-speaking Wallonia and a northern-oriented Flanders.

This would take to its logical conclusion the idea of a 'two-tier' Europe which has been the talk of European capitals in the wake of the progressive collapse of the Exchange Rate Mechanism.

The critical question would be the position of France, which still sees itself as being in the same 'tier' as Germany. As argued earlier, it cannot afford to be either isolated from Germany or subordinated to it. It has extensive southward-oriented interests as well. Its choice would boil down to leading a weak bloc separate from and, in some instances, in confrontation with the DM zone, or being integrated into a German-led alliance. The strategy of using economic integration to tie Germany down is now bankrupt. Warwick Lightfoot, an adviser to British Chancellors of the Exchequer, invoked a pungent historical analogy when he commented that 'the notion that a single currency can limit German influence, as a necessary part of a policy of economic containment . . . is likely to prove a financial Maginot Line'.[39]

For Germany, a bloc without France would mock Bonn's ambitions to be a world power, diminish its military resources and deprive it of a political cover for expansion, so it will not let France go lightly. Yet if the price of French inclusion is losing control of the common currency, the German government may just find that too high. Hence Kohl's potent mixture of demands for belt-tightening to meet the deadline for a common currency with threats of a war danger if there is a failure to bring in the 'euro' on time.

But even a two-bloc Europe is too neat. Russia's new establishment has its own demands, centred around a re-extension of Russian power into the former Soviet republics to its west and a veto over the extension of formal German influence into the USSR's erstwhile allies in eastern Europe – precisely the present targets of German hegemony.

The Russian perspective was outlined by *Financial Times* journalist Bruce Clark in his book on the rise of the new Russian imperialism. Within the Russian security establishment

> there was a renewed stress on trying to secure a *de facto* division of the world into spheres of influence. This was Russia's counter-proposal in the face of the US effort to promote a new world order in which the leading Western nations, and their values, would hold sway everywhere.[40]

In almost pontifical style, Russian extreme nationalist leader Vladimir Zhirinovsky outlined his own specific proposals to Western journalists. 'America and Russia can come to an agreement. By this, I mean we could divide the spheres of influence', he said.[41] Under this scheme, western Europe gets Africa, the US Latin America and the Pacific rim, while Russia gets the former Soviet republics, Iran, Turkey and Afghanistan. Eastern Europe and India Zhirinovsky left curiously unassigned. Zhirinovsky's policies are sometimes dismissed as the rantings of a madman, but it would probably be more accurate to see him as presenting brazenly and outrageously what more sober elements in the Russian ruling class are contemplating.

And then there is Britain. John Major went some way towards making the Connolly thesis his own at the EU summit in Madrid in December 1995, which christened the common currency 'euro'. He spelt out British fears that moving in this direction would only lead to more conflict rather than co-operation. The British government is most unlikely to join either a 'northern empire', a 'southern empire' or any fusion of the two. Indeed, it may actually try to wreck any attempt to create a united French-German grouping. The leader of the British Tory Right, John Redwood, declared bluntly that 'it is not in Britain's interest that Germany and France should merge. If they do abolish the franc and mark and have one economic policy, they are half way to a single country.'[42] Britain will remain an advocate of the loosest possible form of union consistent with a unified free-trade zone, since that is the set-up which offers the fairest prospect for the City of London. As Connolly put it:

> London is essentially a global financial centre. It is vital for it to be able to compete with New York and Tokyo . . . Within a single-currency area ruled by a would-be Bundesbank, it simply could not do that. An EMU with Britain in it would mean terminal decline for London. But if EMU happened and Britain stayed out, London would be perfectly placed to cash in on the inevitable decline of Paris and Amsterdam within 'Europe' . . .[43]

The flutters of investor interest in the Swiss franc as a stable store of value (at the expense of the 'euro'-compromised Deutschmark), precisely because it is outside the European monetary project, indicate that there is some truth in this.

In pursuit of this option, Britain will continue to make up to the French in an effort to draw them out of the German orbit, may try and build links with the new rulers of Russia and will otherwise pursue the will-o'-the-wisp of a refurbished globalism, an international condominium of the great powers, with Britain playing a central role.

And the US clearly retains the capacity to intervene in European politics, as its role in the conclusion of the Yugoslav civil war indicated. At present, that weight is being brought to bear for an integrated, German-led EU which remains open to US capital.

So the Europe of the end of the twentieth century only presents variations on the themes of the start of it. Far from moving inexorably and peacefully to a fusion of capitalist interests in one united continent, the prospect is of two, two-and-a-half or three-and-a-half blocs and spheres of influence, with sometimes clashing ambitions.

Middle East

If the big powers stand together against the oppressed nations – say, in the Middle East – it is only in order to fight over the spoils once they are secured. The Middle East is, in fact, already a volatile arena for commercial and political competition in the wake of the 'united front' of the great powers displayed in the Gulf War. While all the big powers work to prop up the reactionary and corrupt Saudi royal dictatorship, they manoeuvre against each other to win the orders which King Fahd and his family deal out. Many of these are arms contracts, a faintly surreal trade since in the event of any actual menaces being made towards Saudi Arabia, as in 1990, the Saudi princes are not actually expected to fight for themselves, despite all their fine weaponry, but instead call out the armed services of their weapons suppliers – the US, Britain and France. The US would probably welcome renewed military tension in the area as a means of reasserting through arms the strategic hegemony it is losing through economics. Some of these contradictions are coming to the surface in the battle over the succession to King Fahd. Britain and the US both support the maintenance of the feudal dictatorship, but Britain supports the new leadership of Prince Abdullah, while Washington's man is defence minister Prince Sultan.

German interests are encroaching on the region, upsetting previous power relationships. Washington is, in particular, indignant at Germany's increasingly close ties with Iran (it is now the Islamic Republic's largest trading partner), which remains demonised in the US. An article in the US magazine *Foreign Affairs* noted that, whereas once Iran had been one of Washington's main client states and most important business partners, it was now shut out of the market while 'the list of German firms doing business in Iran includes the cream of the Federal Republic's industry: Siemens, Mannesmann, Krupp, Daimler-Benz'. German banks have also helped bail out the Iranian government, rather than bringing it to its knees, as Washington would wish. The head of the foreign intelligence service of 'terrorist' Iran has been received in Chancellor Kohl's office in Bonn, much to Washington's anger. 'The German dalliance with Iran typifies the kind of issue that may work to loosen, if not sever, transatlantic ties.'[44]

Such divergent interests were behind Washington's unilateral decision to impose sanctions on foreign businesses (mainly German and Italian) trading with the Iranian or Libyan oil industries. Such firms were deemed liable to face penalties under US law similar to those imposed earlier on foreign businesses trading with Cuba. The EU reacted angrily to this extension of US jurisdiction outside its own borders. Evidently it had much less to do with 'fighting terrorism' than with opposing Third World radicalism and gaining advantage over European business interests in the Middle East. The resistance of the European powers to Washington's dictat underlined, however, that the US can no longer call the political shots in the regime.

France, likewise, has maintained its links with Iraq, despite US hostility to any contact with Saddam. Together with Russia (the latter influenced by the commercial interests of its vast Lukoil monopoly), France has been pushing for an end to sanctions against Saddam Hussein. British business also remains active and particularly influential in the princely statelets – and resentful of Washington's efforts to exclude it from the post-Gulf War round of arms deals with the sundry sheiks. The centrality of the Saudi market to the British arms industry (itself the decisive element in

British manufacturing) has been vividly demonstrated in London's repeated submission to royal Saudi interference in British affairs.

For its part, the US has started to push into countries which were formerly exclusively in the French sphere of influence, like Algeria (where US companies have won a large number of oil concessions in recent years) and Morocco.[45]

US officials have spoken out against the Europeans trying to create a 'fortress Mediterranean' in the region. No sooner had the US organised a Middle East/North Africa economic summit then the EU held its own, larger, get-together, without US involvement. Not that the European powers are all pulling in the same direction. France has recently stepped up arms sales and military advice to Jordan, long in the British sphere of influence. Gradually, the Middle East is being drawn into the European bloc, at the expense of US interests, but its future will surely depend to some extent on the fissures within Europe itself.

The process of redividing the world into spheres of influence is already passing beyond the stage of economic reorganisation. Each bloc is, to some degree or other, riven; and there is no community of interest, in general, between the powers heading each. No corner of the world will be immune from the conflicts the developing redivision of power engenders, since capitalism has threaded the globe into one market. The overall picture is of Germany and Japan pushing most actively for a new division of spheres of influence, while the US tries to hang on grimly to the remains of its global suzerainty. Russia, recovering from its prostration, must surely seek a rearrangement to allow it to regain some of its former position and China's integration into the world economy must ultimately lead to a clash of interests with Japan. The reorganisations which this implies cannot be, and have never been, achieved peacefully.

Let the last word on the European bloc, and the whole consequence of the struggle for position in the world economy, come from Henry Kissinger's memoirs, in which the US geopolitical strategist relates an encounter he had with the embodiment of French nationalism:

> I asked how France proposed to keep Germany from dominating the Europe he had just described. Obviously, de Gaulle did not consider this query to merit an extensive reply. 'Par la Guerre' he replied curtly – a mere six years after he had signed a treaty of permanent friendship with Adenauer.[46]

History supplies the necessary translation.

CHAPTER 10

The Technology of War

All conflicts, even serious ones, do not necessarily lead to shooting matches. Were it otherwise, there would never be a day of peace. To make a serious divergence of interest a war, to bring underlying antagonisms and contradictions to the level where they can only be addressed by military means, requires three things – a military ability to pursue the armed solution, immediate issues to trigger it and the political capacity to do so. This chapter examines war from the military technical angle.

It is true, of course, that war is not simply a military phenomenon, it is a political and social one. Bows and arrows, revolvers, tanks, battleships and nuclear missiles have not caused wars; ruling classes pursuing their conflicting interests have. At the height of the 'second Cold War' in the early 1980s, there was a lot of scientifically founded speculation about the possibility of a nuclear exchange between the US and the USSR being triggered by some sort of satellite/computer error, leaving high-powered information technology blankly confronting itself while humanity irradiated around it. Nevertheless, the fact was that the computers were programmed by scientists on the basis of political assumptions. For example, it was hypothetically possible that a Pentagon satellite/computer system might have mistaken an explosion in a Siberian nuclear power plant for a Soviet missile launch and triggered a response accordingly. The same system would have responded differently to the detection of an identical accident in France.

The idea that nuclear weapons in and of themselves pose a threat to world peace has now receded. Their use would, and could, make the consequences of war much worse – under certain circumstances, terminally so for much or all of humanity. But we would not have the weapons to blame if the worst came to pass. The real role of weaponry is different. It can help shape the possibilities of war, of who fights whom, where and how. It is never more than peripheral in answering the question as to why. Superior military technology on the part of the US-led coalition dictated the outcome of the war in the Gulf in 1991, for example. If the US had lacked such high-tech weaponry, or if Iraq had mastered it, then military action might have been much delayed and its outcome different.

For two generations, military technology suspended the possibility of world war by giving both the superpowers roughly equivalent resources in the field of nuclear missiles, a fact conceptualised in the potent acronym of MAD, for Mutually Assured Destruction. The real dynamics of the Cold War were, of course, rather more complicated. When the US had a nuclear weapons monopoly, their number was too small and delivery systems too precarious for it to be sure of destroying the USSR's military infrastructure before the latter had converted its vast conventional military superiority 'on the ground' into a decisive defeat for NATO in Europe. The breaking of the US nuclear monopoly made the calculation still more complicated, and the attainment of strategic parity by the Soviet Union in the 1960s finally meant that the US could not launch a nuclear war to 'roll back communism' without risking total self-immolation in the process. Reagan's desire to develop the 'star wars' Strategic Defence Initiative (SDI) to protect the US against oncoming missiles was the first serious attempt to regain a first-strike capability. In reality, SDI proved more effective at bankrupting the Soviet Union through the expense of meeting the challenge presented by it than it was in girdling the American homeland with protective lasers – much of the technology remains speculative, if not completely implausible.

This situation effectively reduced the number of powers able to start a world war to two – the US and the USSR – and made it very difficult for either to do so, had they wished to. This mirrored the geopolitical reality of the time – the main contradiction in the world was between socialism and capitalism, the former having no desire or need to start a war, the second having no ability to do so at an acceptable cost. Even the other 'official' nuclear powers, Britain, France and China, effectively lacked any capacity for independently using nuclear weapons except in the most remote contingencies.

As in every other field, the end of the US–Soviet stand-off has changed the situation. In a sense, it has democratised war-making, bringing the possibility of fighting a greater range of conflicts within the reach of a greater number of countries. The hitherto unthinkable may now be readily thought by many more political leaders. As the 'Armageddon option' of an all-out exchange of nuclear-armed intercontinental ballistic missiles recedes, the possibility of lesser wars comes to seem more reasonable.

The Gulf War is one example. Ten years earlier, the Soviet Union might have restrained an Iraqi government from a military annexation of Kuwait. Had Iraq nevertheless gone ahead, the Soviet government might have deterred the US-led powers from resolving the issue by military means. One can envisage a score of variations on that theme – conflicts which could never happen within the logic of the Cold War confrontation, but now become possible.

This does not stem solely from the ending of the possibility of strategic nuclear warfare between the US and the USSR. It is also a consequence of the dwindling of the US hegemonic military presence in many parts of the world. The US has pulled out of the Philippines and is under pressure to quit Japan, which would leave South Korea as the only remaining significant US deployment in Asia. In Europe, there have been massive troop cut-backs and base closures. Only in the Middle East has the US military presence actually expanded.

When this goes in parallel with the build-up of the forces of other countries – Japan, most strikingly – it is clear that, from the purely military angle, the balance of power (and, consequently, the range of war-fighting possibilities) has shifted decisively. The field in which the US military remains pre-eminent – nuclear weaponry – is of limited use in most of the war-fighting scenarios thrown up by the reality of the 'new world order'.

For sure, some wars remain unlikely. Neither Japan nor anyone else is likely to begin an assault on the vital interests of the US by means of a direct attack on the American military or the US homeland, for fear of provoking an overwhelming and possibly nuclear response. The 'Pearl Harbor' scenario is implausible, since few states will begin a war they have next to no chance of winning. Furthermore, relations between the US and Russia will remain regulated, although to a diminishing extent as nuclear arsenals are drawn down, by the ability of each to deal a crippling nuclear blow to the other.

However, the number of potential points of entry to a nuclear conflict have multiplied – the number of apparently lesser wars which could now be started and could then lead to the use of nuclear weapons which are, in any case, in the possession of a growing number of countries. In addition to the 'official' nuclear powers, Israel, India, Pakistan, South Africa and maybe other states are already so equipped, despite the official doctrine of nuclear non-proliferation. The list will certainly grow longer, and with it the number of regional conflicts which could start some form of nuclear exchange.

The US is in the lead in searching for new ways to use nuclear weapons. It has urged the development of low-yield weapons which 'could be very effective and credible counters against future third world nuclear threats' and could 'neutralise mobs' – nuclear crowd control, as it were. The head of the US Strategic Command has also called for the creation of a 'nuclear expeditionary force' for use in the Third World.[1] Clearly, the spread of such weapons would make it easier for a larger number of states to engage in 'local' wars with relative impunity.

Under such circumstances, it is scarcely surprising that nuclear non-proliferation is becoming harder to enforce politically. Indeed, almost any form of arms control is coming slap up against the realities of the new world rivalry. For example, the big US chemical monopolies are hostile to any agreement limiting the production of chemical weapons, because the international inspection regime such an agreement would require would allow a variety of inspectors from foreign countries into their factories, creating plenty of opportunities for the economic espionage now emerging as a regular part of international relations.[2]

Nor are these the only relevant form of technology. The military machines of the major powers are increasingly built on sophisticated, computer-driven weapons systems rather than vast armies or navies, let alone vast nuclear arsenals. If only two great powers could sustain nuclear parity, the number which could sustain a plausible technological parity is much greater – a dozen or more, including all the major powers (except perhaps China, and even there the deficiency will not endure much longer) whose policies have been discussed in this book.

This has led to a rethinking in the world's defence ministries as to how and when to fight wars. The Pentagon is, unsurprisingly, in the lead, faced as it is with the need to project a global power in new circumstances within much more limited budgets. Its war games now read like futuristic fiction: 'Satellite-guided antiship missiles showered the US fleet, which was naked to Chinese surveillance sensors high in space. As fast as the US could blind the small, inexpensive satellites, the Chinese launched more. American aircraft carriers were forced to stay too far off China's coast to do much', according to one account of a recent Chinese–American 'conflict' played out at the US Naval War College.[3]

The Pentagon is preparing for what it calls the warfare of the 'Information Age'. Its chief planner believes that the next 30 years will see the end of what he calls the 'industrial era' of attrition warfare. The features of the new warfare include smaller, more technically skilled armies fighting from great distances, direct satellite control of front-line combat personnel and an erosion of the classic military division of armed forces into land, sea and air arms as high-powered weaponry would allow a ship, for example, to fire missiles deep inland.

Still deeper into the world of science fiction becoming fact, the Pentagon is plotting offensives without soldiers or missiles at all:

> First, a computer virus is inserted into the aggressor's telephone switching stations, bringing about a total failure of the

'phone system. Next, computer logic bombs, set to activate at pre-determined times, destroy the electronic routers that control rail lines and military convoys . . . meanwhile, enemy field officers obey the orders they receive over their radios, unaware the commands are phony . . . US planes, specially outfitted for psychological operations, then jam the enemy's TV broadcasts with propaganda messages that turn the populace against its ruler. When the despot boots up his PC, he finds that the millions of dollars he has hoarded in his Swiss bank account have been zeroed out. Zapped. All without firing a shot.[4]

Thus *Time* magazine's account of the officers in the US Army's Intelligence and Security Command waging war against an imaginary 'aggressor', although one might point out that the US has not waited for a declaration of war before jamming up television screens around the world with propaganda messages, courtesy of Hollywood. The rationale behind the new Pentagon thinking is clear: now that the size of the US military has dwindled (its army is only the world's eighth largest, although its budget remains the biggest) it will have to rely on its technological edge to retain a war-winning capacity.

For all its gee-whizzery, this is a risky strategy. Firstly, the US edge in science is nowhere near as conclusive or overwhelming as its nuclear weapons hegemony once was. As has been noted earlier, the US has no significant lead over Japan in technological application – indeed, it is possible that it may fall behind. Other potential rivals are not much worse off.

Secondly, it is much easier for another power, or even a highly skilled group of people, to break into and disrupt the sort of techno-warfare described above than it would be to steal a nuclear missile, or even a tank. For example, the Pentagon estimates that outsiders try to break into its military communications systems around 500 times a day – and once you have broken into one US military computer you can break into 90 per cent of them, since they will recognise the first computer as having legitimate access. This is, ironically, a legacy of the ease-of-access of the Internet, which was created by the Pentagon itself.

Of course, the switch to new forms of war-fighting is far from making all powers equal as yet. The US retains a decisive edge in most fields sufficient to deter many potential adversaries. Yet, when one sets the trend towards a technological 'democratisation' of war-making capability away from the two erstwhile superpowers alongside the parallel trend towards the fragmentation of the existing military blocs and alliances, it seems clear that more states than ever before can consider launching a wider variety of wars to attain initially limited strategic objectives.

And, of course, there is no shortage of arms monopolies vying to equip all and sundry. Indeed, such competition has grown only fiercer with the end of the Cold War, and the consequent shrinkage of the guaranteed home markets of the arms suppliers in the US, Britain, France, Russia and elsewhere. Naturally, the weapons are pouring into the most volatile regions. As the *Financial Times* put it, rather euphemistically, 'the two largest export markets for western manufacturers – the Middle East and Pacific rim – are showing signs of strength'.[5]

Arms businesses in both Europe and the US have recently been swept by a wave of mergers, consolidating capital in the industry into a small number of giants struggling fiercely for markets between them. Arms industry monopolies are also playing a larger and larger part in the politics of the big powers, quite sufficient to override any moves towards curbing the weapons trade which any politician or party may from time to time propose. The net effect is to ensure that anyone wanting to begin a conflict – even one directed against 'Western interests', like Iraq's invasion of Kuwait – will not falter for want of Western arms. For all the occasional huffing and puffing over various arms exports scandals, the trade has become so central to the industrial economy of the big powers that the pursuit of it will come before all else – even traditional notions of freedom and free speech, as the Saudi Arabian dissident Masari found out when his criticisms of the royal regime, directed from his London base in exile, began to make life difficult for arms exporters like Vickers and British Aerospace. The ruling class which had been self-confident enough to play host to Karl Marx immediately began moves to deport the critic of the corrupt House of Saud.

To conclude, nuclear warfare was a very big and very dangerous option, to be even hypothetically contemplated only by the few. The era of the rapid-reaction force, information-driven battle groups, high-tech sabotage and arms for all places the war option in the hands of the many.

CHAPTER 11

Flashpoints

A clash of interests, and the capacity to settle it by military means, do not a war make, at least on their own. The great wars of the modern age have been caused by the opposing interests of nation-states in general, but they have actually been triggered by specific crises and incidents, as World War I was ignited by the assassination of the Austrian Archduke Franz Ferdinand and his wife by a Serbian nationalist in Sarajevo.

Such 'flashpoints' do not exist separately from the underlying contradictions between states and blocs – the same assassination at another time might have warranted no more than a police operation, rather than setting in motion vast armies which only ceased their struggle four years and millions of dead later. The spark must fall on dry grass to cause the conflagration.

Hence, we must search for the issues which might provoke a third world war in those parts of the globe where the interests of different powers most obviously collide, and where the potential for seeking an armed resolution of that clash is greatest. Even then, it is a risky business to identify a particular *casus belli* in advance. It was obvious to almost everyone, for example, that Hitler's ambitions would almost certainly lead Nazi Germany into war. But it was far from certain in, say, 1937, that Hitler's war would be caused by an invasion of Poland, rather than of Austria or Czechoslovakia or Lithuania or the USSR; or that when the conflict came it would pit Germany against Britain and France, and find the former allied with Italy.

The most that can safely be done is to identify the faultlines, the places in the globe were the mixture of factors making for war is most potent. Flashpoints will arise when the redivision of the world already in progress finds powers roughly equivalent in strength (or at least one not overwhelmingly more powerful militarily than the other) striving to control the same markets and territories, having no other profitable outlet for their surplus capital, and these rival interests intersect with nationalist or other political grievances in the disputed zones. At first or second time of asking, the clash may abate short of the outbreak of war, thanks to some form or other of patched-up negotiated settlement, a papering over of differences and pledges of co-operation. But, in the end, it is in places like these that war will start.

There are some clashes of interest which, while profoundly affecting the evolution of world politics, will not trigger a war in themselves, even if they subsequently reinforce and shape the conflict. For example, the new divergence in the positions of the French and German ruling classes is a major development which this book has discussed in some detail. Nevertheless, it is hard to envisage any war *starting* with German troops pouring over the French border, as happened very early in both the world wars we have endured to date.

The three regions of the world with the clearest potential for breeding flashpoints are eastern Europe (including the most western of the former Soviet republics), the Far East and the Middle East. However, the nature of the power struggle in the world today ensures that any conflict starting in any of these zones would swiftly draw in the rest of the world. The US and all the European powers were involved, in one way or another, in the limited Gulf War, for example. The special menace of these three regions is that a war starting in one of them would be almost impossible to localise, and would trigger a chain of responses which would drag the whole world, more or less, into the proceedings.

Eastern Europe/Balkans

It is in Eastern Europe that the world's most dramatically expanding power (in terms of economic and political strength), Germany, meets the most deeply dissatisfied, Russia, still recovering from the 'Versailles plus' national humiliation of the collapse of the socialist system of states in Europe and the destruction of the USSR.

The region into which the influence of these two states seeks to expand – stretching from the Polish/German border over to the Ukrainian/Russian border, and from Estonia down to the Balkans – is aflame with local rivalries and enmities, in particular over a host of national questions, and has by and large unstable political situations. Many of these countries have large and aggrieved national minorities and unresolved border disputes with their neighbours. The crisis in Yugoslavia is the most dramatic and obvious expression of this, but it is not necessarily unique. The region of the former Yugoslavia has only enjoyed anything like peace and stability during the 40 years or so of socialist government, and its present predicament has been the result both of the restoration of a capitalist system and the disintegration of the multi-national federation into five successor states, each with

issues outstanding both with their fellow ex-Yugoslav republics
and with other neighbouring countries.

The world's attention has been fixed on the crisis in Bosnia and
the tripartite clash of Serb, Croat and Bosnian Muslim forces. But
beyond that conflict in the region, we find Slovenia in dispute
with Italy, Serbia with Albania, Serbia with Macedonia, Macedonia with Albania, Macedonia with Greece, Bulgaria with Macedonia, Hungary with Serbia, Albania with Greece and Greece with
Turkey. Turkey allies with Azerbaijan against Armenia, which
depends on Russian support. Hungary has points of friction with
Slovakia and with Ukraine, and so on.

It is into this cockpit of conflict that Germany is extending
its economic empire. As German historian Michael Sturmer has
observed: 'Germany has no natural frontiers ... Germany was not
designed by God and centuries of history but has always had to
design itself. In the epoch of nation-states this is a problem, for
Germany is always too small to impose its hegemony, and too big
to yield to an equilibrium.'[1] It is in the east that Germany's ruling
class is trying to resolve this contradiction by fashioning its own
'equilibrium'.

The Deutschmark's drive eastward has already been described.
Many of the states mentioned above, and more besides, are being
incorporated into a DM zone, with the critical economic decisions
being taken in Frankfurt and Bonn (soon to be replaced as Germany's capital by Berlin, in a symbolic move eastwards). These
decisions will be taken with only the interests of German big
business in mind. After Yugoslavia, another relatively strong
multi-national state – Czechoslovakia – has already crumbled
before the German-inspired redivision of Europe. The wealthier
Czech Republic has clearly been drawn into Germany's orbit. At
present, Russian influence remains stronger in Slovakia, a circumstance Bonn is unlikely to find acceptable for long. Everywhere,
the successor states, sometimes little more than statelets, have no
greater real capacity for independent action, or to follow their own
policy, than has a local subsidiary of General Motors.

The next stage in German policy is to draw the somewhat
stronger states in the region – Poland, the Czech Republic, Hungary and Slovakia – into the EU and, later, NATO. Since there is,
at present, no 'Soviet threat' for defence ministers to fling themselves out of windows over, the only rationale for such a move is
the extension of Germany's military–political hegemony, in the
wake of its economic position, at the expense of Russia's.

Yet such a move would certainly be regarded as good grounds
for war by large elements of the Russian establishment, from Boris
Yeltsin to the 'moderate' nationalist Alexander Lebed and the
'extreme' nationalist Vladimir Zhirinovsky. All of them have said

as much, although the dispiriting performance of the Russian military against Chechen hostage-takers would indicate that there is a way to go before the new 'tsars' will have an instrument able to sustain their rhetoric.

More likely the critical point will be reached when the extension of German power (possibly trailing the institutions of NATO and the EU in its wake) reaches into the heart of the old USSR itself. Moldva, where General Lebed cut his nationalist teeth promoting the interests of the Russian minority, is one potential flashpoint. The majority of the ex-Soviet republic was, before 1940, part of Romania, which has not renounced hopes of retrieving its lost territories one day, an aspiration supported by some politicians in Moldva itself. If the Russian minority like the idea of being citizens of an independent Moldva little, they like the idea of being Romanian citizens still less. Like Serbia before it, Moldva could be a chain which pulls larger powers into a locally initiated conflict.

To take another example, if Poland should be incorporated in a military alliance with Germany and Moscow does not make good on its threats at that point, might Warsaw not be tempted to seek the restoration of territory it lost to Lithuania during World War II? Not only would that appear to be an easy target for a demagogic Polish leader, it would also increase the possibilities of Germany re-annexing the Kaliningrad (formerly Konigsberg) enclave of the Russian republic itself, surrounded as it is by Lithuanian and Polish land.

The biggest prize, however, must remain the Ukraine. The extension of Germany's influence into a country which most Russians regard as part of their own has already been noted. The Ukraine is an agriculturally rich and industrialised land divided between a generally pro-Soviet east with a large Russian minority and a 'Western', nationalistic west, based around Lvov and other lands which were part of the Polish state until 1939. Of all the new 'nation-states' the Ukraine holds the greatest capacity for dramatic fragmentation, and is the object of the greatest interest by outside powers. Russia cannot accept Ukrainian independence, still less its incorporation into a German bloc, without accepting its own permanent relegation to the second rank of powers and denying its privatised giant industrial companies the most obvious 'external' market to attach. Yet without the Ukraine, Germany's domination of Europe would remain attenuated and provisional, always at the mercy of a Russian resurgence. The splits amongst the Ukrainian people, reflecting different histories and culture, could provide any number of internal pretexts and possibilities for external intervention. Moreover, the working-class movement in both countries is in favour of a closer union of the two states as part of the re-creation of the socialist Soviet Union in opposition to Russian and Ukrainian nationalists (and the Western powers) alike.

It is becoming increasingly clear that the international alignments which the next Russian–German war would create will be different from those of the last one. Britain is most likely to oppose any extension of German power, an attitude prefigured in the Yugoslav crisis. France may share Britain's fears about a German-dominated Europe, but its capacity for extending its desire for independent action *vis-à-vis* Germany into the military sphere is not so great. The US, however, would seem overwhelmingly more likely to back Berlin in any conflict to the east, hoping to share in the post-war spoils with its new number one 'strategic partner'.

There are other lesser-known sideshows of European political life (not necessarily directly involving Germany or Russia) which have similar potential, given the wrong congregation of circumstances. Slovenia, for example, has congratulated itself on making a relatively bloodless exit from the Yugoslav Federation, and avoiding the wars to its south. Yet its application for associate membership status of the EU was blocked, not by Serbia, but by Italy.

Rome is demanding that its tiny neighbour liberalise its rules on foreign property ownership and address no fewer than 20,000 outstanding claims for the restoration of property lost by Italian citizens who left Italian territory handed over to Yugoslavia (now Slovenia) at the end of World War II. Having long forgotten about the issue, Italy revived the claims in 1991 as part of its contribution to the 'new world order'. Slovenia's President Milan Kucan (who played a major role in the destruction of Yugoslavia) has accused Italy of behaving 'as if the war never ended'. To dramatise Kucan's point, the leader of Italy's resurgent fascist party, Gianfranco Fini, placed hundreds of bottles in the sea off Slovenia containing messages pledging an Italian return to its lost territories. Fini is fast becoming one of the most influential political leader in Italy, so clearly it is not the last war which Kucan should be worrying about so much as the next one.

If extended, Rome's behaviour could lead to the reopening of a host of similar claims in eastern and central Europe. Indeed, Germans are already making similar claims against the Czech government arising from the end of World War II, the expulsion of three million Sudeten Germans from the then Czechoslovakia in 1945 being another unresolved issue. Despite desperate efforts at appeasement of the Germans (already dominant economically in the Czech Republic), the Bonn government has become increasingly belligerent. Even Washington has (along with Britain and Russia) had to disassociate itself from Germany's reading of the 1945 peace settlement.[2]

And *Financial Times* columnist Ian Davidson has pointed out that Hungary, which lost much of its territory at the end of World War I, 'could one day be a cause of another military conflict as the substantial Hungarian minorities in neighbouring countries, such as Slovakia, pursue self-determination'.[3]

The dispute between Greece and Turkey is better known, and reflected in the different positions taken by the two powers on almost every conceivable international issue, despite their shared membership of NATO. The possibility of their disputes over Cyprus, divided since a Turkish invasion in 1974, and over contested islands in the Aegean reaching boiling point was displayed when the two countries had a naval stand-off over some uninhabited islets in January 1996.[4] Greece has also declared a 'common defence space' with Cyprus, enhancing the possibility of a clash on the island escalating into a wider war.[5] In its disputes with Turkey, Greece has the unvarying support of Russia, and a measure of sympathy from Britain, France and Italy. The US and Germany, on the other hand, line up behind Turkey, with which Washington, in particular, enjoys the closest of relationships. Every few years war threatens to break out between the two nominal allies in the Aegean and eastern Mediterranean, and the progressive deterioration of the solidity of the NATO alliance must make each stand-off more fraught with danger than the one before.

The seriousness with which other powers take the situation was reflected in Washington's dispatch of its top trouble-shooter, Richard Holbrooke, fresh from supervising the post-Yugoslav settlement in Dayton Ohio, to sort out the Turkish–Greek dispute. This is a testimony, above all, to the capacity of conflict between the two countries to embroil larger powers on one side or another – it is all too easy to envisage Russia intervening against Turkey if the latter was in conflict with Greece, a move which would almost certainly bring in Germany on Ankara's side, and possibly the US as well.

This does not exhaust the list of possible flashpoints in Europe at present. But it is sufficient to indicate that the potential for war in Europe has not been exhausted with the Yugoslav 'peace'. The significance of each of these hypothetical wars is that they would swiftly bring in bigger powers to some extent or other, very much in the manner of August 1914, on the basis of the divergent great-power interests analysed previously.

Far East

Still less does one need a crystal ball to perceive the outline of the next war in the Pacific, with China apparently on the brink of seeking the reunification of the rebel province of Taiwan, for 50 years a US protectorate, with the mainland by whatever means seem necessary. Taking advantage of the power vacuum opened up in the Far East, and enraged by Taiwan's increasingly assertive campaign to be recognised as effectively independent (encouraged by many elements in the US), the leaders of the People's Republic of China have made it ever clearer that the military option for securing reunification not only remains alive, but appears to be moving up the menu. There is even talk of a 'timetable' for re-unification having been agreed in Beijing. China has started firing missiles in the seas around its rebellious province, and the US, in turn, has resumed sailing the Seventh Fleet through the Taiwan Straits in a show of force.

There can be little doubt that an actual Taiwanese declaration of independence, or a large measure of US-sponsored international recognition – a *de jure* partition of China – would lead to a military conflict.

How will Japan respond to the second (after Hong Kong) of the 'four tigers' becoming integrated with its main rival for the posi-tion of economic hegemony in the fastest-growing economic region in the world? Will Washington accede in a reunification which, however accomplished, would be the clearest signal yet of the passing of its unique superpower status? It remains very hard to see how China exercising its right to reintegrate its internation-ally recognised sovereign territory would not lead to an escalation of confrontation on the part of the great powers in the direction of war, despite the studied ambiguity of Washington's position on the issue.

What is harder to be definite about is how the three powers would align against each other. The legacy of Cold War politics would pit Japan and the US against China, as would a mutual fear of the latter's rising power. Contemporary economic rivalry could tempt Japan into a strategic alliance with China to the exclusion of the US, an attempt at a modern re-creation of the 'Greater East Asia Co-Prosperity Sphere' of the 1930s. The US could prefer to see the two Asian powers slug it out, leaving American interests to re-establish themselves in the aftermath – this being what Harry Truman hoped to see as the outcome of the German–Soviet con-flict when it started in 1941. Only a US–Chinese alliance against Japan seems unlikely, although if the Beijing government were to renounce communism (not something which seems imminent), even this could not be excluded.

There are other possible sites for the outbreak of an Asiatic war, too, given the tensions over the South China Sea and its potential oil deposits (China, Vietnam and the Philippines), between China and India, and on the Korean peninsula. The latter, particularly, could bring in all the three powers in the region, again with uncertain alignments between them. A conquest of North Korea could give a mighty boost to South Korea's campaign to be at the top table of twenty-first-century nation-states, but would almost certainly meet with Chinese opposition.

Less likely, but still possible, is a conflict between Japan and South Korea. Relations between the two countries have deteriorated markedly in recent years. The two countries are in dispute over small islands lying between them; a row over the issue provoked anti-Japanese demonstrations and a show of military force by the Seoul government in February 1996.[6] Japan and South Korea have a range of other issues, substantive and symbolic, dividing them, as has already been mentioned. A new factor in the islands incident was the absence of any US leadership, such as would have been applied in the days of the Cold War, to calm the dispute down.

The stage has been clearly set for a three-power struggle for supremacy in Asia. The political and institutional bonds which might retard the onset of war are weaker than they are in Europe, the military options more extensive. This is a continent without a 'peace dividend' – over the last ten years defence spending has risen by 58 per cent in Japan, 59 per cent in South Korea, 32 per cent in Thailand, 37 per cent in the Philippines and 31 per cent in Taiwan (though in China it has risen by less than 7 per cent).[7] And there is no lack of friction between these powers.

Middle East

The third, and perhaps most obvious, place where war could break out in the near future is in the Middle East – indeed, war has broken out there in the near past. Saddam Hussein's attempted annexation of Kuwait is not likely to be the last attempt by an Arab leader to redress the vast imbalances of wealth created by the domination of the region by external powers. Even if the possibility of military conflict between the Arab states and Israel appears to have abated, other crises are coming in to sharper focus.

As in Africa, although perhaps less noticed by the world at large, imperialist-drawn borders in the Middle East have created dozens of anomalies and friction points. Many of the states in the region owe their shape and their existence in their present form to the interests of British and French diplomats, financiers, oil bosses, generals and politicians who took advantage of the disintegration of the Ottoman Empire in the late nineteenth century to reorder the map to their own specifications. The dispute over Kuwait is far from an exception. The struggle for Arab unity will continue to appear as a mortal threat to the interests of the US, Britain and France. On its own it provides a variety of flashpoints which, as discussed in Chapter 9, could bring in the external powers on different sides – Germany close to Iran, France to Iraq, Britain and the US competing in Saudi Arabia, etc.

Russia has re-emerged as a major political force in the Middle East, allying itself with both Iran and Iraq in defiance of protests from the Clinton administration. Soviet troops occupied northern Iran for a period at the end of the World War II and, for the sake of securing its position in Azerbaijan and its oil fields, if for no other, Russia today may seek to revive some sort of spheres of influence agreement over Iran.

In the event of any future Iran–Iraq war, or inter-Arab conflict, not only is it unlikely that the big powers would act in concert, it is even possible that they could be brought in, to some degree or other, on different sides. Conversely, should war break out in Europe, it could easily extend to the Middle East as a second theatre.

Of course, the scenarios outlined above do not go anywhere near covering all the possible wars which could break out at any moment in the new world order. But they are the conflicts which could provide the first steps towards drawing the big powers into struggle for their own interests – the local conflicts which are the start of world war.

CHAPTER 12

The Third World War

Wars can and do start unexpectedly, in unforeseen ways and places, but they do not start by accident. The decision to go to war is, in the end, a matter of policy. What has been described so far is the tendency towards war in the contemporary world situation, the progressive disappearance of those factors which militated against war breaking out, and the emergence (or re-emergence) of factors which make it more likely.

However, none of this can actually lead to war until and unless the state is reorganised for war. There can be no division between foreign policy and domestic politics here. If the logic of capitalist competition is to reach its highest expression in conflict between nation-states, the same force must overcome the domestic impediments to war. Put simply, the 'war party' must prevail in at least some of the powers sufficiently to set a match to the combustible international environment.

It is sometimes argued on the Left that, under capitalism, war is inevitable. It would be more accurate to say that the tendency towards war is inevitable. It can be impeded, temporarily diverted, for a time frozen (as it has been for 50 years or so), but it cannot be negated. Whether or not a particular war starts, however, is very much in the hands of humans. As a result, the issue will increasingly become the main one in the internal politics of states – the furore around recent remarks by German Chancellor Kohl, Russian President Yeltsin and Chinese President Jiang Zemin shows that this is already becoming so.

A war can only break out, if, finally, the internal balance of forces in the powers permits it. If, for example, in 1914 the Socialist International had made good on its pledge to call a Europe-wide general strike in the event of an attempt to start the war, the conflict would have ground to a halt. That would not have laid the war danger to rest, since the factors which created the drive to war pre-1914 would have remained. Only an overturning of the whole great-power system could have uprooted the war danger, but the mobilisation of people against war by means of a general strike could have arrested the immediate menace.

The same factors are relevant today. Whatever the danger of war may be, it is within the power of people to avoid it in any given

situation. War is about politics: the politics of the ruling classes
and the politics of the mass of ordinary people. The latter lives in
the shadow of the former in 'normal times', but whatever such
times may have been, we are sailing away from them.

Clearly, the end of the Cold War has had a major impact on the
internal politics in all the major states. For over 40 years anti-
communism and anti-Sovietism were the main focus of ruling-
class policy in most of the big powers. They formed the glue
holding parties and entire establishments together. The diminu-
tion or disappearance of that factor has set in train a process of
political recomposition in the main powers: in Italy this has
amounted to a virtual melt-down of the political establishment
and the reorganisation of politics around apparently new forces; in
Japan it has meant a reshuffling of parties and the end of the
Liberal Democrats' 40-year uninterrupted hold on office. The
extent of the post-Cold War change varies greatly at present, but
there are trends common to all.

We have already seen that the rising forces are those of nationalism, of unilateral diplomatic and political action, of '(insert
country of choice) First'. In some cases this reaches a form of neo-
fascism. Everywhere it is associated with a breakdown in the post-
war 'consensus' and, usually, with the political and electoral
decline of social democratic parties, which have played such a big
part in politics throughout the post-war period. Within the ruling
classes, despite all talk of 'globalisation', it is the parties which
represent multilateralism, international co-operation and peaceful
resolution of disputes which are in decline.

Those seeking comfort in the face of this may turn to the old saw
that 'democracies do not go to war unless attacked'. There is a
sense in which this is true, a sense in which it is not, and a sense in
which it misses the point. Firstly, it is true that the greater freedom
people are allowed, the more the opportunities for expression and
organisation, the harder it is for a government to embark on a war
– its diplomacy is scrutinised, its policies challenged, people are
mobilised against the conflict. Public opinion is a factor which
cannot be dismissed – this is perhaps most relevant in considering
Germany today, where revulsion against militarism and against
any war policy remains very strong, particularly among the young.

Yet one also has to note, secondly, that this is no more than a
relative truth. The big capitalist democracies have forever been
starting wars, mainly against Third World countries (including
sometimes those which have democratic governments). And the
difference in political systems was hardly central to the start of
World War I, for example. Today, the development of a more
democratic society in South Korea has aggravated its relations
with Japan, rather than ameliorated them – politicians find it

electorally useful to pander to anti-Japanese sentiment, even though it makes conflict more likely.

But most importantly, the drive towards war invariably also engenders a drive against democracy. If it is difficult for a democracy to start a war, then those wanting to start one are as likely to remove the democratic impediment as the latter is to thwart their plans – was not Hitler's elimination of Weimar democracy a necessary precondition for his later international aggressions?

The menace to freedom and the menace of war stem from the same source because the big business groups which are, in the end, the only ones which may hope to benefit from carrying competition to the level of arms, are also the decisive element in the real power structures of a capitalist society. No candidate for the presidency of the United States can even leave the starting blocks without massive support from big business; in Japan both major party 'blocs' are in hoc to the *keiretsu* monopoly groups; in Europe socialist parties now vie with their traditional conservative or Christian democratic adversaries in seeking to express the interests of 'their own' establishments.

The 'war party' does not appear today in any country as the party calling, literally, for war. It is rather the dominant tendency of politicians who, seeking to ensure that their domestic corporations come out on top in the competitive jungle, follow a particular line leading in the direction of conflict. The common features this trend displays in all the major powers include fighting for a reduction in the share of the nation's wealth going to working people in the form of wages and social benefits, a foreign policy aimed at putting the business interests of their own country first in an increasingly militant fashion, support for keeping the Third World 'in its place', and demands for 'order' in social life, the moral sphere, etc.

As it further develops, this trend merges into a more thorough-going authoritarianism on social questions, campaigns against immigrant and ethnic minority workers, an extreme tariff policy and measures against left-wing or dissident groups. In its final form (which is not to say it necessarily has to reach this stage everywhere), the 'war party' becomes the expression of outright nationalism, virtual dictatorship and international aggression. It is impelled in this direction by the need to step up the exploitation of working people and to conquer new markets for secure super-profits, excluding all rivals.

In each big power, we can see this process unfolding. It cannot, however, be traced simply to the electoral fortunes of one or another political party, since the advance of these reactionary trends sweep up, to some degree or other, all the parties tied to the establishment, making of them one whole, in all essentials. What

leading Labour member of the British parliament Tony Benn said
of the national politics of his own country – that 'the consensus
amongst party leaders who regard the process of globalising capital
as both inevitable and desirable is effectively leading to a one-
party state'[1] – has a more general application.

Throughout western Europe, for example, both government and
opposition (normally conservative and socialist respectively) support the same policy on the crucial questions. Everywhere, both
parties are partisans of less spending on people's welfare, of privatisation of industry, of low taxation, of support for the free market
and of whatever else is required to help 'their' country 'win' in the
international competition for investment. Within each country,
both parties tend to follow the same policy towards the EU, as well.
In Britain, both are reserved (and divided) about monetary union
and a federal Europe. In France and Italy, both are partisans of it.
In Germany, both have moved towards a new scepticism on the
issue. The point is that, within each state, the major parties follow
one, national, policy in all essentials.

The same is even more clearly true in the US and Japan. In the
latter, the Social Democrats provided a prime minister for the first
time in 1995 at the head of a coalition dominated by the conservative LDP. The premier, Murayama, then reversed socialist
policy on just about everything, merging his long-dissident party
into the national 'bloc'. As big business integrates with the nation-
state, so also do conservatism, liberalism and social-democracy
lose their sharp distinctions and follow the same line. They
struggle not with each other (despite all the excitement of elec-
tions) but as one against other countries.

This 'consensus' on policies which bear down hard on millions
of working people is inevitably causing dissatisfaction, and creating the grounds for the emergence of still more right-wing and
nationalistic elements. This is emerging clearly in the US at
present. Barely had President Clinton won election on the most
right-wing platform advanced by a Democratic Party nominee for
70 years or more than he was politically superseded by a right-
wing Republican take-over of Congress, led by Newt Gingrich, on
a policy of aggressive attacks on the welfare state and a more
assertive, 'America First', approach to the rest of the world.
Gingrich himself came under fire from the right-wing of the
Republican Party for being too soft. The campaign for the Republican presidential nomination in 1996 saw the front-runner,
Senator Dole, a man devoted body and soul all his political life to
the pursuit of the interests of American big business, competing
with tax-cutting multi-millionaire Steve Forbes and xenophobic
authoritarian Pat Buchanan.

The more extreme of these elements are not yet decisive in US political life, but already they are helping to move the whole centre of gravity to the Right. These positions have limited popular support at present – around half of adult Americans do not vote at all – but they are likely to find an increasing hearing in a society where real wages have been falling, where job insecurity is rife and where the population is unaccustomed to the idea of relative economic and political decline. As elsewhere, there is a growing political backlash at the consequences of international economic developments which make conventional politics seem powerless.

Throughout Europe, the same forces are at work. In Italy, the leader of the country's neo-fascist party, Gianfranco Fini, is fast becoming a leading force in the right-wing coalition – he who has pledged to take territory back from neighbouring Slovenia. In France, the National Front is an established force electorally and on the streets, pursuing openly racist policies and influencing the stance of 'mainstream conservatives' in turn, as well as building international alliances with the likes of the Russian fascist Zhirinovsky. In Germany, where neo-Nazism is at present a phenomenon of the streets rather than respectable political circles, the ruling parties have nevertheless launched one attack after another on the rights of the left-wing Party of Democratic Socialism. Even in Britain, historically the most stable of the democracies, the Conservative Party is increasingly falling into the grip of its nationalistic, flag-waving, foreigner-baiting wing. In all these countries, the political establishment is broadly united on the need to spend less on benefits for the aged, the unemployed and the poor, less on health, and on the need to squeeze wages downwards.

In such a situation, all that is certain is that resistance will arise and that the forces of the far right will have a chance to flourish, capitalising both on people's discontents and society's fear of disorder.

Of course, the rise of far right movements and opinions (and we do not mean just neo-fascist groups, which will generally not play a leading role) is not yet a dominant trend, and it does not represent a definitive shift in international politics at this stage. It is, however, a rising trend, just as the parties and policies of international social democracy are on a downward glidepath. Under the capitalist system, tomorrow seems to belong to Gingrich and Buchanan in the US, Lebed and Zhirinovsky in Russia, Fini in Italy, Le Pen in France, Ishihara in Japan and Lamers and Schauble in Germany. Whatever electoral zigzags there may be, the 'war party' is on the hoof.

Some are surprised by the decline of the more pacific social democrats in this situation (although it cannot be denied, given the actual political fortunes of socialist parties these last 15 years or so). The London magazine *Prospect* agonised recently:

Isn't the European welfare state now in crisis? Do we not need social democracy again? Indeed, are not other classically social democratic themes re-emerging? For example, mass unemployment, or the widening gap . . . between the haves and the have-nots. This is the paradox. There are a whole range of social democratic *questions*, but under the new rules of economic globalisation hardly anyone still believes in the possibility of social democratic *answers* . . .[2]

This presentation clearly points to the reason for the apparent 'paradox' of social democracy's waning appeal. If one accepts that the main aim of national policy must be to win capital investment from the trans-national corporations and financial institutions (the meaning of 'economic globalisation'), then one is immediately locked into a bidding war in which welfare spending, high wages and government deficit spending to create jobs are encumbrances rather than advantages. When in office, as in Sweden and Spain most recently, socialist governments have followed basically neo-conservative policies. Italy's Socialist Party did not survive the end of the Cold War at all, and its most eminent leader, Bettino Craxi, is on the run from corruption charges. In Japan, the social democratic party entered government only to negate everything it had ever purported to stand for. The French Socialist Party has been reduced to an electoral rump following a decade of policies aimed at accommodating the interests of big business.

Special mention must be made of the situation in wounded Russia. Its political scene increasingly resembles that of Weimar Germany, with the same appeals to a humiliated nationalism and the same economic misery for millions. The coalition which restored capitalism and broke up the Soviet Union is floundering, despite uniting for electoral purposes around the vodka-sodden person of President Yeltsin.

Western comment on the situation is invariably misleading, painting the political struggle as being between 'reformers' and 'extremists', lumping in Communists and nationalists together under the latter heading, while regarding Yeltsin, the butcher of the Chechens, as the leader of the former.

The truth is that the division lies between those championing capitalist restoration, who are increasingly moving towards nationalistic positions as well, and those who stand for a restoration of socialism and see the re-creation of the Soviet Union (the only basis for durably reuniting the other ex-Soviet republics with Russia) as being a peaceful and voluntary process. For example, Zhirinovsky, the extreme nationalist, almost Hitlerite leader, has made it clear that he supports 'reformers' like Yeltsin and his team in preference to the Communists. Unlike the Communists, he supported Yeltsin over Chechnya. The more moderate nationalist, General Lebed, plumped for an alliance with Yeltsin rather than the Communists – perhaps not surprisingly, since his role model is apparently Chile's General Pinochet, a murderer of communists *inter alia*. These leaders may indeed be 'anti-Western', and play on the deep sense of shock amongst Russians over the disintegration of the USSR. But they are, like Yeltsin, political representatives of the new big business bosses running Russia. Not unlike Hitler before them, both national and social questions are tools to be manipulated in order to cover a more aggressive policy of business-driven expansion. The more moderate 'reformers' who briefly dominated the political scene after 1991 are either falling in behind the new nationalism or departing for private business, mourning, in the words of economics minister Yevgeny Yasin, that 'people want someone to pay for the hard times they are going through and it is quite impossible to explain to the simple people that the ones to blame aren't Yeltsin and [top reformer] Chubais' but the Soviet system. Quite.[3]

The Communist Party of the Russian Federation, on the other hand, is an alliance between politicians like its leader, Zyuganov, who accept to some extent the restoration of capitalism but wish to mitigate its effects and curb its internal and international excesses, and more militant elements opposed to the whole course of recent developments. Still firmer communist groups are active to the left of the CPRF. The continued hegemony of either the Yeltsin 'reformers' or the nationalists will represent the triumph of Russia's 'war party', with only the speed at which subsequent conflict arises at issue; the victory of the Left would mean a turning back of Russia from the course of the aggression which has already spread its wings in Chechnya. In Russia, more than in any other of the major powers at present, the whole direction of the state is contested. While the forces of nationalism and aggression are more lurid and strident than elsewhere, their position in society is also more precarious and provisional. The question of Russia's future is, in that sense, the most vital question of war and peace today.

It would be wrong to present the political initiative as being solely in the hands of the ruling classes of the world. Even in the US, which has never boasted an influential socialist movement, masses of people are looking for an alternative to the eternal moving-right show of capitalist politics. *Business Week* editorialised that while

> most Americans have tended to blame Big Government for their economic woes . . . [now] their anger may be shifting in some measure toward Big Business. The role of the corporation in society is being challenged. Only the foolish would

ignore the signs. Who benefits from the new high-tech global economy? That is the question both right and left are asking. Their answer is virtually identical: despite big gains in productivity and profits, most employees are not sharing in the rewards, while shareholders and option-laden corporate officials most definitely are.[4]

This is a global and not just an American truth. Steadily, the worldwide basis for political support for the prevailing world economic system is being eroded. In 1975, it would have been true to say that almost everyone in the world was living better than they had been 30 years previously – the extent and durability of the improvement might vary wildly, but the great bulk of humanity would have felt that things had improved at least somewhat, and would have been fairly confident that their children would enjoy better living standards still.

But how many in 1997 can say that they live better than in 1977? Even within the most developed countries, the return of mass unemployment, the stagnation in real wages in many states, the growth in inequality, mean that far from everyone is better off now than 20 years ago. In the Third World, whole nations have fallen back enormously; while in the former socialist countries, only the smallest number of spivs and racketeers, bureaucrats and an element of the intelligentsia have moved ahead. Perhaps 80 per cent of the world's population live no better or actually worse than they did 20 years or so ago.

Yet the same period has seen not only the vast, epic-scale, accumulation of profits in the centres of the world economy – the nation-states whose policies have been discussed in this book – but also a comprehensive and historic renewal of the technological base of economy, and the movement of that economy on to a potentially higher plane of scientific production. Taking the world economy as a whole, the accumulation of wealth and power at one pole and of poverty and marginalisation at another has never before seemed so pronounced.

In the end, this cannot but determine the shape of world politics. Already this is happening. The most significant struggles around the world over the last two years or so bear this out: the Chiapas insurrection in Mexico, directed against the economic aggression of the US; the vast strikes in France against the process of social immiseration in the name of a common currency in Europe; the worldwide movement against nuclear weapons testing by France; the united miners' strikes in Russia and the Ukraine (displaying the durability of working-class solidarity in the ex-USSR); the campaign to expel the US military presence in Okinawa (Japan); and the actions against the imperialist presence in Saudi Arabia. All these stand out in sharp contrast to the general movement to the right in ruling-class politics. And all are, in the end, directed against the 'war party' in world affairs, because they all oppose the logic of developments leading in that direction – addressing chronic symptoms before the disease reaches a higher form.

There is a danger, however, of a sort of paralysis in the face of events, to which the struggles mentioned above are the exception. Bad as things may be, people often cast around for an alternative in vain. Perhaps this is the result of searching for better ways to manage the present situation, rather than fighting for the comprehensive alternative inherent in the polarisation of the world economy mentioned above. Free trade or import controls? A penny on the tax or cuts in public spending? European monetary union now or in ten years time? These are all choices rooted in the unbending reality of private control of the world's means of production, the very reality which has not only created a planet in which millions starve in the shadow of the vast accumulation of wealth but is also impelling millions more to death in future wars.

The simplest answer to the politics of poverty and war was given by German social democrat Rudolf Hilferding in 1910:

> The proletariat avoids the bourgeois dilemma – protectionism or free trade – with a solution of its own; neither protectionism nor free trade, but socialism, the organisation of production, the conscious control of the economy not by and for the benefit of capitalist magnates but by and for society as a whole . . . Socialism ceases to be a remote ideal, an 'ultimate aim' which serves only as a guiding principle for 'immediate demands' and becomes an essential component of the immediate practical policy of the proletariat.[5]

The development of the world economy today brings Hilferding's words back to life. More than ever before, the gigantic international socialisation of the wealth-creating process by the great corporations has generated a situation in which the private control of that process is a barrier to the fullest utilisation of the technology and machinery in which so much has been invested. How else to explain the massive deterioration in the circumstances in which millions live, next to the continuing revolutionisation of technology and production?

Every step taken in the direction of taking power out of the hands of the present rulers of the world economy – of imposing the priorities of humanity over those of private profit – is a step away from war. That is not to say that other measures cannot be taken, short of socialism, to prevent the outbreak of conflict:

- The principle of non-intervention in the affairs of other countries should be upheld (against liberal 'internationalism' *à la*
  Somalia as much as against blatant aggression *à la* Grenada).
- The arms trade should be curbed, and military budgets cut,
  with some of the savings going to defence conversion in order
  to protect jobs and develop socially useful production.
- The United Nations Security Council should be restructured
  to include large Third-World countries like India and Brazil
  as permanent members with veto powers.
- The International Monetary Fund and World Bank should be
  controlled by all the states of the world on an equal basis, ending their role as wedges for great power interests – American,
  above all.
- Controls should be placed on the export of capital, and also on
  the abuse of 'foreign aid' by donor powers.

These measures – many of which are already the subject of broad
campaigns in a number of countries – would at least go some way
towards eroding the war-makers' present rising advantage in world
politics. It is clear, however, that they would not on their own
uproot the causes of war, which are buried deep in the system.

In the end, this must bring us back to the question of the nation-
state. We have argued that it has far from disappeared, and every
development on the world scene today tends to reinforce that view.
However, the growing internationalisation of the economic life of
humanity must point in the direction of the nation-state's ultimate
abolition under different economic and social circumstances.

In principle, this would be a good thing. Humanity is, after all,
one, with common problems and common hopes. The nation and
the state alike are, finally, passing episodes in the social development of humanity. The only issue is which road will take us to that
destination: change or conflict? Lenin addressed the issue in 1916,
at another moment when speculations about all the capitalist
powers eventually merging into one united whole were being cast
around by German socialist leader Karl Kautsky:

> There is no doubt that the development is going in the direc-
> tion of a single world trust that will swallow up all enterprises
> and all states without exception. But the development in this
> direction is proceeding under such stress, with such a tempo,
> with such contradictions, conflicts and convulsions – not only
> economical, but also political, national etc. etc. – that before
> a single world trust will be reached, before the respective
> national capitals will have formed a world union of 'ultra-
> imperialism', imperialism will inevitably explode, capitalism
> will turn into its opposite.[6]

One can understand the point still more clearly today. The problem with capitalism is not that it is obliterating the nation-state, but that it cannot. Every step it is compelled to take in that direction leads towards and, eventually, through war between blocs of nation-states – the highest expression of economic competition.

And if the prospect of war issues forth from capitalism, it can only call forth in turn the prospect of its 'opposite' – socialism, which, by abolishing economic rivalry and competition, creates the conditions for laying the nation-state to rest in a world at peace.

Notes

Introduction

1. *Independent*, London, 18 January 1995.
2. *Wall Street Journal Europe*, 15 July 1994.
3. *Financial Times*, London, 24 March 1995.
4. *Newsweek*, 6 March 1995.
5. *Guardian*, London, 31 December 1994.
6. *Financial Times*, London, 6 January 1995.
7. *Wall Street Journal Europe*, 11 March 1996.
8. Eric Hobsbawm, *Age of Extremes*, Michael Joseph, London, 1994, p. 3.
9. Rather than adopt terms like 'the West' (geographically incorrect) or the 'free world' (politically inaccurate) the capitalist countries are described here as – capitalist. Likewise, the Soviet Union and associated states are described as what they were, socialist, rather than what they were called, but only aspired one day to be – communist.
10. The longest periods of great-power peace in capitalist Europe were from 1815 until 1854 (Crimean War) and from 1871 to 1914. The post-1945 peace is therefore the longest, even if one counts as its demise the civil war in the former Yugoslavia, an event which has at time of writing not caused a wider conflict.
11. Frank Füredi, *The New Ideology of Imperialism*, Pluto Press, London, 1994, p. 107.
12. *Wall Street Journal Europe*, 5 April 1995.

Chapter 1

1. Corelli Barnett, *The Collapse of British Power*, Alan Sutton, Gloucester, 1972, pp. 85–6.
2. Ralph Fox, *The Class Struggle in Britain*, Martin Lawrence, London, 1932, pp. 17–19.
3. R. Palme Dutt, *Crisis, Tariffs, War*, CPGB, London, 1931.
4. James Allen, *World Monopoly and Peace*, International Publishers, New York, 1946, p. 19.
5. Sarmila Bose in *Spectator*, London, 19 August 1995.

6. William Roger Louis, *Imperialism at Bay*, Oxford University Press, Oxford, 1977, pp. 7–9.
7. Stalin, 'Economic Problems of Socialism in the USSR', in *Works 16*, Red Star, London, 1986, p. 329.

Chapter 2

1. Quoted in John Rees, *Marxism and the New Imperialism*, Bookmarks, London, 1994, p. 103.
2. C. J. Bartlett, *The Global Conflict*, Longman, London, 1984, p. 87.
3. *Financial Times*, London, 30 September 1994.
4. *Wall Street Journal Europe*, 7 October 1992.
5. See William Pfaff, *The Wrath of Nations*, Touchstone, New York, 1993, p. 15.
6. *The Economist*, London, 23 December 1995.
7. Anthony Brewer, *Marxist Theories of Imperialism*, Routledge & Kegan Paul, London, 1980, p. 280.
8. Samir Amin, *Empire of Chaos*, Monthly Review Press, New York, 1992, p. 46, pp. 11 and 105. It should be noted that Amin does not himself expect these contradictions to lead to a repetition of 1914 or 1939, seeing the main problem in world political economy as being relations between 'the core' and 'the periphery'.
9. Kenichi Ohmae, *The End of the Nation-state*, HarperCollins, London, 1995, p. 80.
10. *Wall Street Journal Europe*, 21 December 1995.
11. *Financial Times*, London, 9 April 1990.
12. UNCTAD figures, quoted in *Wall Street Journal Europe*, 7 December 1995, and by Richard Kozul-Wright, 'Transnational Corporations and the Nation-State', in Jonathan Michie and John Grieve Smith (eds), *Managing the World Economy*, Oxford University Press, Oxford, 1995, pp. 146 and 158.
13. *Business Week*, 24 July 1995.
14. Martin Wolf in *Financial Times*, London, 13 February 1996.
15. *Wall Street Journal Europe*, 18 May 1995.
16. *Wall Street Journal Europe*, 9 November 1995.
17. *Wall Street Journal Europe*, 8 January 1996.
18. N. Bukharin, *Imperialism and World Economy*, Merlin Press, London, 1972, p. 61.
19. *Financial Times*, London, 13 February 1996.
20. *Independent*, London, 22 March 1995.
21. *Wall Street Journal Europe*, 1 July 1994.
22. *Wall Street Journal Europe*, special report, September 1992.
23 *The Economist*, London, 7 October 1995.
24. *Wall Street Journal Europe*, 9 March 1994.

25. *Business Week*, 13 March 1995.
26. *Financial Times*, London, 6 February 1996.
27. Noam Chomsky, *World Orders, Old and New*, Pluto Press, London, 1994, p. 183.
28. Bukharin, *Imperialism*, p. 87.
29. A. Sivanandan in *Race and Class*, vol. 30, no. 4, London, 1989, p. 12.
30. All figures from *Business Week*, 10 July 1995.
31. See Paul Hirst and Grahame Thompson, *Globalization in Question*, Polity Press, Cambridge, 1996, pp. 76–99, for a full discussion of MNCs and globalisation.
32. *Foreign Affairs*, November/December 1995.
33. *Foreign Affairs*, January/February 1996.
34. Figures from International Trade Administration, US Department of Commerce.
35. Mathew Horsman and Andrew Marshall, *After the Nation-State*, HarperCollins, London, 1994, p. 53.
36. Paul Kennedy, *Preparing for the 21st Century*, HarperCollins, London, 1993, p. 225.
37. Ohmae, *The End*, p. 87.
38. Horsman and Marshall, *After*, p. 142.
39. *Business Week*, 19 February 1996.
40. Rudolf Hilferding, *Finance Capital*, Routledge & Kegan Paul, London, 1985, p. 369.

Chapter 3

1. Gail Reed, *Island in the Storm*, Ocean Press, Melbourne, 1992, p. 53.
2. Lenin, *Speeches at Party Congresses*, Progress, Moscow, 1971, p. 69.
3. Felix Chuyev, *Molotov Remembers*, Ivan Dee, Chicago, 1993, p. 253.
4. C. J. Bartlett, *The Global Conflict*, Longman, London, 1984, p. 200.
5. Noam Chomsky, *World Orders, Old and New*, Pluto Press, London, 1994, p. 69.
6. The most vivid account of the disintegration of the CPSU leadership has been written from 'within', by Gorbachev's deputy in the early years of *perestroika*, Yegor Ligachev. See Y. Ligachev, *Inside Gorbachev's Kremlin*, Pantheon, New York, 1993. Ligachev is particularly forthright on the role of Alexander Yakovlev, who he appears to view as a more or less conscious and deliberate advocate of the restoration of capitalism.
7. M. Gorbachev, *October and Perestroika: The Revolution Con-*

tinues, Novosti Press Agency, London, 1987, pp. 50–1. Gorbachev expanded on this position in his better-known address to the United Nations a year later, which consigned the October Revolution, along with the French Revolution, to history.
  8. Karl Marx, *Capital, Volume One,* Penguin, London, 1976, p. 926; *Business Week,* 15 April 1996.
  9. *World Employment 1995,* ILO, Geneva, 1995, pp. 107–12.
 10. *Wall Street Journal Europe,* 1 November 1994.
 11. *Financial Times,* London, 16 September 1994.
 12. *Wall Street Journal Europe,* 15 November 1994.
 13. *Wall Street Journal Europe,* 22 June 1994.
 14. John Lloyd, *Spectator,* London, 27 August 1994.
 15. *Wall Street Journal Europe,* advertising supplement, 9 November 1992.
 16. *Wall Street Journal Europe,* 2 December 1992.
 17. *Financial Times,* London, 4 May 1995.
 18. *Newsweek,* 17 April 1995.
 19. *Wall Street Journal Europe,* 1 January 1994.
 20. *Independent,* London, 30 March 1994.
 21. *Time,* 23 October 1995.
 22. *Guardian,* London, 3 October 1995.
 23. *Wall Street Journal Europe,* 31 March 1995.
 24. *Wall Street Journal Europe,* 1 January 1994.
 25. *Wall Street Journal Europe,* 22 September 1995.
 26. *Guardian,* London, 3 October 1995.
 27. *Financial Times,* London, 25 March 1994.
 28. Ludo Martens, *Non a l'Europe Imperialiste, Militariste, Allemande,* PTB, Brussels, 1992, p. 49.
 29. *Financial Times,* London, 19 December 1994.

Chapter 4

  1. Henry Kissinger, *Diplomacy,* Simon & Schuster, London, 1994, p. 805.
  2. Paul Kennedy, *The Rise and Fall of the Great Powers,* Fontana Press, London, 1989, p. 563.
  3. Lester Thurow, *Head to Head,* William Morrow, New York, 1922, p. 30.
  4. *Fortune,* 26 July 1993.
  5. *New Statesman,* London, 21 July 1989.
  6. OECD National Accounts 1960–1993.
  7. Thurow, *Head,* p. 157.
  8. *Wall Street Journal Europe,* 29 October 1992.
  9. *Financial Times,* London, 21 July 1993.
 10. *Time,* 28 September 1992.
 11. *Financial Times,* London, 4 September 1992.

12. *Business Week*, 15 August 1994.
13. *Wall Street Journal Europe*, 26 May 1995.
14. *International Herald Tribune*, 9 March 1992.
15. *Time*, 18 May 1992.
16. *Guardian*, London, 21 September 1989.
17. *International Herald Tribune*, 24 July 1995.
18. Noam Chomsky, *World Orders, Old and New*, Pluto Press, London, 1984, p. 111.
19. *Newsweek*, 6 March 1995.
20. Farkeed Zakaria, *World Policy Journal*, summer 1995.

Chapter 5

1. This point is developed in Jeremy Leaman, *The Political Economy of West Germany 1945–1985*, Macmillan, Basingstoke, 1988, p. 13, and in the foreword to Volker Berghahn, *The Quest for Economic Empire*, Berghahn Books, Providence, 1996.
2. *Independent on Sunday*, London, 15 July 1990.
3. *Wall Street Journal Europe*, 11 October 1995.
4. *Spectator* (London), 6 May 1995.
5. David Marsh, *Germany and Europe*, Heinemann, London, 1994 p. 201.
6. Leaman, *Political Economy*, p. 197.
7. Marsh, *Germany*, p. 201.
8. Leaman, *Political Economy*, p. 199.
9. *Spectator* (London), 30 November 1991.
10. *Business Week*, 29 May 1995.
11. *Financial Times*, London, 3 February 1993.
12. Andrew Murray, *Europe – Continent in Crisis*, Camden Communists, London, 1992.
13. *Business Week*, 25 March 1996.
14. *Wall Street Journal Europe*, 8 December 1994.
15. *Business Week*, 7 November 1994.
16. *Fortune*, 21 September 1992.
17. *Wall Street Journal Europe*, 30 August 1993.
18. *Financial Times*, London, 11 November, 1992.
19. *Financial Times*, London, 14 November 1992.
20. Marsh, *Germany*, p. 141.
21. *International Herald Tribune*, 5 December 1995.
22. *Wall Street Journal Europe*, 9 June 1995.
23. Bernard Connolly, *The Rotten Heart of Europe*, Faber, London, 1995, p. 389.
24. Misha Glenny, *New Statesman*, London, 20 December 1991. Glenny accurately predicted, in the same article, the bloodbath in Bosnia which would follow from this policy.
25. *Wall Street Journal Europe*, 19 June 1995.

26. *Wall Street Journal Europe*, 9 September 1993.
27. *The Times*, London, 4 August 1995.
28. *Independent*, London, 4 January 1996.
29. *Daily Telegraph*, London, 7 September 1995.
30. *Financial Times*, London, 31 October 1995.
31. *Financial Times*, London, 24 November 1995.
32. *Financial Times*, London, 26 February 1996, and in Berghahn, *The Quest*.
33. *Wall Street Journal Europe*, 3 October 1991.
34. *Time*, 9 January 1995.
35. *Financial Times*, London, 24 February 1995 and 9 February 1995.
36. *Business Week*, 10 May 1993.
37. *Financial Times*, London, 24 June 1987 and 12 December 1985.
38. *Guardian*, London, 13 January 1994.
39. *Wall Street Journal Europe*, 11 May 1995.
40. *Newsweek*, 12 April 1993.
41. *Wall Street Journal Europe*, 23 July 1993.
42. *Wall Street Journal Europe*, 24 September 1992.
43. *Wall Street Journal Europe*, 4 August 1993.
44. *Business Week*, 10 July 1995.
45. *Financial Times*, London, 20 January 1995.
46. *Wall Street Journal Europe*, 24 November 1995.
47. Central Statistical Office, *Economic Trends 1992*, Central Statistical Office, London, 1992.
48. Central Statistical Office, *The Pink Book 1992*, Central Statistical Office, London, 1992.
49. Stephen Woolcock, Michael Hodges and Kristin Schreiber, *Britain, Germany and 1992*, Pinter, London, 1991, p. 82.
50. Ohmae, *The End of the Nation-state*, HarperCollins, London, 1995, p. 131.
51. *Wall Street Journal Europe*, 29 November 1995.
52. John Plender and Paul Wallace, *The Square Mile*, Hutchinson, London, 1985, pp. 26–7.
53. Central Statistical Office, *Annual Abstract of Statistics 1991*, Central Statistical Office, London, 1991.
54. CSO, *Economic Trends 1992*.
55. Nicholas Costello, Jonathan Michie and Seumas Milne, *Beyond the Casino Economy*, Verso, London, 1989, p. 81.
56. *Wall Street Journal Europe*, 28 December 1995.
57. Noam Chomsky, *World Orders, Old and New*, Pluto Press, London, 1994, p. 6.
58. *Financial Times*, London, 14 September 1995.
59. *Daily Telegraph*, London, 4 September 1995.
60. *Wall Street Journal Europe*, 1 December 1994.
61. *Wall Street Journal Europe*, 8 February 1995.

62. *Wall Street Journal Europe*, 7 July 1995.
63. Both articles are from *Spectator*, London, 12 September 1992.
64. An interview in the *Spectator*, quoted in the *Financial Times*, London, 18 July 1990.
65. *Wall Street Journal Europe*, 4 July 1994.
66. *Observer*, London, 4 February 1996.
67. Her Majesty's Stationery Office, *Statement on the Defence Estimates 1992*, HMSO, London, 1992, p. 14.
68. *Socialist Economic Bulletin*, London, November 1995.
69. *Daily Telegraph*, London, 28 March 1995.
70. *Aid is Not Enough*, report of the Independent Group on British Aid, London, 1984, p. 1.
71. *Financial Times*, London, 10 April 1995.
72. *Central European Economic Review*, July/August 1995.
73. *Business Week*, 8 May 1995.
74. *Wall Street Journal Europe*, 1 December 1995.
75. *Financial Times*, London, 10 April 1995.
76. *Financial Times*, London, 1 March 1996.
77. *Prospect*, January 1996.
78. *Wall Street Journal Europe*, 6 March 1996.
79. *Business Week*, 1 April 1996.
80. *Business Week*, 8 May 1995.
81. *Financial Times*, London, 10 April 1995.
82. *Wall Street Journal Europe*, 25 October 1995 and 21 March 1996.
83. *Wall Street Journal Europe*, 25 September 1995.
84. *Financial Times*, London, 17 May 1995.
85. Bruce Clark, *An Empire's New Clothes*, Vintage, London, 1995, p. 208.
86. *The Economist*, London, 7 January 1995.
87. *The Economist*, London, 16 March 1996.

Chapter 6

1. *Financial Times*, London, 31 May 1989; quotation from James Fallows.
2. *Workers' Rights, Human Rights and the Democratic Control of Multinationals*, Zenroren (National Confederation of Trade Unions), Tokyo, 1994, pp. 3–4.
3. *Business Week*, 10 July 1995.
4. Zenroren, *Workers*, p. 3.
5. Lester Thurow, *Head to Head*, William Morrow, New York, 1922, p. 127.
6. Zenroren, *Workers*, p. 4.
7. Ryoshin Minami, *The Economic Development of Japan*, Macmillan, Basingstoke, 1986, p. 417.

8. Thurow, *Head*, p. 127.
9. Michael Montgomery, *Imperialist Japan*, Christopher Helm, London, 1987, p. 511.
10. *Wall Street Journal Europe*, 18 February 1987.
11. *Time*, 13 April 1987.
12. *Financial Times*, London, 27 January 1987.
13. Shintaro Ishihara, *The Japan That Can Say No*, Simon & Schuster, New York, 1991, pp. 20–1.
14. Ishihara, *Japan*, p. 23.
15. Clyde V. Prestowitz Jr., *Trading Places*, Basic Books, New York, 1989, pp. 176–7.
16. *Financial Times*, London, 21 January 1992; microchip sizes advance in multiples of four – one, four, sixteen, sixty-four and so on.
17. *Wall Street Journal Europe*, 7 December 1995.
18. Terutomo Ozawa, *Multinationalism, Japanese Style*, Princeton University Press, Princeton, NJ, 1982; p. 195.
19. George Friedman and Meredith Lebard, *The Coming War with Japan*, St Martin's Press, New York, 1992, p. 283.
20. Ozawa, *Multinationalism*, p. 77.
21. Jon Halliday and Gavan McCormack, *Japanese Imperialism Today*, Monthly Review Press, New York/London, 1973, pp. 238–40.
22. *Financial Times*, London, 15 November 1995.
23. Zenroren, *Workers*, p. 5.
24. Ibid., pp. 5–6.
25. *Business Week*, 10 April 1995.
26. Ishihara, *Multinationalism*, pp. 106 and 56.
27. *Financial Times*, London, 17 October 1995.
28. *Fortune*, 6 May 1991.
29. *Nikkei Weekly*, April 12 1993.
30. *Financial Times*, London, 8 December 1995 and 23 March 1995.
31. *International Herald Tribune*, 31 July 1993.
32. *The Economist*, London, 23 December 1995.
33. *Wall Street Journal Europe*, 2 August 1994.
34. *Fortune*, 18 May 1992.
35. *Time*, 15 June 1992.
36. *Financial Times*, London, 18 November 1993.
37. *Wall Street Journal Europe*, 15 November 1995.
38. *Financial Times*, London, 18 July 1995.
39. *Business Week*, 15 May 1995.
40. *The Economist*, London, 29 July 1995.
41. *Time*, 31 July 1995.
42. *International Herald Tribune*, 24 July 1995 and 1 August 1995.
43. *Daily Telegraph*, London, 2 June 1995.

44. *Guardian*, London, 3 January 1995.
45. Anne Applebaum in *Spectator*, London, 23 September 1995.

Chapter 7

1. Michael Parenti, *Against Empire*, City Lights Books, San Francisco, 1995, p. 100.
2. *Guardian*, London, 17 September 1990.
3. *Sunday Times*, London, 3 February 1991.
4. Sandhurst is the British equivalent of West Point, the major training school for army officers.
5. See Andrew Murray, *British Imperialism Today*, Communist Publications, North Shields, 1987 and Mike Toumazou, *No War in the Gulf*, Straight Left, London, 1990.
6. *Guardian*, London, 17 October 1992.
7. *Wall Street Journal Europe*, 28 July 1995.
8. *Wall Street Journal Europe*, 9 February 1993.
9. Warren Zimmerman in *Foreign Affairs*, March/April 1995.
10. See Christopher Bennett, *Yugoslavia's Bloody Collapse*, Hurst & Co., London, 1995, pp. 178–9.
11. *Guardian*, London, 29 January 1996.
12. *International Herald Tribune*, 4 August 1995.
13. See James Petras and Steve Vieux, 'Lethal Power Play in Bosnia', *New Left Review*, No. 218, July/August 1996.
14. *Financial Times*, London, 19 July 1995.
15. *Wall Street Journal Europe*, 2 June 1995.
16. *Independent*, London, 6 July 1994.
17. *Wall Street Journal Europe*, 26 July 1994.
18. The Rwandan Community in France, *Rwanda: L'Operation Turquoise: Un Modele de Manipulation et de Desinformation*, Les Dessins Caches de L'Operation Turquoise, Paris, 1994.
19. 'Working for National Reconciliation in Rwanda', remarks by Dr Theogene Ruchasinga to the Socialist Campaign Group of Labour MPs, London, 1994.
20. *Wall Street Journal Europe*, 7 December 1992.
21. *Wall Street Journal Europe*, 8 January 1993.
22. *Wall Street Journal Europe*, 21 January 1993.
23. Parenti, *Against*, pp. 122–3.
24. *Newsweek*, 6 March 1995.
25. *Time*, 12 December 1994.
26. *Time*, June 1992.
27. *Financial Times*, London, 2 December 1994.
28. *Financial Times*, June 1995.

Chapter 8

1. *Wall Street Journal Europe*, 21 April 1995.
2. *Time*, 20 March 1995.
3. Ibid.
4. W. L. Givens, *Foreign Affairs*, July/August 1995.
5. Nicholas von Hoffman, *Spectator*, London, 23 February 1991.
6. *Wall Street Journal Europe*, 17 March 1995.
7. *Financial Times*, London, 25 March 1995.
8. Diane Kunz, *Foreign Affairs*, July/August 1995.
9. Quoted by Mica Panic, 'The Bretton Woods System: Concept and Practice', in Jonathan Michie and John Grieve Smith (eds), *Managing the World Economy*, Oxford University Press, Oxford, 1995, p. 39.
10. Bernard Connolly, *The Rotten Heart of Europe*, Faber, London, 1995, p. 180.

Chapter 9

1. Frederick Rolfe, *Hadrian the VII*, Wordsworth Editions, Ware, 1993, pp. 327–8.
2. *Time*, 23 January 1995.
3. *Financial Times*, London, 13 March 1992.
4. *Wall Street Journal Europe* (supplement on world business) September 1992.
5. *Financial Times*, London, 29 January 1992.
6. *Wall Street Journal Europe*, September 1992.
7. *People's Voice*, Canada, April 1993.
8. *Time*, 16 January 1995.
9. *Caribbean Times*, London, 18 February 1995.
10. *Business Week*, 13 February 1995.
11. *Wall Street Journal Europe*, 30 May 1995.
12. *Wall Street Journal Europe*, September 1992.
13. *Time*, 14 September 1992.
14. *Financial Times*, London, 11 January 1993.
15. *Financial Times*, London, 30 January 1990.
16. *Wall Street Journal Europe*, 16 November 1995.
17. *Business Week*, 11 May 1992.
18. *Fortune*, 5 October 1992.
19. *Time*, 14 September 1992.
20. *Wall Street Journal Europe*, 5 April 1995.
21. *Wall Street Journal Europe*, 18 January 1995.
22. *Business Week*, 1 May 1995.
23. Mark Taylor in *Foreign Affairs*, November/December 1995.
24. *International Herald Tribune*, 24 July 1995.

25. Brahma Chellany in *International Herald Tribune*, 26 January 1996.
26. Hemant Kumar in Zenroren, *Workers*, pp. 26–40.
27. *Financial Times*, London, 15 February 1995.
28. *Wall Street Journal Europe*, 12 May 1993.
29. *Independent*, London, 18 January 1994.
30. *Newsweek*, 15 November 1993.
31. *Time*, 18 March 1996.
32. *Newsweek*, 15 November 1993.
33. Bernard Connolly, *The Rotten Heart of Europe*, Faber, London, 1995, pp. 395, 396 and 230–2 for the comparisons with the Nazis' plans.
34. *Wall Street Journal Europe*, 21 March 1996.
35. *Observer*, London, 4 February 1996.
36. See Andrew Marr in the *Independent*, London, 6 February 1996.
37. See John Keegan in the *Daily Telegraph*, London, 7 February 1996, and Roger Scruton in *Wall Street Journal Europe*, 8 February 1996.
38. Connolly, *Rotten Heart*, pp. 326–30
39. *Wall Street Journal Europe*, 20 January 1995.
40. Bruce Clark, *An Empire's New Clothes*, Vintage, London, 1995, p. 285.
41. *Wall Street Journal Europe*, 13 February 1996.
42. *Wall Street Journal Europe*, 20 December 1995.
43. Connolly, *Rotten Heart*, p. 399.
44. Charles Lane in *Foreign Affairs*, November/December 1995.
45. *Wall Street Journal Europe*, 20 December 1995.
46. Henry Kissinger, *Diplomacy*, Simon & Schuster, London, 1994, p. 604.

Chapter 10

1. Noam Chomsky, *World Order, Old and New*, Pluto Press, London, 1994, p. 73.
2. Peter Schweizer in *Foreign Affairs*, January/February 1996.
3. *Wall Street Journal Europe*, 15 July 1994.
4. *Time*, 21 August 1995.
5. *Financial Times*, London, 5 December 1995.

Chapter 11

1. William Pfaff, *The Wrath of Nations*, Touchstone, New York, 1993, p. 42.

2. *Wall Street Journal Europe*, 1 December 1995 and 22 November 1995.
3. *Financial Times*, London, 7 February 1996.
4. *Financial Times*, London, 9 February 1996.
5. *Wall Street Journal Europe*, 31 October 1995.
6. *Wall Street Journal Europe*, 21 February 1996.
7. *Observer*, London, 11 February 1996.

Chapter 12

1. *Morning Star*, London, 6 February 1996.
2. Robert Leicht in *Prospect*, January 1996.
3. *Wall Street Journal Europe*, 12 January 1996, 7 February 1996 and 13 February 1996.
4. *Business Week*, 19 February 1996.
5. Rudolf Hilferding, *Finance Capital*, Routledge and Kegan Paul, London, 1985, pp. 366–7.
6. Lenin, Introduction to N. Bukharin, p. 14.

Index

Abdullah, Prince, 148
Adenauer, Konrad, 60
Aegean Sea, 67, 161
Afghanistan, 41, 42
Africa, 36, 40
Airbus Industrie, 33
Akihito, Emperor, 140
Albania, 2, 49, 158
Algeria, 72, 145, 149
    see also France
Allianz Holdings, 32
America, see United States of
    America
Amin, Samir, 23
Amoco, 48, 115
Angola, 42
Archer Daniel Midland, 30
Argentina, 132, 134
Armenia, 48, 85, 158
Aristide, Jean-Bertrand, 116
Asea Brown Boveri, 32
Asia, 36, 40, 55
    and Russian economy, 85
    economy of, 89–103, 135–40
    Japanese investment in, 95
    manufacturing, 131
    Asiatic war, 161–3
    defence spending, 163
Asia-Pacific Economic Confer-
    ence, 57, 96, 130, 135–40, 136
Attlee, Clement, 74
Audi, 62
Australia
    and Britain, 80
    Japanese investment in, 96
    and APEC, 135
Austria, 22, 63, 64
Austria-Hungary, 12
AutoVAZ, 82
Azerbaijan, 47, 85, 158, 164

Balkans, 108, 110, 157–61
    see also Eastern Europe
Balladur, Eduard, 74
Baltic Republics, 2, 55, 64
    see also Eastern Europe
Barings Bank, 27
Bavaria, 66
Belgium, 22, 63, 64, 113, 127, 145
    and Rwanda, 112
    industrial disputes, 141
Benn, Tony, 168
Berlin Wall, 38, 59, 74, 104, 131
Bernstein, Eduard, 18, 37
Blinder, Alan, 26
Boeing, 30, 33
Bosnia, 7, 57, 109, 158
    see also Balkans/Yugoslavia
Brazil, 124, 132, 134, 174
Bretton Woods, 16, 120, 126
Brewer, Anthony, 21
Britain
    Navy, 5, 74, 77
    Empire, 6, 53, 104, 129
    industrial development, 7, 10–
    11, 75–7
    Anglo-German rivalry, 10–12,
    66, 74
    Atlantic Charter, 15
    India, 15, 139
    the great powers, 51
    GNP, 52
    and Deutschmark bloc, 59
    and France, 70
    and Yugoslavia, 70, 75, 110–12
    and US, 70, 74–5, 78–81
    City of London, 74, 75–77, 120,
    147
    Foreign and economic policy,
    74–81, 142–7
    UN Security Council, 75

Britain *cont.*
  Gulf War, 75, 78, 107
  Falklands, 75, 80
  European Union, 75, 78, 79,
    131, 142–7, 168
  transnational corporations,
    75–6
  Stock Exchange, 75, 78
  Libya, 78
  defence spending, 81
  Pergau Dam, 81
  Japan, 89, 90–9
  Arab states, 107
  and New World Order, 117
  Bank of England, 121
  world trade, 121
  World War One, 121
  IMF, 124
  Hong Kong, 140
  Exchange Rate Mechanism, 144
  Middle East, 148–9, 164
  nuclear/military technology,
    151
British Aerospace, 34, 155
British Gas, 48
British Petroleum, 48, 114
Brzezinski, Zbigniew, 80
Buchanan, Pat, 168, 169
Bukharin, Nikolai, 27, 31
Bulgaria, 61, 48, 158
Bush, George, 43, 55, 106, 108,
  121, 132
  Gulf War, 105–6
  pan-Yugoslav policy, 110
  Somalia, 114

Cambodia, 99, 101
  see also Kampuchea
Canada, 37, 51, 132–5, 137
Castro, Fidel, 38, 41
Catholic Church, 112
Caucuses, the, 45, 46, 104, 158
Central Bank (China), 122
Central Intelligence Agency
  (USA), 3, 55, 71, 85, 98, 110
Charette, Herve de, 68
Chaudhuri, Nirad C., 14
Chechnya, 3, 47, 49
Chernomyrdin, Victor, 82
Chevron, 115

Chiang Kai-shek, 15
Chile, 87, 136, 171
China, 3, 15, 51, 129
  economic and foreign policy,
    19, 89, 99–103, 125, 139–40
  nation state, 23
  trade barriers, 29
  USSR, 42, 47, 101
  US, 55, 58, 101–3, 162
  India, 101, 139
  Japan, 101, 103, 136, 139–50,
    149
  Spratley Islands, 101–2
  Taiwan, 102, 140, 161
  navy and air force, 103
  Pakistan, 139
  Mongolia, 140
  Thailand, 140
  Myanmar (Burma), 140
  Hong Kong, 140
  nuclear/military technology,
    151, 153
  defence spending, 163
Chirac, Jacques, 69, 70, 71
Chomsky, Noam, 31
Christian Democratic Union
  (Germany), 66
Churchill, Winston, 4, 15, 104
Claes, Willy, 72
Clark, Bruce, 146
Clinton, Bill, 30, 54, 55, 57, 168
  National Economic Council,
    56
  Taiwan, 102
  Haiti, 116
  trade policy, 130
  Mexico, 133–5
  APEC summit, 136
Coal and Steel Community, 68
Coca-Cola, 32
Codevilla, Angelo, 115
Cold War, 6, 40–1, 69, 74, 75, 93,
  108, 121, 124
  British defence spending, 81
  Japan, 99
  Yugoslavia and USSR, 109
  Second Cold War, 150–1
  Mutually Assured Destruction,
    151
  end of, 155, 166

Commonwealth of Independent
    States, 87
Communaute Financiere
    Africaine, 73
Communist Party (China), 100,
    101
Communist Party (Russia), 129,
    170, 171
Communist Party (Soviet Union),
    42
Connolly, Bernard, 141, 144, 145,
    146, 147
Conoco, 115
Conservative Party (Britain), 169
Costa Rica, 134
Craxi, Bettino, 170
Croatia
    Deutschmark bloc, 59
    Utashe, 109
    US and German support, 110
    see also Balkans/Yugoslavia
Cuba, 36, 38, 40, 41, 148
Currency, 119–26
Cyprus, 2, 67, 80, 105
Czech Republic, see Czecho-
    slovakia
Czechoslovakia, 1, 63, 64
    Deutschmark bloc, 59
    Germany, 61, 158, 160

Daewoo Research Institute, 137
Daimler-Benz, 32, 148
Daiwa Bank, 27
Davidson, Ian, 111, 117, 161
Defence Science Board (USA), 92
Democratic Party (USA), 54, 168
Deng Xiaoping, 4, 100–1
Denmark, 63, 64
Department of Defence (USA), 94
Dole, Bob, 168
Dole Food Co., 115
Dornbusch, Rudi, 44

East Asia Economic Caucus, 136
Eastern Europe
    Restoration of capitalism, 38, 44
    Potential for conflict, 157–67
    Germany, 157–61
    see also Balkans
El Salvador, 42

England, see Britain
Estonia, 87, 157
Ethiopia, 42
European Assembly, 1
European Union, 17, 22, 61, 63,
    64, 66, 68, 69, 71, 72, 73, 75,
    129, 130, 131, 168
    council of ministers, 1
    free trade, 31, 46
    eastward expansion, 55, 59
    Germany, 62
    European Free Trade Area
        states, 65
    Exchange Rate Mechanism, 73,
        74, 120, 152–7
    Maastricht Treaty, 74, 142–7
    Japan, 95
    Slovenia and Croatia, 109
    Yugoslavia, 111
    Rwanda, 112–14
    economic integration, 124,
        142–7
    Ecu, 124
    economic interests, 141–7
    convergence criteria, 143
    Euro, 143
Exxon Crop., 56, 114
Eyal, Jonathan, 74

Fahd, King, 147
Farben, IG, 14
Far East, 57, 135
    economy and power relations,
        89–103
    Japanese trade bloc, 135
    Potential for conflict, 157,
        161–3
Federal Reserve (USA), 26, 121,
    134
Fini, Giancarlo, 2, 51, 143, 160,
    169
Finland, 64
Forbes, Steve, 168
Ford Motor Co., 30, 114
Fokker, 33
France
    Germany, 6, 59, 68–74
    industrial development, 7, 10
    World War One, 11
    Franco-German cartels, 22

France *cont.*
  overseas development, 26
  USSR, 43
  Russia, 45
  great powers, 51
  GNP, 52
  economic and foreign policy,
    68–74
  nuclear weapons testing
    (Mururoa Atoll), 68, 74, 172
  Gaullism, 69
  Vichy regime, 69
  Britain, 70
  Yugoslavia, 70, 111–12
  Balkans, 71
  Mediterranean, 71
  internal political situation, 71,
    141, 172
  Yalta order, 71
  CIA, 71
  West European Union, 71, 117
  Algeria, 72
  colonialism, 73, 112–14
  Maastricht, 74
  Gulf War, 107
  Exchange Rate Mechanism, 120
  European Union, 142–7, 168
  Latin Monetary Union, 145
  Middle East, 148–9
  Iraq, 148, 164
  nuclear/military technology,
    151
Fuji Xerox Co., 97
Furedi, Frank, 6
Furet, Francois, 69

G7 countries, 24, 32, 51, 59, 84,
  120
Garten, Jeffrey, 33
Gaulle, General Charles de, 70,
  121
GAZ, 82
General Agreement on Tariffs and
  Trade, 27, 28, 74, 103
General Electric Co. (USA), 30
General Motors, 30, 56, 62, 158
Georgia (ex-Soviet republic), 47,
  85
German Democratic Republic, 43,
  62, 123

Germany
  Deutschmark zone, 6, 59, 121–
    6, 128, 143, 158–61
  development of capitalism, 7,
    10–11, 60–2
  Empire, 10
  Anglo-German rivalry, 10–11
  World War One, 12
  Nazi Soviet pact, 14
  West Germany re-established,
    16, 63
  overseas investment, 26, 61–2
  annexation of GDR, 43
  Russian investment, 45
  Former Soviet republics, 46,
    62
  great powers, 51
  GNP, 52
  economic and foreign policy,
    55, 59–68, 129, 141–7, 168
  Kaiserism, 60
  Weimar republic, 60, 167
  Nazism, 60
  Federal Republic, 61
  car industry, 61–2
  rise of neo-fascism, 62, 169
  eastward expansion, 62–3, 66,
    158–61
  reunification, 64
  Bundesbank, 65, 123, 126, 128,
    142
  Yugoslavia, 66–7, 70, 109
  Turkey, 67, 161
  Somalia, 67
  Franco-German relations, 68–
    74
  Eastern Europe, 96, 158–61
  Gulf War, 106
  UN Security Council, 117
  economic integration, 124
  manufacturing, 131
  Middle East, 148–9, 164
Gingrich, Newt, 55, 168, 169
Global 1000, 32, 36
Globalisation, 18, 20, 130, 166
Goebbels, Josef, 60
Goering, Hermann, 60
Goldsmith, James, 30
Gorbachev, Mikhail, 42, 43, 85

Greater East Asia Co-Prosperity
Sphere, 97, 128, 162
Greece, 2, 48, 67
Turkey, 67, 158, 161
Yugoslavia, 111
Grenada, 105, 135, 174
Gulf War, 151, 157
see also Britain, France,
Germany, Iraq, Japan,
Kuwait, Soviet Union, US

Haiti, 55, 104, 116
Healey, Denis, 124
Henderson, David, 19
Hilferding, Rudolf, 37, 173
Hirst, Paul, 33
Hitachi, 92
Hitler, Adolf, 60, 104
rise of, 13, 171
fear of communism, 39
new order, 109
ambitions, 156
Poland, 156
Weimar, 167
Hobsbawm, Eric, 38
Holbrooke, Richard, 161
Hong Kong, 89, 102, 136, 140
Horsman, Mathew, 34
Howell, David, 79
Hugo Boss, 62
Hungary, 63, 64, 158
insurrection, 41
Deutschmark bloc, 59
German exports, 61

India, 100
China, 101, 129, 139
Asia, 136, 138–9, 162
economy, 138–9
NAFTA, 139
nuclear policy, 152
UN Security Council, 174
Indonesia, 96, 137
Institute of Directors (Britain), 79
International Business Machines,
56
International Labour Organisa-
tion, 44
International Monetary Fund, 16,
23, 41, 73, 124, 132, 139, 174

Internet, 8, 154
Iran, 42, 58
Russia, 87, 164
China, 140
Germany, 148
Iraq, 78, 87, 164
Gulf War, 104–8, 150–1, 155
Saddam Hussein, 105, 108, 148,
163
France, 148
Ireland, 59
Ishihara, Shintaro, 93–4, 97, 98,
169
Israel
and former Soviet republics, 46
occupation of West Bank, 105
nuclear policy, 152
Arab states, 163
Italy, 64, 72, 166
GNP, 52
Deutschmark bloc, 59
economy, 124, 168
EU, 130, 142, 143, 160
Latin Monetary Union, 145
Yugoslavia, 160

Japan, 7, 21, 44, 51, 58, 128, 129
company mergers, 22
nation state, 23
economic downturn, 24, 98
overseas investment, 26, 95–6
GNP, 52
position in Asia, 89, 135–40,
149
economic and foreign policy,
90–9, 121–6, 135–40
keiretsu, 90, 167
trade unions, 91
US, 92, 99, 137, 152
Okinawa US bases, 97, 172
Gulf War, 98, 106
nuclear policy, 98–9, 152
China, 102–3, 139–40, 162
UN Security Council, 117
protectionism, 119
yen bloc, 125, 129, 130
manufacturing, 131
military, 152
Russia, 152

Japan *cont.*
  South Korea, 163
  defence spending, 163
Jiang Zemin, 165
Johnson, Paul, 115
Juppe, Alain, 69

Kampuchea, 42
  see also Cambodia
Kautsky, Karl, 174
Kazakhstan, 47, 86
Kennedy, Paul, 35, 56
Kinkel, Klaus, 74
Kissinger, Henry, 51, 102, 139,
  149
Kitchener, Lord, 115
Kohl, Helmut, 4, 59, 63, 65, 66,
  144, 146, 148, 165
Korea, 38, 162
Korea, North, 55, 58, 162
  US, 54, 98
  South Korea, 138
Korea, South, 35, 89, 103
  economy, 136, 137–8
  US, 152
  Japan, 163, 166
Korean Institute for Defence
  Analysis, 138
Kozyrev, Andrei, 84
Kravchuk, Yevgeny, 43
Krupp, 148
Kucan, Milan, 160
Kuwait, 1, 41
  Emir 104–8
  Iraqi annexation, 151, 155, 163

Lamers, Karl, 67, 80, 169
Laos, 42
Latin America, 36, 40
  economy, 133–5
Latvia, 87
Laughland, John, 69
Lazard Freres, 123
League of Nations, 7
Lebed, Alexander, 1, 87, 158, 159,
  169, 171
Lenin, V. I., 38, 174
Liberal Democratic Party (Japan),
  166

Liberal Democratic Party
  (Russia), 84
Libya, 58
  bombing of, 78, 105
Lightfoot, Warwick, 145
Lithuania, 87, 159
Lockheed (company), 30
Luce, Henry, 104
Luddendorf, General, 60
Lvov, 1–8, 159

Maastrict Treaty, 74, 142–7
Macedonia, 2, 109, 158
Mahathir, Mohamad, 135, 136,
  138
Major, John, 19, 70, 78, 146
Malaysia, 96, 135, 136, 137, 138
Mannesmann, 148
Marion, Pierre, 33
Marr, Andrew, 144
Marshall, Andrew, 34
Martin Marietta (company), 30
Marx, Karl, 44, 155
Massari, Mohammad al-, 155
McLarty, Thomas, 134
Mediterranean, 71, 72, 131
Mexico, 7, 35, 36, 96, 123, 124,
  133–6, 172
  US and NAFTA, 72, 129, 130,
  131–2
Michie, Jonathan, 77
Microsoft, 32, 56
Middle East, 36, 41, 55, 80
  Russia, 87
  Gulf War, 104–8
  Japan, 140
  US, 147–9, 152
  arms exports to, 155
  potential for conflict, 157,
  163–4
  Ottoman Empire, 163
Milne, Seumas, 77
Mitterand, Francois, 3, 4, 64, 69,
  71
Molotov, V. M., 39
Morgan Stanley (bank), 63, 64–5
Morocco, 72, 149
Mother Teresa of Calcutta, 114
Ministry of Defence (Britain), 80,
  107

Ministry of International Trade and Industry (Japan), 94
Mitsubishi, 91
Moisi, Dominic, 71
Moldva, 48, 85, 159
Mongolia, 140
Montgomery, Michael, 91
Morita, Akio, 93–4, 97, 98
Mozambique, 42
Mulroney, Brian, 132
Murayama, Tomiichi, 168
Myanmar (Burma), 140

NAFTA, 30, 53, 57, 72, 123, 128, 129, 130
Mexico, 131–5
and India, 139
Nagorno-Karabakh, 48
Nation-states, 20–37, 119, 174–5
National Economic Council (USA), 56
National Front (France), 169
NATO, 3, 6, 7, 16, 43, 46, 48, 54, 67, 70–1, 72
founding of, 78
Russia, 84, 87, 117
China, 103
Yugoslavia, 110–12
decay, 117–18
Cold War, 151
Germany, 158–9
Naval War College (USA), 153
NEC (company), 92
Nestlé, 32
Netherlands, 63, 64, 65, 127
New World Order, 3, 8, 44, 52, 77, 104–18
New Zealand, 81, 135
Nicaragua, 41, 42, 105, 135
Nigeria, 73

OECD, 19
Ohmae, Kenechi, 25, 35
Oman, 107
OPEC, 106
Opel, 62

Pakistan
China, 139
nuclear policy, 152

Palestine, 41
Palme Dutt, R., 13
Palmerston, Lord, 4
Panama, 43, 55, 105, 135
Paraguay, 132
Pareti, Michael, 105
Party of Democratic Socialism (Germany), 169
Pennzoil, 48
Pergau Dam, 81
Perot, Ross, 30
Peugeot, 29
Philippines
Pentagon, 57
Japanese investment, 96
US withdrawal, 97, 152
China, 101, 102
defence spending, 162, 163
Philips (company), 115
Pinochet, General Augusto, 87, 171
Pol Pot, 42, 101
Poland, 1, 2
Germany, 59, 61, 158, 159
economy, 63, 64, 124
Lithuania, 159
Portugal
Deutschmark bloc, 59
Latin Monetary Union, 145
Prestowitz, Clyde, 94

Quayle, Dan, 1, 3

Reagan, Ronald
arms race, 39, 42, 52, 53, 123
National Security Council, 56
Star Wars (Strategic Defence Initiative), 93, 151
Japan, 93–4
trade and budget deficits, 121
Cold War, 121
Red Cross, 114
Redwood, John, 146
Reed Elsevier, 32
Republican Party (USA), 54, 168
Rhodes, Cecil, 33
Richthofen, Baron Hermann von, 117
Ridley, Nicholas, 80
Rifkind, Malcolm, 78

Roberts, Paul Craig, 125
Roche (company), 32
Rohatyn, Felix, 123
Rolfe, Frederick, 127–9
Roman Empire, 20
Romania, 159
Roosevelt, Franklin D.
    Stalin, 15
    Chiang Kai-Shek, 15
Royal Dutch/Shell, 26, 32
Ruchasinga, Theodore, 113
Ruehe, Volker, 67
Ruggiero, Renato, 28
Russia, 6, 51
    Tsarist Russia, 11–12, 20
    restoration of capitalism, 19, 44,
        45, 81
    nation state, 23
    GDP, 44–5
    ILO, 44–5
    crime, 45
    State Duma, 45
    German investment, 45–6
    Chechnya, 47, 84, 85, 159, 170,
        171
    economic and foreign policy,
        81–8
    internal political situation,
        83–8, 170–1, 172
    Comecon, 85, 87
    former Soviet Republics, 85,
        146
    Belarus, 86
    Soviet Black Sea Fleet, 86
    Russian left, 86, 171
    Rouble zone, 87
    Yugoslavia, 111
    new world order, 118
    EU, 146, 149
    Russian-German conflict,
        157–61
    Greece, 161
    Middle East, 164
    see also Soviet Union, Ukraine
        and other former Soviet
        Republics
Rwanda, 73, 104, 112–14, 117
    Tutsis and Hutus, 112
    Operation Turquoise, 112, 113
    Rwandese Patriotic Front, 112

Sakhrai, Sergei, 84, 86
Sanwa Bank, 32
Saudi Arabia
    House of Saud, 41
    Gulf War, 105, 147
    anti-imperialism, 173
Schauble, Wolfgang, 169
Schmidt, Helmut, 60, 65
Serbia, 2, 109, 158, 159
Shevardnadze, Eduard, 42, 85
Siemens, 62, 148
Simes, Dimitri, 41
Singapore, 89, 136
Sivanandan, A., 31
Skoda, 62
Slovakia, 59, 64, 109, 158, 161
Slovenkia, 22, 64, 109–12, 158, 160
Smith, Adam, 29, 82
Social Democratic Party
    (Germany), 65
Social Democratic Party (Japan),
    168, 170
Socialist International, 18, 165
Socialist Party (France), 170
Socialist Party (Italy), 170
Somalia, 3, 36, 55, 67, 104, 114–17,
    129, 174
Somalifruit, 115
South Africa, 37, 152
South America, 37, 133, 136
South Ossetia, 49, 85
Soviet Union
    Moscow archives, 5
    formation, 12
    Nazi-Soviet Pact, 14, 88
    anti-Soviet alliance, 16
    restoration of capitalism, 19
    demise, 25, 40, 85, 89, 106, 122,
        129, 138
    rift with China, 42, 101
    arms race, 42
    Gulf War, 43, 105, 151
    Comecon states, 85, 87
    Yugoslavia, 109
    Siberia, 128
    Soviet bloc, 129
    Cold War, 150–1
    Strategic Defence Initiative,
        151
    re-creation of, 170

Soviet Union *cont.*
  see also Russia and other former
    Soviet Republics
Spain, 170
  Deutschmark bloc, 59
  rapid reaction military unit, 72
  economy, 124
  Latin Monetary Union, 145
Stalin, J. V., 15, 16
Sturmer, Michael, 158
Suez crisis, 16
Sultan, Prince, 148
Sutherland, Peter, 28
Sweden, 63, 64, 143, 170
Switzerland, 64

Taiwan, 3
  China and US, 102
  economy, 136, 137
  defence spending, 163
Tajikistan, 47, 49, 85
Talbott, Strobe, 99
Tamberlaine the Great, 48
Thailand, 96, 138, 140, 163
Thatcher, Margaret, 3, 42, 60, 64,
    74, 77
Third World
  debt, 24, 35, 100
  and big powers, 41, 166, 167
  US, 114
  economies, 131, 132, 172
Thompson, Graham, 33
Tito, Josip Broz, 109
Toshiba, 91, 92
Toyota, 32, 91, 114
Trans-Atlantic Free Trade Area,
    135
Trans-national corporations, 31,
    36, 139
Truman, Harry, 162
Turkey, 2, 7, 46
  former Soviet Republics, 46
  oil pipeline, 48
  Germany, 67
  Greece, 67, 158, 161
  US, 105
  Yugoslavia, 111

Ukraine, 1, 43, 49, 85, 86, 109,
    118, 158, 159–60, 172

Unilever, 32
United Energy System (com-
    pany), 82
United Fruit, 34
United Kingdom, *see* Britain
United Nations, 5
  Security Council, 6, 7, 8, 51, 70,
    75, 101, 115, 136, 174
  armed forces, 23
  US, 23
  Third World, 35
  Africa and Middle East, 70
  Cambodia, 99
  Yugoslavia, 111
  Somalia, 114–17
United States of America, 6, 7
  Japan, 8, 15, 54, 89, 90–9, 102,
    117–18, 123, 136, 152
  industrial development, 10,
    121, 131
  World War Two, 15
  Vietnam, 16, 38, 42, 121
  company mergers, 22
  nation state, 23
  overseas investment, 26
  trade disputes, 30, 90–9
  Mexican border, 35
  anti-Communism, 40
  USSR, 40, 41, 121, 150
  foreign policy, 41, 54–8, 70
  Gulf War, 43, 47, 56, 57, 98,
    104–8, 117, 123, 150
  Panama, 43
  former Soviet republics, 46
  oil interests, 47–8
  economy and economic policy,
    51–8, 121–6, 129, 148
  Monroe doctrine, 66
  Britain, 70
  military research, 91, 150–5
  semiconductors dispute with
    Japan, 93–4
  Taiwan, 102
  Yugoslavia, 110
  Haiti, 116
  Mexico, 129–35
  APEC, 130, 135
  Canada, 132–5
  Costa Rica, 134
  European Union, 142, 147

United States of America *cont.*
　Middle East, 148–9, 152, 164
　Algeria and Morocco, 149
　Philippines, 152
　Third World, 152
　Turkey, 161
　China, 162
　US socialism, 171
Uruguay, 132
USSR *see* Soviet Union

Vickers, 34, 155
Vietnam, 162
　economy, 19
　war, 38
　defeat of US, 42
　Chinese invasion, 89, 101
Volkswagen, 62, 114

Waigel, Theo, 143
Warsaw Pact, 43, 87
Waterloo, Battle of, 11
Wilhelm, Kaiser, 60, 128
World Bank, 16, 23, 132, 133, 174
　see also IMF
World Trade Organisation, 8, 24,
　28, 30, 71
World War One, 121
　Archduke Franz Ferdinand, 4,
　156
　origins, 11, 166
　Tsarist Russia, 11, 38
　Hungary, 161
World War Two, 52, 59
　developments towards, 13–15,
　156

World War Two *cont.*
　Anti-Communism, 13, 39
　Nazi-Soviet Pact, 14
　Red Army, 41
　Warsaw Pact, 43
　Vichy, 69
　Yalta, 71
　Croatia/Serbia German policy,
　109
　Japan and Germany, 130
　anti-Japanese legacy, 136
　Japan and China—Akihito's
　apology, 140
　Poland and Lithuania, 159
　Italy and Yugoslavia, 160
　Czechoslovakia, expulsion of
　Sudeten Germans, 160
Worsthorne, Peregrine, 78

Yakovlev, Alexander, 42
Yasin, Yevegeny, 171
Yeltsin, Boris, 3, 42, 49, 63, 82, 84,
　87, 88, 158, 165, 170–1
Young, Thomas, 48
Yugoslavia, 2, 4, 7, 25, 48, 55, 104,
　108–12, 119, 147
　Germany, 64, 66–7
　France and Britain, 70–4
　Tito, 109
　potential for conflicts, 157–61
　see also Balkans/Eastern Europe

Zhirinovsky, Vladimir, 84, 86–7,
　146, 158, 169, 170–1
Zyuganov, Gennadi, 86, 88, 171